Observing Acceleration

Peter W. Roberts • Saurabh A. Lall

Observing Acceleration

Uncovering the Effects of Accelerators on Impact-Oriented Entrepreneurs

Foreword by Randall Kempner

palgrave
macmillan

Peter W. Roberts
Goizueta Business School
Emory University
Atlanta, GA, USA

Saurabh A. Lall
University of Oregon
Eugene, OR, USA

Foreword by
Randall Kempner
Aspen Network of Development Entrepreneurs
Washington, DC, USA

ISBN 978-3-030-00041-7   ISBN 978-3-030-00042-4   (eBook)
https://doi.org/10.1007/978-3-030-00042-4

Library of Congress Control Number: 2018962928

Cover design: Fatima Jamadar

This Palgrave Macmillan imprint is published by the registered company Springer Nature Switzerland AG
The registered company address is: Gewerbestrasse 11, 6330 Cham, Switzerland

Foreword

When I ask entrepreneurs what they need to make their businesses grow and positively impact the world, the answers usually touch on three major challenges: money, talent, and networks. In all three of these areas, accelerators offer support, promising to help entrepreneurs fill the gaps in their financial, technical, and social resources as they seek to scale. How accelerators endeavor to do so varies significantly around the world. But in general, accelerators aim to help startups hone their strategy, identify market opportunities, strengthen their management teams, and connect to potential investors. In so doing, accelerators also play an important role in identifying and supporting the most promising ventures.

Many in the international community have looked to the rise of Silicon Valley as a source of inspiration. They see startups as the way forward in promoting sustainable economic development around the globe. As the world tries to identify the next startup hot spot, accelerator programs like Silicon Valley-based Y Combinator have emerged as a model to help entrepreneurs take their innovative ideas to market. And new accelerator programs are popping up all over the world. Of the more than 500 accelerators that we know of, more than half launched in 2014 or later. With varying structures, methods, and intended outcomes, and with funding from corporations, foundations, and governments, business acceleration is emerging as a sector of its own.

As the executive director of the Aspen Network of Development Entrepreneurs (ANDE), a global network of organizations that support entrepreneurship in emerging markets, I have seen acceleration develop into one of the most popular approaches to bolster entrepreneurship in developing economies. Currently, of our more than 290 member organizations, more than 30 percent identify themselves as accelerators or incubators.

While the number of accelerators has grown, the evidence base for their impact lags. A series of essential questions remain. For example, at the most basic level, do they work? Do accelerators have a meaningful effect on the businesses they support, or would these businesses have excelled no matter what? More specifically, do certain types of acceleration programs work best in certain contexts and for certain types of entrepreneurs?

Five years ago, the sector was only beginning to ask these questions. Acceleration was hardly studied. There were almost no published papers on acceleration, little data existed, and there was no clear consensus on what defines an accelerator. Anecdotes of quickly scaling ventures sent positive signals, but there was almost no hard evidence to say if this was due to the accelerators themselves. And if it was, there was even less research to support whether this solution could transfer to emerging markets and sectors outside technology. Data about the cost-effectiveness of acceleration were basically non-existent.

These questions drove ANDE, Emory University, and a consortium of public and private funders to come together to make a concerted effort to expand the evidence base. This work, led by ANDE's research director at the time, Saurabh Lall, and Peter Roberts, academic director of the Social Enterprise Center at Emory University, is designed to ask the hard questions. Out of this partnership, the Global Accelerator Learning Initiative (GALI) was formed. GALI is the first initiative to gather data that can speak to the effectiveness of acceleration programs.

So what do we know now that we did not know five years ago?

Our research shows that, on average, accelerators work. That is, they have identifiable effects on the growth trajectories of early-stage businesses, or ventures, as they are referred to in the book. Accelerated ventures are outperforming their counterparts in terms of revenue earned, employees hired, and financing secured, and there seem to be positive effects across a range of geographies and sectors. Whether this growth is a product of selection, technical assistance, mentoring, or some secret combination of all three, is yet to be determined.

By collecting the same kind of data from thousands of entrepreneurs over time (as opposed to a one-off survey), we now have the ability to address these—and other—important questions. GALI to date has partnered with more than 175 acceleration programs, collecting data from over 13,000 entrepreneurs that operate in more than 150 countries around the world. Academics and accelerators alike have been digging into the data to ask what 'success' in acceleration means and what are the best ways to measure it. Most importantly, we can now say that we have useful data and that we have raised the bar for accelerators and funders to be data-driven in evaluating their impact.

The ultimate goal of GALI is to help accelerators run better programs and to guide resources to the most effective types of support. We should do this for the entrepreneurs that need this critical support, and in the end, to foster a stronger and more inclusive global economy.

In this book, Peter and Saurabh continue to press into complex subjects in acceleration. They want to know—what types of acceleration programs work best? Which types of ventures and sectors are best suited for this type of fast-paced growth? Is acceleration effective in emerging markets? Is it leveling the playing field for women-founded startups? While there are still many questions left to answer, I'm proud to introduce Peter and Saurabh's work, and hope that it encourages more academics and practitioners to pursue evidence-based answers to difficult questions around startup acceleration.

Aspen Network of Development Entrepreneurs   Randall Kempner
Washington, DC, USA

Acknowledgments

It is difficult to settle on the right order in which to thank the many people who had more than just a hand in producing this book. If we start with the reason that the book was written in the first place, then we have to thank the innumerable impact-oriented entrepreneurs who work around the world to tilt businesses and markets away from their singular obsession with making more money for investors who arguably have enough money already. Many of you are implicitly thanked by the short references and examples that are scattered throughout the book. The rest of you will have to be satisfied with our general but heartfelt thanks for your amazing energy, efforts, and impacts.

If we start with the people who are the actual focus of the book, then we have to shout out to the accelerator program founders and managers who not only see the potential that is inherent in these impact-oriented entrepreneurs, but also know that the business world is not yet ready for most of them. Our thanks start with our friend and mentor Ross Baird, who allowed us to become affixed to, and fixated on, the early evolution of Village Capital. These thanks extend to the many other people who work to ensure that Village Capital continues to grow its influence by accelerating many impact-oriented ventures around the world: Dustin Shay, Heather Matranga, and too many others to be named individually. Our thanks then go out to many other friends and colleagues who do similarly great work: people like Paul Basil and P.R. Ganapathy at Villgro, C'pher Gresham at SEED SPOT, Ayesha Khanna and Megan Christenson at CivicX, Oscar Ortiga (and his team) at Impulsa Tu Empresa, Carrie Rich (and her team) at the Global Good Fund, Abigail Sarmac at IMPAQTO, and Rodrigo Villar (and his team) at New Ventures. We are grateful for the opportunity to work with you all as partners in the Entrepreneurship Database Program (EDP) and Global Accelerator Learning

Initiative (GALI) initiatives, and for approaching all of our collaborations with generosity and curiosity—clearly, this is the best way to learn together.

We could also start this list of acknowledgments with the people who are (or were) instrumental in ensuring that we have the data required to make these various observations possible. The EDP would not have launched at all without the amazing early work of Sara Johnson and then Sean Peters. It would not have made it out of its infancy without the confidence expressed by the Argidius Foundation and the Kauffman Foundation. It would not have found a home in the context of the GALI without the support and votes of confidence from Randall Kempner and Jenny Everett from the Aspen Network of Development Entrepreneurs (ANDE). (Thanks again to you Randall, for writing the foreword to the book.) In truth, the list of ANDE people who must be thanked is a very long one: Stephanie Buck, Katia Dumont (and many other ANDE regional chapter managers, past and present), Vicky Hume (for your splendid work on the figures and tables), Kate McElligott, Mary Mwangi, Aditya Pant, and Rebeca Rocha. And, because GALI would not be possible without the vision of several founding supporters, we owe a huge debt of gratitude to our colleagues at USAID (Matt Guttentag and Rob Schneider), the Argidius Foundation (Nicholas Colloff and Harry Devonshire), the Lemelson Foundation (Carol Dahl), the Omidyar Network (Mike Kubzansky), and the Kauffman Foundation (Amisha Miller and Alicia Robb).

We might also start our acknowledgments with the people who we most directly and regularly leaned on over the last two years. Emily Eastman, Brent Ruth, and Josh Zhou know that curating application and follow-up data from scores of accelerator programs around the world is hard enough without our continuous stream of requests to check and contextualize our many observations. Thank you—over and over again—for your many efforts, and for making sure that the EDP and GALI programs continue to develop so that we can continue learning more about impact-oriented acceleration. And, because the EDP does not exist in isolation from the bigger team at Social Enterprise @ Goizueta, we also thank Aelish Benjamin-Brown, Tiffany Campbell, Giselle Carias, Brian Goebel, Erin Ingleheart, and Jacob Watt-Morse—for the work you all do, making markets work for more people, in more places, and in more ways, and for your comments and suggestions on earlier drafts of our various chapters.

A final round of thanks goes to two of our academic colleagues: Li-Wei Chen and Wes Longhofer. As the EDP database manager, Li-Wei has been responsible for turning the various streams of application and follow-up data into one unified river of data. As our co-author in several research papers, Li-Wei also develops the more complex econometric models that help us understand entrepreneurs' needs and preferences, as well as accelerators' selection practices. We hope that any topical interest that we cultivate by publishing this book will immediately transfer to the great work that is housed in your published and soon-to-be-published papers. As for Wes, there is no better or smarter colleague to think about issues at the nexus of business and society. We are thankful to you for sharing many of these thoughts with us, and for your feedback on multiple versions of our surveys and chapters.

Of course, if we really want to do this right, we would start by thanking two people who, in an alternate universe, would be recognized as co-authors of this book: Abigayle Davidson and Genevieve Edens. Abby and Genevieve are thanked as 'ghost co-authors' in several places throughout the book, most notably Chaps. 5 and 9. This book would not have been possible, and this intellectual journey would not have been nearly as pleasant, without our regular conversations and collaborations. For this reason, we not only thank you both. We also dedicate our book to you—our amazing friends and colleagues.

Now that we have settled on the many possible options for thanking the people who helped make this book possible, we must also thank the special people who make our work possible. Peter thanks his wife and kids—Tania Herbert and Ellis and Oliver Roberts—not so much for what they put into the book, but for what they put up with while the book was being written. Saurabh is grateful to his parents Ajay and Priti Lall, an endless source of encouragement, even from 8000 miles away; and to his wife, Naila Bhatri, whose own work at an impact-oriented enterprise is continually inspiring.

Finally, we want to be sure to thank our editor, Marcus Ballenger, and the amazing team at Palgrave Macmillan; in particular, Jacqueline Young and Lucy Kidwell. You have all been supportive and patient throughout this process; supportive in guiding us through our first book project, and patient with the corresponding stream of naïve questions and requests from two newbies. We hope that you are satisfied that our book represents an adequate return on these much-appreciated investments.

Contents

1 Introduction   1

2 Entrepreneurs, Ecosystems, and Accelerators   13

3 The EDP Data   31

4 Is Acceleration Working?   59

5 Driving the Net Flow of Funds   75

6 Building Application Pipelines   93

7 A Closer Look at Entrepreneur Selection   107

8 Programming to Close Knowledge, Network, and Capital Gaps   119

9 Acceleration in Emerging Markets   135

10 Where's the Equity for Women Entrepreneurs?   161

11 Accelerating Learning About Accelerators   187

Glossary   203

Index   205

List of Figures

Fig. 2.1   Accelerator programs in the GALI database   20
Fig. 2.2   New accelerators in the GALI directory by founding year   21
Fig. 2.3   Primary funding sources for GALI accelerators   23
Fig. 2.4   Primary funding sources for GALI accelerators   23
Fig. 2.5   Investor engagement approaches in (a) emerging markets and (b)
            impact-oriented programs   24
Fig. 3.1   EDP accelerators, 2013–2016   34
Fig. 3.2   EDP partner organizations and programs, 2013–2016   36
Fig. 3.3   Accelerator benefits ranked #1 by EDP applicants   43
Fig. 3.4   EDP applicants seeking private and philanthropic investment
            support   44
Fig. 3.5   Prior-year revenues and investment for participated and rejected
            ventures   48
Fig. 4.1   Accelerator participation and negative-, no-, and positive-growth
            ventures   64
Fig. 5.1   The range of NFF and its four components   78
Fig. 5.2   (a) Average NFF and NFF for high-NFF and low-NFF programs
            (b) Average NFF and NFF components for high-NFF and
            low-NFF programs   82
Fig. 5.3   One year changes in full-time employees for high-NFF and
            low-NFF programs   83
Fig. 5.4   World Bank regions for high-NFF and low-NFF programs   85
Fig. 5.5   Average cohort size for high-NFF versus low-NFF programs   86
Fig. 5.6   Accelerator benefits ranked #1 by high-NFF versus low-NFF
            programs   87
Fig. 6.1   Average number of applicants for high-NFF versus low-NFF
            programs   94

Fig. 6.2   Average flow of funds in the prior year for high-NFF versus
            low-NFF programs   95
Fig. 6.3   Source of applicants for high-NFF versus low-NFF programs   97
Fig. 6.4   Program focus for high-NFF versus low-NFF programs   99
Fig. 6.5   Preference for women and minority applicants for high-NFF
            versus low-NFF programs   102
Fig. 7.1   Number and gender of selectors for high-NFF versus low-NFF
            programs   110
Fig. 7.2   Selector emphasis by high-NFF and low-NFF programs   114
Fig. 8.1   Use of a structured curriculum among high-NFF and low-NFF
            programs   122
Fig. 8.2   How participants spend their time in high-NFF versus low-NFF
            programs   124
Fig. 8.3   Mentor backgrounds for high-NFF versus low-NFF programs   127
Fig. 9.1   Accelerator benefits ranked #1 across three country groups   147
Fig. 9.2   Probability of program participation across three country groups   150
Fig. 9.3   Accelerator participation and negative-, no-, and positive
            (a) revenue-growth ventures, (b) equity-growth ventures,
            (c) debt-growth ventures, and (d) philanthropy-growth ventures
            across three country groups   152
Fig. 9.4   Accelerator benefits ranked #1 for India, Kenya, and Mexico   157
Fig. 9.5   Accelerator participation and negative-, no-, and positive
            (a) revenue-growth ventures and (b) equity-growth ventures for
            India, Kenya, and Mexico   158
Fig. 10.1   Founding teams by gender category   164
Fig. 10.2   Outside equity since founding by founding team gender   166
Fig. 10.3   Outside equity since founding by founding team gender—
            differences broken down   168
Fig. 10.4   (a) Sources of outside equity by founding team gender; (b) Levels of
            outside equity conditioned on access to source   169
Fig. 10.5   Twelve-month investment aspirations by founding team gender   174
Fig. 10.6   Accelerator benefits ranked #1 by founding team gender   177
Fig. 10.7   Accelerator participation and negative-, no-, and positive equity-
            growth ventures by founding team gender   182

List of Tables

Table 2.1	Sector focus for GALI accelerators	22
Table 3.1	EDP partner organizations with 2+ programs, 2013–2016	37
Table 3.2	Reported IRIS impact objectives	39
Table 3.3	Ventures and entrepreneurs in the EDP sample	41
Table 3.4	Revenues, employment and investment, averages and correlations	47
Table 4.1	Year-over-year growth, participated versus rejected	62
Table 4.2	Negative-growth, no-change, and positive-growth ventures	63
Table 4.3	Isolating the top-50 growth outcomes	65
Table 4.4	Simple regression equations that control for prior-year performance	67
Table 4.5	Accelerator bumps across different types of ventures	68
Table 4.6	Average growth in key variables by program, participated ventures only	70
Table 5.1	The program-level sample	77
Table 5.2	The NFF and its four components	78
Table 5.3	Correlations among the four NFF components	79
Table 5.4	The NFF by dominant component	80
Table 5.5	Cost, duration, and human capital inputs for high-NFF versus low-NFF programs	86
Table 6.1	Venture stage targeted for high-NFF versus low-NFF programs	100
Table 6.2	A closer look at gender in high-NFF versus low-NFF programs	103
Table 7.1	The background diversity of selectors used by high-NFF versus low-NFF programs	111
Table 7.2	Selection steps taken by high-NFF versus low-NFF programs	112
Table 8.1	Topics covered and emphasized in high-NFF versus low-NFF programs	123

Table 8.2   Time spent with mentors in high-NFF versus low-NFF
               programs   126
Table 8.3   NFF before and after accounting for direct investments   129
Table 9.1   World Bank country categories   138
Table 9.2   Where do entrepreneurs apply?   139
Table 9.3   Reported IRIS impact objectives across three groups   140
Table 9.4   Commonly held beliefs about entrepreneurship and acceleration
               in emerging markets   142
Table 9.5   Venture differences across three groups   143
Table 9.6   Founding team differences across three groups   146
Table 9.7   Ecosystem differences across three groups   149
Table 9.8   Average accelerator effects across three groups   151
Table 9.9   Resources spent on accelerator programs   153
Table 9.10   Differences across India, Kenya, and Mexico   156
Table 10.1   Reported IRIS impact objectives by founding team gender   165
Table 10.2   Other investment sources by founding team gender   167
Table 10.3   Ventures by founding team gender   172
Table 10.4   Women versus men founders   175
Table 10.5   Founding teams by gender category   176
Table 10.6   Explaining equity since founding by gender category, with and
               without controls   179
Table 10.7   Average accelerator effects on investment by founding team
               gender   181

1

Introduction

This book is about the interplay between entrepreneurship, entrepreneurial ecosystems, and accelerators. A quick run through the Wikipedia website orients the reader to this trio of concepts. Entrepreneurship is 'the process of designing, launching and running a new business.'[1] It tends to take place in the context of local ecosystems, which are 'the social and economic environment[s] affecting the local/regional entrepreneurship.'[2] When there are problems with these local ecosystems, promising entrepreneurs often rely on accelerators, which are 'fixed-term, cohort-based programs that include seed investment, connections, mentorship, educational components, and culminate in a public pitch event or demo day to accelerate growth.'[3] When the typical reader reads these three definitions, she envisions the founder of a company like Uber working in a place like Silicon Valley, leaning on the support programming offered by accelerators like Techstars or Y Combinator. This is a perfectly fine place to begin thinking about entrepreneurs, ecosystems, and accelerators. After all, Uber recently had its market valuation pegged at roughly $50 billion,[4] while Silicon Valley has become self-caricaturing when it comes to spawning high-tech companies.[5] Moreover, prominent accelerators like Techstars and Y Combinator are regular fixtures on published lists of top programs, while their founders—Paul Graham and Brad Feld—are quoted regularly in the media for their views on entrepreneurship and acceleration.[6]

While it makes sense to begin by thinking about these prominent accelerators, it is not acceptable to stop there. There is simply too much else that is, and should be, happening around the world when it comes to accelerating entrepreneurship. Consider, for instance, the programs run by Village Capital,

© The Author(s) 2019
P. W. Roberts, S. A. Lall, *Observing Acceleration*,
https://doi.org/10.1007/978-3-030-00042-4_1

Points of Light, and GrowthAfrica. Since its founding in 2011, Village Capital has engaged numerous partners to run accelerators in sectors and regions around the world. To support promising entrepreneurs who tackle social and environmental challenges, they run programs in the agriculture, education, energy, financial services, and healthcare sectors in the United States, India, Kenya, Mexico, and South Africa. In a typical program, Village Capital works with 10 to 12 ventures and deploys a peer-review model that allows participating entrepreneurs to select the ventures that receive seed funding from Village Capital and its co-investors. The Points of Light Civic Accelerator (CivicX) operates out of Atlanta, Georgia, and supports for-profit and nonprofit ventures that want to solve critical social challenges around the country. Since running its first program in 2012, CivicX has provided mentoring, education, and post-program support to more than 100 ventures. Each of their programs consists of three four-day sessions and spans ten weeks. In the end, two ventures from every cohort receive investments of $50,000 each, structured as convertible notes for the for-profit ventures or revenue-share agreements for the nonprofits. GrowthAfrica is headquartered in Nairobi and runs programs in Kenya, Uganda, and Ethiopia. Although the organization was established in 2002 with the broad goal of enhancing business development in Africa, its first accelerator ran roughly one decade later. Since 2012, GrowthAfrica has worked with more than 150 ventures across a range of sectors, including agriculture, energy, financial services, and healthcare. In doing so, they partner with like-minded organizations, including other accelerators (e.g., Village Capital), foundations (e.g., Hivos), and networks (e.g., VC4Africa).

Those who know these programs—or any of the other impact-oriented accelerators working around the world—also know entrepreneurs who generate more than attractive financial returns for investors. In many cases, their ventures generate employment or improve incomes for people that currently live in poverty. In other cases, they produce innovative business models that give underserved people access to essential products and services like education, energy, financial services, and clean water. For example, one Village Capital program worked with FINV, Mexico's first sustainable crowdfunding platform.[7] Its mission is to create a bridge between the demand for financing and the supply of capital without the interventions of traditional banks. One of the CivicX programs supported Pentorship, an educational company in the United States that provides skills-based training and tools to incarcerated persons.[8] As they expand, more people will be prepared to thrive when released from prison. GrowthAfrica worked with Wanda Organic, a Kenyan social enterprise that develops organic bio-fertilizers to improve food security.[9] This company provides the latest in biotechnology solutions to medium-scale farmers that protect the soil while increasing farmers' profitability.

Moving from these examples to the hundreds of alumni from scores of impact-oriented accelerators reveals a range of business models and aspirations that are positively disrupting the status quo. It also reveals a range of places that bear little resemblance to Silicon Valley. In the years since the semiconductor industry was propelled forward by the direct and indirect descendants of Fairchild Semiconductors,[10] this region has become the prototype for high-octane entrepreneurial ecosystems.[11] Many books and articles are written about the networks and connections that allow promising entrepreneurs and ideas to flow toward the most able supporters and investors.[12] Now, Silicon Valley is flooded with mentors, angel investors, and venture capitalists. These ecosystem actors are complemented by a number of accelerators—including 500 Startups, Alchemist, Angel Pad, and Y Combinator—that help to identify promising entrepreneurs and ideas and then ensure that their knowledge and network gaps are recognized and closed. These acceleration processes facilitate connections to funding networks so that entrepreneurs also receive the investments required to scale their operations. Combinations of productive ecosystems plus high-quality support programs do not guarantee the success of any one entrepreneur, but they do ensure that the overall probability of success is maximized.

The non-traditional entrepreneurs who work in other places—like the founders of FINV in Mexico, Pentorship in Atlanta, or Wanda Organic in Kenya—face more serious ecosystem challenges. Fewer individuals and organizations are in place to advise and invest in promising ventures. This makes it extremely difficult for entrepreneurs to find and then make positive connections to these critical stakeholders. In reality, there are way too many regions and sectors that are not really conducive to positive entrepreneurial outcomes, and these tend to be the places where the contributions of promising entrepreneurs would be most valued.[13] It is troubling to a lot of people that major entrepreneurial advances are not as common in sectors like health and education as they are in mainstream technology; that underdeveloped regions in East Africa, South Asia, and Central America (and the United States) do not benefit from positive entrepreneurial outcomes as much as the highly developed regions in the United States and Western Europe; and that women and minority entrepreneurs experience greater difficulties turning their promising ideas into prospering companies.

In the midst of all the outsized knowledge, network, and capital gaps that slow the progress of impact-oriented ventures in entrepreneurial dead spaces, the prospect of having a few more accelerators is enticing. This is where we see both good news and bad news. The good news is that a growing number of accelerators—like Village Capital, CivicX, and GrowthAfrica—are taking up the challenges of working in underdeveloped entrepreneurial ecosystems. If they are able to find and effectively support promising entrepreneurs, then more early stage ventures will scale and generate positive impacts for more people, in more places and in more ways.

The bad news is that we really do not know whether these accelerators are working.[14]

Adding Breadth and Depth to Our Observations

The title of this book emphasizes 'observing' for two reasons. The first relates to what typically comes to mind when thinking about entrepreneurship and acceleration. As we said before, it is OK to home in on the most salient and successful instances when orienting to a topic. However, it becomes problematic when observation stops there. After all, inferences are likely to be misleading when researchers only observe those things that are easiest to look at.[15] Consider the impression that is left from the second sentence on accelerators taken from the Wikipedia page cited earlier: 'Most startup accelerators in Silicon Valley and globally are privately funded as an investment fund that take equity and focus on a wide range of industries.' As we will show throughout this book, the accelerator model is being deployed in a range of places, supported by a range of funders and funding types, to support entrepreneurs with a range of aspirations. While many of these founders want to earn attractive financial returns for themselves and their investors, they have parallel interests in building companies that make scalable contributions to society and the environment.

To appreciate the full range of cause-and-effect relationships that are implicated when considering accelerator effects on early-stage ventures, researchers must know about the full range of active accelerators. However, most of the insights that have been generated so far focus on the most prominent accelerators. It is therefore important to move 'past the streetlight' to also observe the impact-oriented accelerators that support marginalized entrepreneurs in challenging ecosystems. To support these additional observations, the Entrepreneurship Database Program (EDP) was started in 2013 by Social Enterprise @ Goizueta within Emory University. This was followed shortly thereafter by the launch of the Global Accelerator Learning Initiative (GALI) in partnership with the Aspen Network of Development Entrepreneurs (ANDE). This joint effort represents the first global initiative to study the broader landscape of accelerators.

The second reason to double down on observing entrepreneurs and accelerators is that we have not been doing enough of it to understand what is and is not working when it comes to acceleration. As we discuss in Chap. 3, the goal of the EDP and GALI programs is to collect detailed data from entrepreneurs who apply to impact-oriented accelerator programs around the world. Pre-program data are collected through customized application surveys. Then, starting one year later, post-program data are collected in follow-up surveys completed by entrepreneurs who participated in programs and those who were rejected. This multi-year effort to collect longitudinal data permits detailed observations of thousands of entrepreneurs who are working on impact-oriented ventures around the world.

We currently know too little about who applies to impact-oriented accelerators, who is selected to participate into those programs, and whether program participation has any systematic effects on venture performance. With our perspective broadened to include the impact-oriented accelerators working in entrepreneurial dead spaces around the word, and with thousands of observations curated over a five-year (2013–2017) period, we are now in a position to ask and address important questions about accelerator effectiveness.

Asking the Right Questions

This book does not obsess about the highest-profile startups; the 'unicorns' that end up with valuations of over $1 billion.[16] Nor does it obsess about the platinum tier of accelerators that work in places where future unicorns are born. Instead, given the broad scope of the EDP and the GALI initiative, the observations in this book are meant to generalize across spaces, including regions where economic development is a high priority, and sectors that place a premium on social and environmental impacts.

While the scope of our observations is broad, we do obsess about addressing a narrow set of questions about impact-oriented acceleration. The many accelerators in the EDP sample, most funded by non-trivial government and philanthropic investments, raise one central question that is yet to be adequately answered—does acceleration actually work? It turns out this is not an easy question to answer, not least of all because entrepreneurs and accelerators have many different objectives. Some work to stimulate economic development and focus on metrics like job creation and income elevation (e.g., Endeavor). Others want ventures to achieve specific social or environmental impacts (e.g., The Toilet Accelerator and its focus on sanitation). Still others have more broad-based societal impacts in mind, like promoting an entrepreneurial culture within a country (e.g., Start-Up Chile) or increasing the representation of women and minorities (e.g., SheEO).

Given this underlying labyrinth of aspirations, our one big question can only be tackled after making it smaller. In the chapters that follow, we not only recognize and respect this plurality of specific aspirations but also assume that most accelerators have a few common conceptions of what it means to be successful. They almost always seek to bolster the commercial and investment foundation of the ventures that they engage. Working with for-profit or non-profit ventures, and with entrepreneurs who are explicitly or implicitly impact-oriented, accelerator program managers know that funds must flow into ventures to pay the costs of operating and thereby generating impact. Looking into the future, they also know that investments are required when some of these outlays predate the inflow of revenues. Adopting this business-oriented line of thinking, this book tackles a more specific version of the above question: do impact-oriented accelerators influence the short-term commercial performance of the ventures that they work with? The EDP data are set up to address this question by allowing us to observe the one-year growth in earned revenues, full-time employees, outside equity investment, debt financing, and philanthropic support.

As a favorable response to this one question begins to emerge, a number of subsidiary questions arise. For instance, are all accelerators equally adept at stimulating short-term commercial and investment growth? Of course not. Every accelerator differs from the average in some way. They attract different financial and non-financial resources to run their programs. They make different choices when building pipelines of applicants. They home in on different factors when selecting entrepreneurs to participate in their programs. Finally, they make different programmatic choices when designing interventions that identify and close the knowledge, network, and capital gaps faced by the entrepreneurs in their cohorts.[17] The detailed observations that we present and discuss in the various chapters of this book respond to the many smaller questions that accelerator program managers, funders, and supporters have been asking over the last several years; all subsumed under the general heading of which accelerator practices correspond with better program outcomes.[18]

The EDP data also give us a unique perspective on acceleration in emerging markets, and on how the gender of founders influences entrepreneurial and accelerator outcomes. These are not new questions. However, we are now able to observe how accelerators are, or are not, moving needles when it comes to channeling resources, including early-stage capital, toward the entrepreneurs who find it most difficult to access them on their own: women and those working in emerging markets.

This book was written to mark the end of the first phase of support for the GALI initiative. Since the first venture-level data were collected in 2013, several summaries, briefs, and reports have been written, addressing many of the questions that people—including entrepreneurs and investors, program managers, philanthropic funders and policy-makers— have asked about accelerators.[19] This wave of questions and answers began with the biggest and most general question: Does acceleration work?[20] As suggested, this one question quickly and predictably morphed into a more nuanced one: Does acceleration *always* work? With preliminary insights about these relatively big questions, and with the accumulation of more detailed data about accelerator programs and the entrepreneurs and ventures that apply to them, we began tackling more specific questions that fall under the general theme of 'what accelerator practices are best-suited to support which entrepreneurs working in which regions and sectors?' By the end of Chap. 10, the reader should have a good sense of the progress that has been made addressing these important questions, and should be armed with a new wave of even more nuanced questions so that the pace of understanding about acceleration can keep up with the impressive range of programming that the EDP accelerators have developed to support impact-oriented entrepreneurs around the world.

The Structure of This Book

To understand the work that these accelerators are being asked to do, it is first necessary to describe the interplay between entrepreneurs and entrepreneurial ecosystems. When navigating the paths from promising ideas to successful companies, entrepreneurs rely on a host of individuals, organizations, and institutions to identify and then close various knowledge, network, and capital gaps. For certain entrepreneurs developing certain business ideas in certain places, the breadth and depth of the local ecosystem allow this to happen; not with absolute certainty but with sufficient regularity to ensure a steady stream of new high-growth companies. However, for thousands of other entrepreneurs aspiring to do different things in different places, underdeveloped ecosystems are not providing the same kind of support. Accelerator programs are springing up in these entrepreneurial dead spaces to build capacity, facilitate market connections, and stimulate capital investments in these promising but otherwise-neglected entrepreneurs and ventures. Chapter 2 describes these impact-oriented accelerators before using recent GALI data to paint a picture of the expanding population of accelerators that are working in various regions and sectors around the world.

Then, to set the stage for the analyses in Chaps. 4 through 10, Chap. 3 describes the venture-level data collected through the EDP. This allows us to see how variables describing the commercial performance of participants and rejected ventures change during the post-application year. In the end, the EDP venture-level sample describes 5614 early-stage companies. A total of 890 of these ventures were selected to participate in the program to which they applied. The analyses in Chap. 4 begin to deploy these EDP data to answer our core question. While there are many ways that accelerators might justify the resources that are spent running them, a common set of expectations relates to their ability to stimulate short-term revenue, employment, and investment growth. The application and follow-up data introduced in Chap. 3 provide evidence of systematic short-term growth advantages for ventures that participate in accelerators compared to those that are passed over during the various selection processes. These accelerator effects are evident when looking at continuous variables measuring average year-over-year growth outcomes and categorical variables indicating positive versus negative growth. They are also evident among the very top-growing ventures in the sample. Even after accounting for the different starting points of participating and rejected ventures, accelerator program effects are still evident in the EDP data.

At the end of Chap. 4, we show that these accelerator effects are uneven across programs. Therefore, the general question of whether acceleration works gives way to more specific questions about which programs and program choices deliver more attractive ratios of accelerator benefits to program costs. Chapter 5 begins by introducing a program-level variable called the net flow of funds (NFF). This NFF variable recognizes the four ways that funds can flow into early-stage ventures; they can be earned, invested, borrowed, or donated. We show that accelerators vary in the extent to which the NFF that they stimulate exceeds the per-venture costs of running programs. After isolating the programs that more than cover their reported operating costs, we begin to look at the various program-level decisions that split the sample into high-NFF and low-NFF programs.

The second part of Chap. 5 lays out three broad categories of work that must be completed for an accelerator to have any systematic effects: building pipelines, selecting promising entrepreneurs and developing, and running programs that close knowledge and network gaps so that entrepreneurs can address their capital gaps. Chapter 6 leverages information gleaned from program surveys to focus on pipeline-building. The various observations show whether differences in the number and sources of applicants, or the type and quality of entrepreneurs and ventures, help us understand which programs end up delivering superior support when it comes to funding entrepreneurs.

Most accelerator program managers believe that best way to ensure the maximum returns to their human, social, and financial capital investments is to ensure that these resources are directed to ventures with the best chance of delivering and scaling impacts. Therefore, they invest an immense amount of time and effort selecting the most promising entrepreneurs into their cohorts. However, programs that end up delivering solid results are often accused of simply cherry-picking entrepreneurs and ventures that would have succeeded any way. This matters most when it comes to presenting evidence to potential funders and supporters. If left unchallenged, the desire to demonstrate accelerator effects through the lens of randomized or pseudo-randomized experimentation overlooks a critical part of the work that accelerators do. Rather than considering selection as a problematic confound, Chap. 7 frames it as critical element of accelerator work and examines several discrete selection strategies employed by high-NFF and low-NFF programs to see which practices seem to correlate with better accelerator outcomes.

Much of the work that accelerators do relates to the design and implementation of their programs, which offer a range of services to close knowledge, network, and financial capital gaps. Chapter 8 looks at how high-NFF and low-NFF programs differ in terms of these program choices. We pay close attention to how much time entrepreneurs spend in the program, to the structure of their mentoring programs, to demo days, and to whether the programs offer direct funding to entrepreneurs.

If it is important to accelerate impact-oriented ventures in places where economies are developed and per capita incomes are high, then it is doubly important to do so in emerging markets. However, along with an increased need for more positive entrepreneurial outcomes are amplified shortcomings in these local ecosystems. Therefore, a large number of the programs identified in Chap. 3 work to accelerate early-stage ventures that operate in countries across Africa, Latin America, South Asia, and Southeast Asia. However, it is not yet clear how well the accelerator model, which originated in well-developed entrepreneurial ecosystems, works in more challenging country contexts. After using the World Bank classification to organize the EDP ventures into those operating in high-income countries versus emerging markets, Chap. 9 shows how the emerging-market ventures and entrepreneurs that seek acceleration are different from their high-income country counterparts. The chapter closes by showing that the effects of acceleration are still evident, but are somewhat muted, among two groups of emerging-market ventures.

Chapter 10 shifts focus once again to home in on a group of entrepreneurs whose potential and performance tend to be under-appreciated: women. Specifically, EDP data are used to illuminate the issues that women entrepreneurs face when it comes to attracting outside equity investment. Roughly half of the ventures in the sample report at least one woman among their top three founders; most on mixed-gender founding teams. A look at outside equity investment across three groups of ventures—founded by men, mixed-gender teams and women—reveals a troubling cascade that favors men. The ensuing analyses show that this cascade is not fully explained by obvious venture or entrepreneur differences across the three groups. The chapter closes by showing that accelerators may not be as helpful as many would hope when it comes to addressing equity inequities face by women entrepreneurs.

This brings the many observations of entrepreneurs, ventures, and accelerators to a close. Chapter 11 gathers these insights into a coherent set of conclusions about what we think we know about acceleration. Spoiler alert … we conclude that there are still more questions than answers, but that the questions that we have at the end of the book are better than the ones we started with. For instance, accelerators seem to have a systematic effect on short-term commercial growth outcomes. In this respect, accelerators are accelerating. However, we cannot say whether these short-term accelerator-induced bumps in revenues, employees, and investment will continue into the future. Nor can we say that the bumps in commercial and investment performance translate into the social and environmental advances that the world is looking for. We are also confident that some accelerators perform better than others. However, we are less clear about the details of the blueprints that tend to produce the superior outcomes. We have some ideas, but are also convinced that there is as much art as science in the design of accelerators, and therefore need more qualitative research to continue providing more answers.

In the end, the purposefully narrow set of questions and therefore observations presented in this book should be seen as a big first step toward a better understanding of the overall effectiveness of impact-oriented accelerators. Therefore, we emphatically state now—and will repeat in the concluding chapter—that we must continue asking the right questions and then designing research strategies that produce observations that speak to these questions. After all, anthropologist Claude Levi-Strauss once told us that 'the scientific mind does not so much provide the right answers as ask the right questions.' This is true for the entrepreneurs who launch impact-oriented ventures and for the accelerator program managers who seek to support them. It is also the least that the rest of us can do to support them.

Notes

1. See https://en.wikipedia.org/wiki/Entrepreneurship (August 2018).
2. See https://en.wikipedia.org/wiki/Entrepreneurship_ecosystem (August 2018).
3. See https://en.wikipedia.org/wiki/Startup_accelerator (August 2018).
4. Breaking Down Uber's Valuation: An Interactive Analysis. Forbes (February 2018).
5. See https://www.hbo.com/silicon-valley
6. The platinum tier of one list includes Alchemist, Amplify LA, AngelPad, MuckerLab, StartX, Techstars, University of Chicago New Venture Challenge, and Y Combinator. Another list of the seven best accelerators includes Techstars and Y Combinator, but also describes 500 Startups, Coplex, Dreamit, MassChallenge, and Plug and Play. A third article, which focuses on the top accelerators for overseas startups, again includes Techstars and Y Combinator along with 500 Startups and PlugAndPlay, but adds Founders Space, Hax, Highway1, InnoSpring, Startupbootcamp, and Techcode to its list of top programs. See Alex Konrad. The Best Startup Accelerators of 2017. *Forbes On-Line* (June 2017); Deep Patel. America's Top 7 Startup Accelerators and What Makes Each Unique. Entrepreneur.com (September 2017); Louise Beavers. Top 10 Global Accelerators for Overseas Startups. Entrepreneur.com (May 2017).
7. See https://finv.mx/
8. See https://www.pentorship.org/
9. See http://www.wandaorganic.org/
10. Steven Klepper. 2009. 'Silicon Valley—a chip off the old Detroit bloc.' In *Entrepreneurship, Growth and Public Policy*: 79–115.
11. Martin Kenney. 2000. *Understanding Silicon Valley: The Anatomy of an Entrepreneurial Region*. Stanford University Press.
12. AnnaLee Saxenian. 1990. 'Regional networks and the resurgence of Silicon Valley.' *California Management Review*, 33(1): 89–112.
13. Ross Baird. 2017. *The Innovation Blind Spot: Why We Back the Wrong Ideas—and What to Do About It*. BenBella Books.
14. Randall Kempner & Peter W. Roberts. Aren't Accelerators Great? Maybe… Wall Street Journal On-Line (April 2015).
15. David H. Freeman. 2010. 'Why scientific studies are so often wrong: The streetlight effect.' *Discover Magazine*, July–August.
16. See https://www.investopedia.com/terms/u/unicorn.asp
17. Susan Cohen. 2013. 'What do accelerators do? Insights from incubators and angels.' *Innovations*, 8 (3–4): 19–25.
18. For examples of these many questions, go to https://www.entrepreneurdata.com/
19. See https://www.galidata.org/
20. Randall Kempner & Peter W. Roberts. Aren't Accelerators Great? Maybe… Wall Street Journal On-Line (April 2015).

2

Entrepreneurs, Ecosystems, and Accelerators

Entrepreneurship is critical to the long-term efficacy of market-based economies because it embodies the dynamism that allows us to continually step up and address new challenges. From Schumpeter's singular 'gales of creative destruction'[1] to Schumacher's many 'smaller and beautiful' innovations,[2] the cumulative effects of entrepreneurship, when it works, provide benefits at many different levels. Consider four (impressive) examples:

- In Togo, Cajou Espoir is the country's first cashew processor, creating jobs in a region where the majority of people live on less than $1 a day. West Africa produces half of the world's cashews, but exports over 95 percent of them as raw nuts. Launched in 2004 with fewer than 30 employees, Cajou Espoir now employs more than 700 people, processing more than 2000 tons of cashews each year for the American and European markets.[3]
- In India, Simpa Networks provides electricity to off-the-grid communities while training local entrepreneurs to install and maintain rooftop solar panels. More than two billion people around the world lack reliable access to electricity, and solar power offers a cheap, clean, and safe option for them. Simpa Networks deploys a pay-as-you-go model so that poorer households can purchase energy in small installments over time.[4]
- In Kenya, Microclinic Technologies provides high-quality, affordable health services in the most rural parts of the country. Founded by Dr. Moka Lantum, who recognized the gaps in supply chains for essential drugs, the company developed a tablet-based software platform that helps clinics track their inventories. These improved systems prevent the need for people to turn to counterfeit medicines.[5]

© The Author(s) 2019
P. W. Roberts, S. A. Lall, *Observing Acceleration*,
https://doi.org/10.1007/978-3-030-00042-4_2

- In the United States, First Step Staffing was started by Greg Block in 2007 to provide jobs and stable incomes for individuals transitioning out of homelessness.[6] Recent estimates suggest that there are more than half a million homeless people in the United States.[7] Grounded in the belief that reliable income is the only reliable path out of homelessness, First Step recently expanded into Philadelphia where they hope to find high-quality jobs for another 1000 people.

These are four examples of the thousands of impact-oriented ventures that are doing amazing things around the world, in sectors and regions with the greatest needs for progress and development. They help us see why many practitioners, policy-makers, and scholars share a fundamental belief in the importance of entrepreneurial experimentation and success for broad-based economic development.[8] Not only do these impact-oriented entrepreneurs create high-quality jobs and reliable incomes, they also develop innovative, market-based solutions to major social challenges, like the lack of access to energy, education, or healthcare.

To appreciate the many benefits that come from more productive entrepreneurial processes and outcomes, start by taking the perspective of the people who start new companies. Entrepreneurship offers them chances to create productive economic roles for themselves that sit outside the current cadre of available employment options. This is important, even for people who have good jobs but dream of doing something bigger. Dr. Lantum, for example, is a trained medical doctor with over 20 years of experience in health service delivery and healthcare management. After working in established companies for many years, he became passionate about improving access to services in the underserved rural areas in Kenya. In this way, while Microclinic provides much-needed health services to others, it also allows Dr. Lantum to reach his own full potential.

Now consider the perspective of the many other people who benefit when innovative new ventures are able to scale their operations. It is widely-believed that new companies make outsized contributions to job creation.[9] Ventures that are growing create new jobs and therefore economic prosperity.[10] This is critically important in regions and communities where jobs are scarce or of low-quality. Cajou Espoir, for example, has created more than 700 new jobs in Togo. Frustrated by the lack of job opportunities, especially for women, founders Francois Locoh-Donou and Maurice Edorh created a business that employs the women who used to cross the border to find work in Nigeria or Benin. The average incomes for these women are now between $70 and $150 per month, which is several times higher than those previous wages.[11]

Successful entrepreneurship also brings new product and service solutions to customers. In rural India, several million people with limited or no access to electricity rely on kerosene and other fuels, which are expensive and dangerous on many levels. Although distributed solar solutions were available, few of the poorest households could afford the upfront costs of installing these systems. Simpa Networks developed their solar offering as a service model, which allows households to pay in small installments using cellphones. With this innovation, many more Indians benefit from clean, safe, and reliable electricity.

Finally, consider the broader benefits for society and the planet. When impact-oriented entrepreneurs go beyond the simple goals of cost minimization plus revenue maximization, their companies join a growing movement that is changing the status quo of businesses as purely profit-maximizing endeavors. And, they end up with companies that restore or replenish valuable human, societal, and environmental resources. In this way, they do more than provide employment, health services, and electricity in a financially sustainable manner. The also enact a fundamental respect for the environment and its resources, while making the ideals of decency and equity more tangible and actionable.

The layered benefits that come from productive entrepreneurial processes require passionate entrepreneurs with promising ideas. However, it takes much more than this. Entrepreneurial potential is often left unrealized due to the many obstacles that early-stage ventures confront. These include gaps in their founders' understanding of markets or basic business functions, a lack of robust market connections, and a paucity of appropriate early-stage finance. When entrepreneurial support processes work, the best entrepreneurs are able to identify and close these knowledge, network, and capital gaps as they transform their ideas into successful companies. Unfortunately, the entrepreneurial ecosystems that provide this support are not working for too many entrepreneurs working on too many problems in too many places.[12]

Actors in the Entrepreneurial Ecosystem

This term—the entrepreneurial ecosystem—is attracting more attention as policy-makers come to realize that the root problem when it comes to stimulating more productive entrepreneurial outcomes relates less to the supply of promising entrepreneurs and more to the context in which they work.[13] Borrowing from the ecological metaphor,[14] entrepreneurial ecosystems are broadly described as a 'set of interdependent actors and factors coordinated in such a way that they enable productive entrepreneurship within a particular territory.'[15] According to researchers at Endeavor Insight, the ecosystem 'describes the way individuals, companies, organizations, and governments interact to influence the development of entrepreneurs and their firms in a single metropolitan area or region.'[16] What benefits do some of these ecosystems provide to entrepreneurs? According to one broad survey, there are three critical factors: providing access to customers and markets, access to human capital workforce support, and access to early-stage finance.[17]

At one point, the world was obsessed about learning from the small number of high-profile ecosystems that do a very good job converting entrepreneurial potential into productive economic outcomes. This produced a spate of advice about the things that must be done to make any region 'more like Silicon Valley.'[18] More recently, researchers have been looking more closely at the less robust ecosystems that characterize entrepreneurial dead spaces. Instead of painting abstract pictures of what other ecosystems look like, these observations show how banks and other lenders can be reluctant to support early-stage entrepreneurs, making debt financing either unavailable or unaffordable[19]; how equity investment is more difficult to obtain in regions with underdeveloped angel and venture capital networks[20]; and how grant funding might—or might not—surrogate for limited debt and equity financing and how its supply is still too low to cover current financing needs.[21] Looking beyond the many issues that relate to capital access, these observations also show how many ecosystems lack established networks of mentors, customers, and other key supporters.

By focusing on these specific problem areas, various individuals and organizations are developing initiatives to augment problematic ecosystems. For example, impact investors and venture philanthropists are stepping up their investments.[22] Philanthropic organizations and new venture capital funds are making better cases for investing in marginalized regions[23] and underestimated entrepreneurs.[24] However, we propose that the most critical of these ecosystem interventions is the impact-oriented accelerator. To stimulate entrepreneurial dead spaces, local ecosystems must help to close knowledge and network gaps so that investment funds can flow to the most promising entrepreneurs and ideas. This is exactly what accelerators were invented to do; and this is what we are asking them to do in underdeveloped ecosystems.

A Brief History of Accelerators

Accelerators arrived on the scene with the launch of Y Combinator in 2005. Since that time, the model has proliferated, with programs spreading across North America and Europe and into Africa, Asia, and Latin America. In reality, the accelerator construct subsumes three different approaches to supporting early-stage entrepreneurs.[25] Private seed accelerators (e.g., Y Combinator) are the most widely known and are oriented to investors with the goal of identifying attractive investment opportunities. According to its founder, Y Combinator was set up to address the chaotic way that seed funding was organized. In the early 2000s, there was limited expertise on either the investor or the founder side of the table, and there were no standardized vehicles for identifying and screening investment opportunities. Since running its initial 'Summer Founders Program,' Y Combinator has evolved into an organizational platform that provides cohort-based mentoring and investment facilitation. These private seed accelerators tend to offer programming plus small amounts of seed capital in exchange for equity stakes in participating ventures. Because they are primarily motivated by the potential returns on these investments, they often favor more mature ventures that work in sectors with relatively high expected profits.[26]

While private seed accelerators focus on technology-sector startups, other organizations have borrowed elements of the accelerator model and adapted them to different purposes. Corporate accelerators, like those operated by Microsoft, Nike, and Barclays, are funded by established companies with the goals of (1) finding innovative products and services, while (2) rejuvenating stagnant corporate cultures by sourcing new entrepreneurial talent.[27]

Although a few private seed and corporate accelerators are mentioned in this book, the third category of accelerators is much more prominent. Impact-oriented accelerators, like Bethnal Green Ventures in England, want to stimulate startup activity because of their underlying interest in economic development. Some of these accelerators work with marginalized entrepreneurs (e.g., women or minorities), some of them work in marginalized cities, countries or regions, and some of them work with entrepreneurs who tackle societal challenges in sectors like agriculture, education, energy, or healthcare. Although they might make equity investments in participating ventures, their main objective is not that of maximizing the financial return on these investments. Instead, they cherish their primary roles as ecosystem builders. As Ross Baird, founder and president of Village Capital, explains, 'entrepreneur support organizations may never be 'revenue-sustainable' in a traditional sense.

That's actually OK! These organizations, when effective, are critical infrastructure for a city or a community, and should be treated as such.'[28]

When they work, impact-oriented accelerators become critical components of underdeveloped ecosystems. In many cases, they are the first and best source of support for their targeted entrepreneurs. Consider Endeavor, which supports high-growth and therefore high-impact entrepreneurship in emerging markets around the world. Endeavor sets up in countries—and more recently cities and regions—with relatively stable macroeconomic growth, but with identifiable barriers to productive entrepreneurial activity. Recognizing the network foundation of their work, Endeavor begins by recruiting five to ten prominent local business leaders who secure the requisite funding while seeding the local mentor network. Participating entrepreneurs, who are selected based on their potential for growth, receive customized support from the Endeavor network. These advisors and mentors help entrepreneurs prepare for growth and then ensure that the requisite investment capital is available to support that growth. As success stories accumulate, Endeavor highlights their alumni as role models, which further stimulates the local entrepreneurial ecosystems.

While people will disagree at the margins, the current wave of accelerators is generally considered to be characterized by three criteria:

- They are cohort-based, typically working with 8 to 15 promising ventures at one time.
- They are time-bound, typically working in periods of three to six months.
- They aspire to connect entrepreneurs with potential investors, typically by offering direct investments and/or hosting pitch nights or demo days.

However, beyond these three definitional criteria, there is considerable programmatic diversity. Some of this relates to how accelerators identify potential program participants. Most accelerators have open applications that involve written applications and interviews. However, as we will see in Chaps. 6 and 7, they make different decisions that influence the size and composition of their applicant pools and their final cohorts. Most accelerators do their work during fixed periods of time. However, they vary in terms of how well they facilitate peer-to-peer engagement and collaboration. They also vary in terms of the specific materials they cover, as well as how (and how well) they make use of mentors. Finally, some, but not all, accelerators provide direct funding to at least some of their entrepreneurs, typically in the form of grants or in exchange for equity. These programmatic differences, and their effects on program effectiveness, are taken up in Chap. 8.

Keeping Track of Accelerators

Since accelerators first arrived on the scene, the number of programs that work around the world has increased dramatically. Estimates of the exact numbers vary widely. According to a recent review article, 'the number of accelerators range[s] from 300+ to over 3,000.'[29] The imprecision of this estimate reflects two challenges associated with identifying accelerators. First, online platforms like F6S and GUST,[30] which tend to produce the largest estimates, allow organizations to self-identify as accelerators and then develop profiles that remain unverified. Many of these organizations do not run programs that have all three of the defining features of accelerators—that is, cohort-based models, time-bound programming, and investment facilitation—but still self-identify as accelerators due to the current hype surrounding the term.[31] Second, many accelerators are run by new organizations that are still working out their many kinks. Because of the well-documented liabilities of newness, many of these organizations run a few programs before folding or simply disappearing.

To appreciate the rapid diffusion of the accelerator model, we must consider the many past efforts to stimulate entrepreneurship, including incubators.[32] According to the National Business Incubation Association, the first incubator was started in 1959 by an egg farmer in Batavia, New York who set up a shared office facility called the Batavia Industrial Complex.[33] From this early experiment, incubators took off, especially in the late 1990s and early 2000s. Current estimates suggest that there are as many as 3000 incubators working around the world.[34] Incubators support startups by providing shared office space, shared business and administrative services, and some educational programming.[35] Some of them also partner with universities and other organizations to provide additional resources like laboratories, maker-spaces, and faculty advisors. Although incubators have been studied extensively, evidence on their efficacy remains mixed. Some studies that emphasize job creation or revenue growth suggest positive, but modest effects.[36] Another study finds marginal benefits when it comes to survival rates.[37]

Accelerators are similar to incubators in their objectives and basic offerings, but differ in several key respects. At the most general level, incubators try to buffer startups from their external environments so they have the time and space to think as they grow. Accelerators tend to intensify these market interactions, encouraging early-stage ventures to engage with potential customers, mentors, and investors.

To our knowledge, GALI represents the most systematic effort to map the global landscape of impact-oriented accelerators using structured criteria and search processes. Potential accelerators are identified through primary and secondary sources by members of the GALI team. This involves online searches plus lists procured from other organizations, including Enclude, F6S, the Global Accelerator Network, Nesta, and Seed-DB. These are supplemented with additional leads gleaned from government agencies, donors that focus on entrepreneurial support programs, and impact investors. Finally, the various individuals affiliated with the ANDE regional chapters in India, Brazil, Central America and Mexico, West Africa, East Africa, and South Africa are asked to identify other organizations that run smaller programs that are not yet on the global radar. These efforts produce a preliminary roster of more than 1000 organizations that run what at least one person calls an accelerator. This roster goes beyond the most prominent organizations to include programs that are critical from a local economic development perspective even if they have not yet received wider recognition.

After casting this wide net, the GALI researchers review the websites and social media of each organization to determine if it is still operational, and whether its programs meet the three criteria outlined above. The organizations that pass these screens are included in the Accelerator Directory published on the GALI website.[38] Figure 2.1 shows the most recent distribution of accelerators working in various regions around the world.[39]

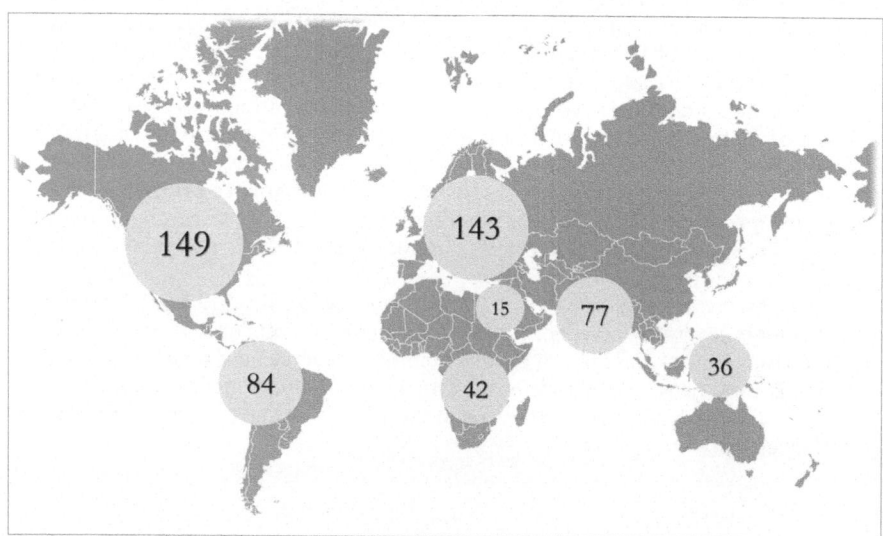

Fig. 2.1 Accelerator programs in the GALI database

Managers from each of these organizations receive surveys asking basic questions about their programs, including questions related to program structure (e.g., program duration) and the types of support provided (e.g., financial support or investor connections). The GALI survey also includes questions about how the accelerator work is organized and funded (i.e., the organization's legal structure and main funding sources). The following observations are based on responses from 164 organizations that run accelerators.[40] Roughly half of these organizations are headquartered in an emerging market, and roughly half of them report having the explicit intention of working with impact-oriented entrepreneurs. This gives us a broad perspective on the global accelerator landscape.

The Global Accelerator Landscape

Consistent with the above summary of the global accelerator movement, accelerators are a relatively recent phenomenon. The majority of organizations that responded to the most recent GALI survey launched their first accelerator on or after 2010, with more than half launching since 2014 (see Fig. 2.2).

Table 2.1 shows that roughly 60 percent of these organizations focus on a particular sector or set of sectors, with the most common sectors being healthcare and life sciences, agriculture and food, and information and communication technology (ICT). In emerging markets, roughly 30 percent (each) focus on healthcare and agriculture. However, these two sectors are also prominent among the dedicated accelerators that run in high-income countries. Programs that focus on water and sanitation (+16 percent), the environment (+10 percent), and energy (+10 percent) are relatively more common in emerging markets than in high-income countries.

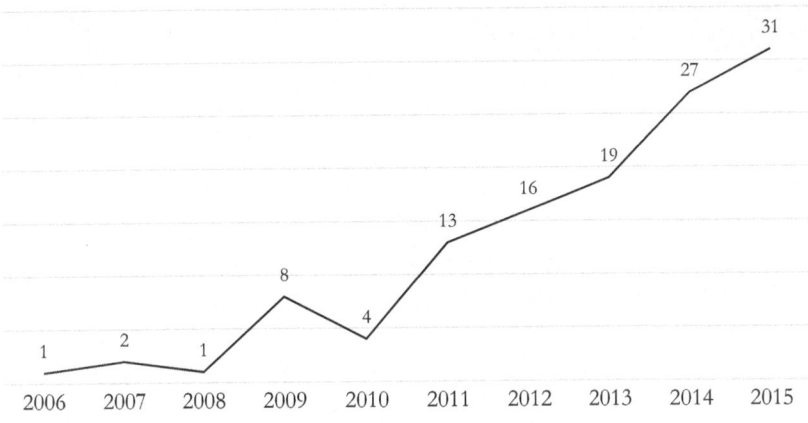

Fig. 2.2   New accelerators in the GALI directory by founding year

Table 2.1 Sector focus for GALI accelerators

	Based in a high-income country	Based in an emerging market
Agriculture and food	23.0%	27.0%
Business services	10.0%	10.0%
Consumer/retail	14.0%	13.0%
Education	12.0%	14.0%
Energy	13.0%	23.0%
Environment	10.0%	20.0%
Financial services	17.0%	16.0%
Health/life sciences	22.0%	29.0%
Hospitality/travel/tourism	8.0%	6.0%
Information and communication technology	17.0%	26.0%
Logistics and distribution	6.0%	10.0%
Media and entertainment	9.0%	7.0%
Real estate	1.0%	0.0%
Water and sanitation	4.0%	20.0%
Other	19.0%	19.0%
No sector focus	37.0%	43.0%

Most accelerators in the GALI sample (roughly 62 percent) run programs that are between 3 and 6 months in duration, with the remainder running programs that last from 1 to 3 months, or 6 to 12 months. In-person programs are the most common (62 percent), although roughly one-third of the sample provides some combination of in-person and virtual-support programming. The median acceptance rate for the various accelerators is roughly 10 percent, although impact-oriented programs have higher acceptance rates (15 percent) compared to those that are not explicitly impact-oriented (8 percent). Nonetheless, when compared to other types of entrepreneurship support programming, such as incubators and business plan competitions, all of these accelerators are highly selective.[41]

We alluded to the fact that governments, donors, and foundations are pouring funds into accelerators, especially those that focus on impact-oriented and emerging-market ventures. The GALI survey supports this notion. Roughly 60 percent of the sampled accelerators report that they rely on two or more funding sources to support their operations. To examine funding sources more closely, the GALI surveys ask each accelerator to identify its main funding source (i.e., one source that covers more than 50 percent of total expenditures). Figure 2.3 shows that roughly 20 percent of the accelerators in the sample rely primarily on corporate support, with similar percentages leaning on philanthropic and government sources. The incidence of corporate support is much higher for programs that run in high-income countries. Only 16 percent of the accelerators in the sample rely primarily on investors to finance their operations.

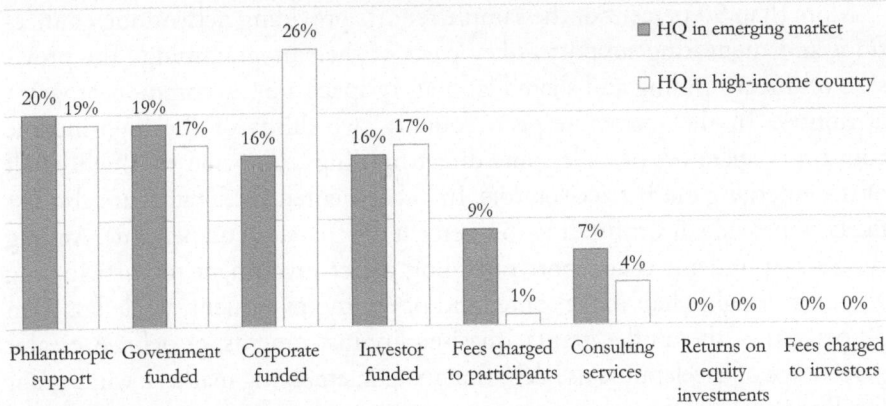

Fig. 2.3 Primary funding sources for GALI accelerators

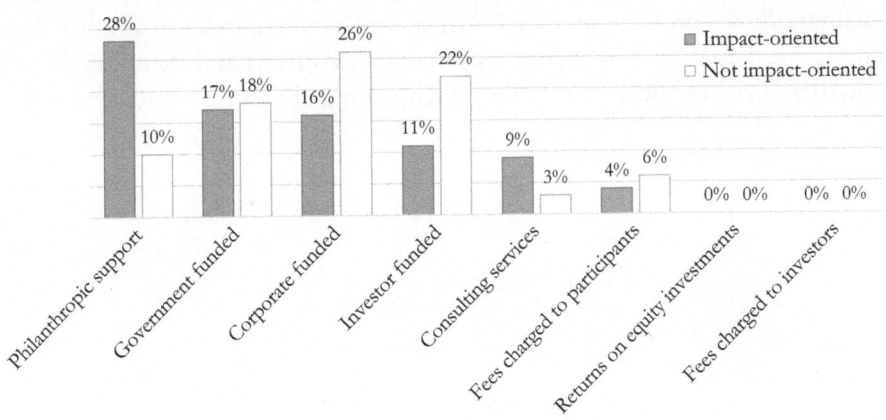

Fig. 2.4 Primary funding sources for GALI accelerators

Importantly, none of the programs rely on funds from prior equity investments as their primary source of income; though about 6 percent of the sample reports having this as a minor source of revenue.[42]

There are important differences in the funding structures for impact-oriented accelerators compared to those that are impact-agnostic (see Fig. 2.4). Understandably, the impact-oriented accelerators have greater reliance on philanthropic funders (28 percent compared to 10 percent). On the other hand, accelerators that do not target impact-oriented entrepreneurs rely more on corporate funding (26 percent compared to 16 percent) and are more likely to be investor-funded (22 percent compared to 11 percent). It is interesting that a similar percentage of impact-oriented and impact-agnostic accelerators rely on government funding as their primary means of support (just under 20 percent in both cases).

More than 90 percent of the sample reports providing networking connections and mentoring support as key parts of their programming. The provision of direct funding and shared laboratory space are less common program attributes. In the former respect, roughly two-thirds of the high-income country accelerators provide some direct funding, compared to roughly half of the emerging market accelerators. Impact-oriented accelerators are also less likely to provide direct funding (51 percent compared to 62 percent). Among the 91 respondents that report providing direct investment to participating ventures, roughly half make some kind of equity investment, while less than 30 percent of them offer grants, quasi-equity instruments, or debt. A greater percentage of accelerators use debt financing in emerging markets, while grant funding is more common among impact-oriented accelerators.

Finally, because one of the defining objectives for accelerators is to connect entrepreneurs to potential investors, we look to see how these organizations facilitate these connections. The GALI survey asks respondents whether they emphasize large investor events, such as pitch contests and demo days, and whether they rely on one-on-one matchmaking. Figure 2.5 provides a few

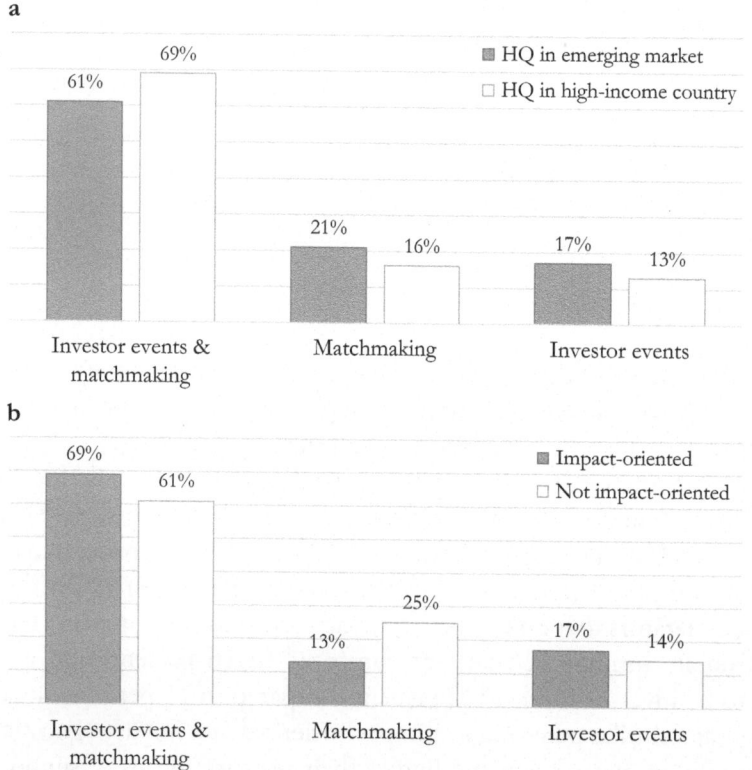

Fig. 2.5 Investor engagement approaches in **(a)** emerging markets and **(b)** impact-oriented programs

interesting observations. Among the 142 respondents that offer access to investors as a service for participating entrepreneurs, roughly two-thirds facilitate these connections using both investor events and one-on-one matchmaking. However, comparing the high-income country accelerators to those in emerging markets, a higher percentage of emerging-market accelerators rely solely on one-on-one matchmaking. There is an opposite skew among the impact-oriented accelerators, with a smaller percentage relying solely on one-on-one matchmaking.

Concluding Remarks

Accelerators have become important fixtures in established and emerging entrepreneurial ecosystems around the world. In the former case, private seed and corporate accelerators work to find and support the promising entrepreneurs who will eventually make attractive additions to investment portfolios or company product and service offerings. In the latter case, impact-oriented accelerators work to find and support the promising entrepreneurs who will eventually produce the economic, social, and environmental benefits that are lacking in places where ecosystems falter.

The tremendous growth in the number of accelerators around the world underscores the importance of this effort to document the scale and scope of the phenomenon, and to understand the specific effects of acceleration on early-stage ventures. The potential for impact-oriented accelerators to produce benefits for entrepreneurs and investors, and for the sectors and regions in which they operate, makes it doubly important to understand their efficacy.

In the following chapters, we move from describing the global landscape of accelerators to a more fine-grained description of how we evaluate and then unpack the accelerator model. As you will see, the fundamental question of whether acceleration works quickly morphs into a series of more nuanced questions of whether and when they are worth the considerable investments of public and private support that they receive.

Looking Ahead: A First Look at the EDP Data

Chapter 1 made the case for the role that accelerators can play when it comes to fortifying the links between entrepreneurship and genuinely broad-based economic development. This latter qualifier means encouraging and supporting entrepreneurs who move beyond a singular fascination with generating captured financial wealth for themselves and their investors. It also means finding and supporting those promising-but-marginalized entrepreneurs, and those who work in neglected regions. Chapter 2 doubled down on these claims by describing the landscape of action and thought when it comes to entrepreneur acceleration. The numbers of accelerator programs are expanding in regions and sectors around the world, and many of these accelerators focus on early-stage ventures that aspire to generate scalable societal impacts. At the same time, the (admittedly limited) academic and practitioner research gives many reasons to believe that these programs can provide promising launch pads for aspiring impact-oriented entrepreneurs, especially those working in challenging ecosystems and those facing biases and barriers that have nothing to do with the underlying quality of their ideas and companies.

These two chapters revisit ground that has already been covered by summarizing the widespread faith in the economic and societal benefits of entrepreneur acceleration. This faith motivates the considerable time, effort, and money that are being spent on accelerator programs. However, it does not provide the evidence required to sustain these investments. This leads to the main purpose of this book; to leverage accumulating quantitative data plus qualitative insights to assess whether the current faith in entrepreneur acceleration as a tool for broad-based economic development is justified. This assessment begins by tackling the main question: Do accelerated ventures demonstrate higher growth rates on key variables during the year in which their programs run?

The next part of the book—which houses Chaps. 3 and 4—provides a series of observations describing thousands of entrepreneurs and ventures that applied to, and in some cases participated in, scores of impact-oriented accelerators working around the world. After describing an ambitious data-collection effort that spans multiple countries and several years (Chap. 3), Chap. 4 presents consistent, albeit preliminary, evidence that accelerator program participation is associated with elevated short-term revenue, employment, and investment growth. While these associations and correlations will not satisfy researchers who seek definitive proof that accelerator program participation causes improved entrepreneurial outcomes, they do provide an optimistic foundation from which further program experimentation and additional research projects can develop.

These observations also provide the foundation to explore, in greater detail, the specific program design choices that correspond with elevated accelerator effects (Chaps. 5 through 8). They also set the stage for more specific analyses that look at the implications of launching and accelerating impact-oriented ventures in emerging markets (Chap. 9), and the role that accelerators play when it comes to overcoming the additional, unnecessary challenges faced by women-led businesses (Chap. 10).

Notes

1. Joseph Alois Schumpeter. 1942. *Socialism, Capitalism and Democracy.* Harper and Brothers.
2. Ernst Friedrich Schuhmacher. 1973. *Small is Beautiful: A Study of Economics as if People Mattered.* Blond & Briggs.
3. See www.whysgbs.org/sgbsinaction
4. See http://simpanetworks.com/
5. See http://www.microclinictech.com/
6. See http://firststepstaffing.com/
7. US Homeless People Numbers Rise for First Time in Seven Years. *BBC News* (December 2017).
8. Wim Naudé. 2010. *Entrepreneurship and Economic Development.* Springer.
9. The Importance of Young Firms for Economic Growth. *The Kauffman Foundation Entrepreneurship Policy Digest* (September 2015).
10. Meghana Ayyagari, Asli Demirguc-Kunt & Vojislav Maksimovic. 2014. 'Who creates jobs in developing countries?' *Small Business Economics,* 43(1), 75–99.
11. See https://www.forbes.com/sites/willyfoote/2013/06/26/cracking-the-nut-on-jobs-qa-with-a-togolese-social-entrepreneur/#14937b7a1989
12. Ross Baird. 2017. *The Innovation Blind Spot: Why We Back the Wrong Ideas—and What to Do About It.* BenBella Books.
13. Entrepreneurial Ecosystem Diagnostic Toolkit. Aspen Network of Development Entrepreneurs (December 2013).
14. Paul N. Bloom & J. Gregory Dees. 2008. 'Cultivate your ecosystem.' *Stanford Social Innovation Review* (Winter 2008).
15. Erik Stam & Ben Spigel. 2017. 'Entrepreneurial ecosystems.' in R. Blackburn, D. De Clercq, J. Heinonen, & Z. Wang (Eds.), *The SAGE Handbook of Small Business and Entrepreneurship.* London: SAGE.
16. The First Thing You Need to Know About Entrepreneurship Ecosystems. *Endeavor Insight* (July 2015).
17. Entrepreneurial Ecosystems Around the Globe and Early-Stage Company Growth Dynamics. *World Economic Forum* (January 2014).
18. How to Create a Sustainable Business Ecosystem 101. *Endeavor Insight.*
19. Paul Robson, Charles Akuetteh, Ian Stone, Paul Westhead & Mike Wright. 2013. 'Credit-rationing and entrepreneurial experience: Evidence from a resource deficit context.' *Entrepreneurship and Regional Development,* 25(5–6): 349–370.
20. Garry Bruton, Susanna Khavul, Donald Siegel & Mike Wright. 2015. 'New financial alternatives in seeding entrepreneurship: Microfinance, crowdfunding, and peer-to-peer innovations.' *Entrepreneurship Theory and Practice,* 39(1): 9–26.

21. Andrew Rogerson, Shelagh Whitley, Emily Darko & Gideon Rabinowitz. Why and How Are Donors Supporting Social Enterprises. *Overseas Development Institute* (April 2014).

22. *Venture Philanthropists and Impact Investors: Sharing Collaboration Successes and Challenges*. Toniic Institute & Shell Foundation (2016).

23. See https://www.revolution.com/entity/rotr/

24. Amy Cortese. Arlan Hamilton: The VC Taking Cold Calls from Underestimated Entrepreneurs. *ImpactAlpha* (January 2018).

25. C. Scott Dempwolf, Jennifer Auer & Michelle D'Ippolito. 2014. *Innovation Accelerators: Defining Characteristics among Startup Assistance Organizations.* Small Business Administration.

26. Charlotte Pauwels, Bart Clarysse, Mike Wright & Jonas Van Hove. 2016. 'Understanding a new generation incubation model: The accelerator.' *Technovation*, 50: 13–24.

27. Thomas Kohler. 2016. 'Corporate accelerators: Building bridges between corporations and startups.' *Business Horizons*, 59(3): 347–357.

28. Ross Baird (2017). How you can help the entrepreneurs you care about succeed: Lessons from 26 Communities worldwide. *Medium* (April 2017).

29. Yael V. Hochberg. 2016. 'Accelerating entrepreneurs and ecosystems: The seed accelerator model.' *Innovation Policy and the Economy*, Volume 16.

30. See http://www.f6s.com/ and https://gust.com/

31. Daniel C. Fehder & Yael V. Hochberg. 2015. Accelerators and the Regional Supply of Venture Capital Investment. Working paper.

32. Sean M. Hackett & David M. Dilts. 2004. 'A systematic review of business incubation research.' *The Journal of Technology Transfer*, 29(1): 55–82.

33. Justin Peters. How a 1950s Egg Farm Hatched the Modern Startup Incubator. *Wired* (June 2017).

34. Eric Stokan, Lyke Thompson & Robert J. Mahu. 2015. 'Testing the differential effect of business incubators on firm growth.' *Economic Development Quarterly*, 29(4): 317–327.

35. Rustam Lalkaka. 1996. 'Technology business incubators: critical determinants of success.' *Annals of the New York Academy of Sciences*, 798(1): 270–290.

36. Frank T. Rothaermel & Marie Thursby. 2005. 'University–incubator firm knowledge flows: assessing their impact on incubator firm performance.' *Research Policy*, 34(3): 305–320.

37. Alejandro S. Amezcua, Matthew G. Grimes, Steven W. Bradley & Johan Wiklund. 2013. 'Organizational sponsorship and founding environments: a contingency view on the survival of business-incubated firms, 1994–2007.' *Academy of Management Journal*, 56(6): 1628–1654; Eric Stokan, Lyke Thompson & Robert J. Mahu. 2015. 'Testing the differential effect of business incubators on firm growth.' *Economic Development Quarterly*, 29(4): 317–327.

38. See https://www.galidata.org/accelerators/directory/
39. Figure 2.1 underestimates the true count of accelerators because new organizations are emerging all the time. Also, the GALI research efforts are constrained by language barriers and so their numbers probably underestimate the number of organizations working in East Asia (and some other regions).
40. Many of the organizations in the GALI sample run multiple programs. However, the GALI survey is administered at the organization level and asks questions about the accelerator programs as a whole.
41. C. Scott Dempwolf, Jennifer Auer & Michelle D'Ippolito. 2014. *Innovation Accelerators: Defining Characteristics among Startup Assistance Organizations.* Small Business Administration.
42. There are some interesting funding differences when it comes to emerging-market accelerators. On average, the organizations that run accelerators from headquarters in high-income countries rely more on corporate funding. On the other hand, emerging-market programs rely slightly more on philanthropic and government support. Emerging-market accelerators also rely more on fees paid by participating ventures (9 percent compared to 1 percent of the high-income country accelerators) and on consulting services (7 percent compared to 4 percent the high-income country accelerators) as their primary source of income.

3

The EDP Data

To expand the societal benefits that flow from market-based activity, more promising early-stage ventures must be encouraged to grow, especially those with explicit social or environmental aspirations, those working in marginalized regions around the world, and those established by otherwise-marginalized entrepreneurs. As we argued in Chaps. 1 and 2, an expanding global population of accelerator programs is working to figure out how to realize the collective benefits provided by these promising entrepreneurs and ventures. The challenge for this book is to provide a systematic examination of the effects that these accelerators have on the entrepreneurs whose ventures are accepted for participation. This requires detailed data describing a range of accelerators, as well as the ventures that show up in their application pools and in their program cohorts.

Almost ten years ago, Short, Moss, and Lumpkin (2009) highlighted the importance of collecting and analyzing data from larger samples of ventures in order to gain a better appreciation of the cause-and-effect relationships that govern impact-oriented entrepreneurship.[1] Unfortunately, while considerable investments of time and money have produced a wide array of programmatic efforts, there has been little in the way of systematic research that tackles questions about what does and does not work when it comes to entrepreneur acceleration.[2] This paucity of research is due, in large part, to a lack of appropriate data.

This is not the same as saying that there are no excellent databases that focus on entrepreneurs. For instance, the World Bank's Doing Business program gathered information on the counts of newly registered companies across a range of countries between 2010 and 2016.[3] These data indicate that almost three million new businesses were registered in South Africa over the

© The Author(s) 2019
P. W. Roberts, S. A. Lall, *Observing Acceleration*,
https://doi.org/10.1007/978-3-030-00042-4_3

11-year period. Roughly 30 percent of the almost 300,000 new limited-liability companies registered in Mexico in 2016 were owned by women. However, these aggregate count data cannot help us understand whether and how entrepreneur support programs like accelerators influence the growth rate of new companies, or whether they are more or less effective in certain countries (e.g., South Africa and Mexico) or for certain groups of entrepreneurs (e.g., women).

The Global Entrepreneurship Monitor (GEM) is another program that collects data describing entrepreneurial activity in more than 100 different countries.[4] For almost 20 years, the GEM has reported on individuals' entrepreneurial behaviors and attitudes, as well as a range of variables that describe the country contexts that might influence them. While GEM data support a number of research papers,[5] they lack the specificity and structure to shine light on the possible effects that accelerator programs have on early-stage entrepreneurs and ventures.

The Kauffman Firm Survey (KFS) is a firm-level database that tracked a representative sample of almost 5000 American companies founded in 2004.[6] Because the KFS is a longitudinal database that captures specific annual information about early-stage companies, it has produced a number of research papers that look at the effects of specific variables (e.g., founders' education levels and gender) on different firm-level outcomes (e.g., growth and investment).[7] However, while the KFS does capture whether a new business received any assistance from the Small Business Association, federal, state, or local governments, other nonprofit or for-profit organizations, colleges or universities, or the chamber of commerce, the data do not indicate whether the focal company sought out or participated in a specific entrepreneur support program, like an accelerator.

Calibrating the effects that accelerators have on impact-oriented ventures requires consistent longitudinal data that track key variables—like revenues, employees, and investment—beginning at least one year prior to the launch of each program. These data must cover all or most of the participating ventures, and not just a handful of obviously successful companies. They must also cover ventures that apply to programs but are rejected during selection processes. Most importantly, these data must come from a large number of accelerators working with a range of ventures and entrepreneurs in different parts of the world. This latter requirement moves us past anecdotal and small-sample evidence toward the more systematic evidence that entrepreneurs, program managers, and program funders require to justify their current and future efforts.

Fortunately, the number of accelerators that are working in what we have called entrepreneurial dead spaces is literally exploding. According to the most recent information on the GALI website, more than 500 organizations now run entrepreneur support programs that fit our description of accelerators.[8] Some of these programs follow the seed investor approach adopted by Y Combinator and support themselves with the returns on investments made in previous cohort ventures. However, as noted in Chap. 2, almost 70 percent of the programs receive funding from corporations, foundations, and governments to cover their costs. For example, Endeavor received roughly $11.7 million worth of philanthropic support in 2008—roughly 97 percent of its total revenues—to run accelerator programs in 12 countries.[9] According to its 990 filing for 2014, Village Capital received more than $1.7 million worth of tax-deductible contributions—almost all of its annual budget—to run multiple programs around the world.[10] An examination of their website suggests that the Points of Light Civic Accelerator receives support from at least eight major sponsors, including the PWC Charitable Foundation and Starbucks, to run its US-based programs.[11]

This reliance on public and philanthropic funding has implications for why and how we assess accelerator program effectiveness. Impact-oriented accelerators that are funded by grants and donations typically need to make structured cases to funders that their efforts are generating the intended effects. Public and philanthropic supporters need this evidence to defend their use of scarce programmatic dollars. This means tracking the entrepreneurs and ventures that participate in funded programs, which requires a commitment to collect preprogram data and to follow up with all participants after program completion. Because funders also want to see evidence of the incremental effects of acceleration relative to some valid base case, this also means collecting pre- and post-program data from the entrepreneurs who applied to programs but were not selected. Finally, funders eventually want to probe beneath the simple 'yes-or-no' question about accelerator effectiveness and ascertain whether they are spending their resources in an efficient manner. This means collecting program-level information about operating costs, as well as information describing the various programmatic choices.

The EDP at Emory University

The EDP at Emory University was launched in early 2013 to support research into the cause-and-effect relationships that relate to accelerating impact-oriented ventures. This multi-year data-collection effort, which is part of GALI, partners with accelerators that operate in various countries around the world (see Fig. 3.1).[12]

Number of Programs

● >35

● 11-15

● 6-10

· ≤5

Fig. 3.1 EDP accelerators, 2013–2016

The EDP is best described with reference to its three key features. The first is a standardized set of core questions that every participating accelerator program asks as part of its application processes. These core questions were developed and then revised based on feedback from initial partner programs and interested university researchers. To ensure comparability with other datasets that describe entrepreneurs and impact-oriented ventures, the application questions were also designed to maximize consistency with questions that are asked and validated in the KFS and in the Impact Reporting Investment Standards (IRIS) program.[13] The EDP application survey consists of roughly 50 questions that cover the following areas (Appendix 1 houses the full set of application questions):

- Basic venture information (e.g., headquarters location and year founded)
- Information about the business model (e.g., operational model, primary clients, and possession/use of technology)
- Information about the venture's goals and targeted social impacts
- Basic financial and operational information (e.g., revenues, profit margins, and employees)
- Information about current venture financing (e.g., equity, debt, and philanthropic investments)
- Information about the use of impact metrics (e.g., IRIS or B Lab)
- Founders' demographics and career backgrounds
- Experiences with and expectations of accelerator programs

The second feature is that partnering accelerators embed these questions into their application processes. Because it is not viewed as a separate survey, the EDP is able to leverage the time that entrepreneurs already spend completing their applications. This greatly increases their responsiveness and allows us to observe (close to) the entire pool of applicants. While addressing the selection and program assessment needs of these partners, the data accumulate to provide comparable information about thousands of entrepreneurs applying to scores of accelerators around the world.

When application and selection processes are complete, program managers record whether each applicant is selected to participate in the program and then transmits this information to the EDP team. For several reasons, gathering comparable application data from both accepted and rejected ventures is a critical feature of the EDP. First, rejected entrepreneurs represent a majority of the entrepreneurs that enter into the database. While acceptance rates vary across programs (a topic explored in Chap. 6), there are almost 10 times more applicants than accepted entrepreneurs. Second, rejected ventures provide an important counterfactual group when assessing the effects of an accelerator program or program attribute; that is, the other entrepreneurs who seek comparable acceleration services. Finally, because applicants have not yet been winnowed out during the various selection processes (a topic explored in Chap. 7), the full applicant pool is more representative of the underlying population of entrepreneurs seeking acceleration services in the targeted geographies or sectors.

The third feature of the EDP is that it tries to collect follow-up data from every entrepreneur who applies to a participating program. In every year following each application window, participating and rejected entrepreneurs are surveyed to capture follow-up information on several key variables (Appendix 2 houses the full set of follow-up questions). These follow-up surveys are administered in February–March, and then again in August–September to pick up additional non-respondents. Because the EDP relies on the support of partner program managers and on the goodwill created during each program, follow-up response rates are relatively high among the entrepreneurs who participate in programs; roughly 72 percent across programs whose applications opened during the 2013–2016 window. This compares to a response rate of roughly 48 percent for rejected entrepreneurs. The overall response rate for these first-year follow-up surveys is 51 percent.

Current Status of the EDP Database

In the middle of 2012, a retrospective pilot survey was developed and adminis-tered to entrepreneurs who applied to one of several Village Capital accelerator programs. Following this initial learning exercise, the EDP formally launched in the middle of 2013 and then quickly expanded (see Fig. 3.2). Growth in the number of partnering organizations and programs was fueled by the services that the EDP offers to its accelerator partners, including detailed reports that describe applicant pools and then compare them to global benchmarks, as well as summaries of what applicants are looking for in their preferred accelerator programs. Partners also receive reports comparing selected versus rejected entre-preneurs, both initially and over time. These latter offerings, which are program-level variants of the analyses presented in Chap. 4, help EDP partners observe and demonstrate where their programs actually make a difference.[14]

The venture-level data used in this book start with every applicant to an EDP partner accelerator that opened applications between 2013 and 2016. Programs with fewer than ten applications are set aside. Because the primary focus is on the implications of accelerator program participation, we also set aside accelera-tors that did not provide their selection information to the EDP, and those for which sufficient data were not collected from both rejected and participating ventures. Finally, we set aside programs that accept entrepreneurs on a rolling basis throughout the year. The remaining entrepreneurs applied to accelerators run by 30 different organizations. Twenty-nine programs were run by Village Capital in various regions and sectors around the world; seven were run by Points of Light in the United States; and four were run by the Unreasonable Institute in Mexico, Uganda, and the United States (see Table 3.1).

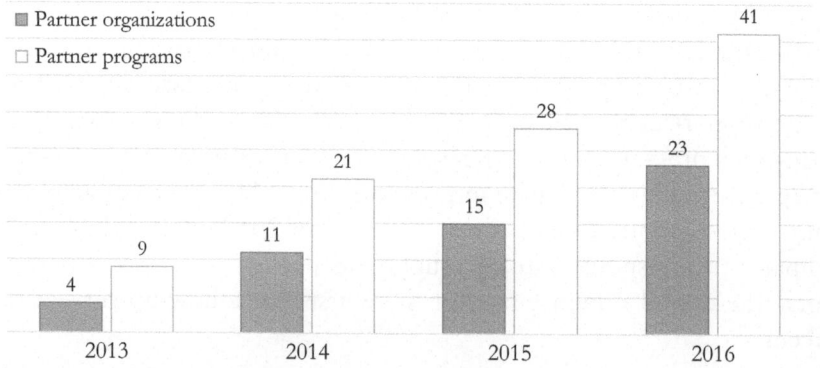

Fig. 3.2 EDP partner organizations and programs, 2013–2016

Table 3.1 EDP partner organizations with 2+ programs, 2013–2016

	Programs run in
Agora Partnerships	Latin America and Caribbean
GrowthAfrica	Kenya and Ethiopia
Impact 8	Canada
IMPAQTO	Ecuador
New Ventures Group	Latin America and Caribbean
Points of Light	United States
Propeller	United States
Startup Cup	Kenya and Zambia
University of South Florida	United States
Unreasonable Institute	Uganda, Mexico, and United States
USADF	Sub-Saharan Africa
Village Capital	India, Kenya, Mexico, Netherlands, South Africa, Sub-Saharan Africa, and United States
Yunus Social Business	Colombia and Uganda

Most of the observations in this book rely on simple t-tests and cross-tabulations. There are also several analysis of variance (ANOVA) and regression analyses. In all cases, we indicate the signal-to-noise value of the observation with reference to its p-value. For cross-tabulations, these p-values come from chi-squared tests of significance. For t-tests and regressions, they are based on two-tailed tests of significance. For the ANOVAs, they come from the associated F-tests. Throughout the book, when the term significant is used without a qualifier, it means that the associated p-value is $p < 0.01$. In cases where statistical significance is weaker, the actual p-value is indicated in parentheses.

The EDP collected data from 6138 entrepreneurs who applied to these programs. For the analyses in this book, 38 of these entrepreneurs provided responses to key survey questions that are considered to be inappropriately high. To ensure that our observations are not unduly influenced by what most would call nonsense responses, we examined the distributions of each of the main variables (i.e., revenues, full-time employees, outside equity, debt, and philanthropic investment) and set aside observations where reported values are clearly outside a reasonable range. For example, ventures are set aside if entrepreneurs reported prior-year revenues greater than $5.1 million at application or in their first follow-up survey. This reduces the sample to 6100 ventures.

The EDP accelerators identify and support ventures that seek some combination of financial returns plus societal impact. This latter stipulation typically means one of two things. Some programs, like the Points of Light Civic Accelerator and the Unreasonable Institute, explicitly seek out impact-oriented ventures whose founders self-identify as social entrepreneurs. For example, one applicant works in the education sector and has a vision is to 'create a world where every entrepreneur is a social entrepreneur, every career is an impact-driven career, and every business is a socially-conscious business.' Other programs, like Village Capital and GrowthAfrica, are open to supporting more typical entrepreneurs whose ventures' impacts are desperately needed in marginalized regions and sectors. An example of this kind of entrepreneur, also from the education sector, aims to 'improve the quality of education by leveraging mobile technology and build value for our investors, partners and co-workers.'

One of the core EDP application survey questions relates to whether the founding team seeks to produce social or environmental impacts: 'Individuals can also have non-financial motives for launching new ventures. Does your venture have the explicit intent of creating social or environmental impacts?' Not surprisingly, a very high percentage—roughly 92 percent of the entrepreneurs in the EDP sample—responds in the affirmative. To ensure that the observations in this book apply to the growing population of ventures that seek to address specific social or environmental challenges, we set aside 486 ventures whose entrepreneurs responded 'no' to this question. For the remaining ventures, the EDP surveys gather information about the targeted impact objectives by asking, 'Which of the following impact objectives does your venture currently seek to address?' Table 3.2 lists the 11 IRIS impact objectives that are identified by more than 10 percent of the ventures in the sample.[15]

Ventures in the EDP sample target a wide range of impact objectives. Roughly one-third of them count employment generation among their specific goals. As the sample mission statement suggests, these ventures typically aspire to cultivate jobs or careers for others. Another objective that is singled out by more than one-quarter of the ventures is income or productivity growth. These ventures try to provide hard and soft infrastructure and support to improve productivity and income-earning capacity in specific sectors or regions. The third most prolific impact objective, community development, is also broad-based but is more social than economic. The most common sector-specific objective is providing access to education. Finally, it is interesting that these top-11 impact objectives are all found on the IRIS list of social impacts. The most prolific objective that comes from the IRIS list of environmental impacts is waste management, an objective for just under 10 percent of the ventures in the sample.

This first look at the EDP sample confirms that the entrepreneurs who seek acceleration services are wide-ranging in their intended impacts. This is exciting because it attests to the broad-based potential that is latent in the global social entrepreneurship movement. It becomes even more exciting if a non-trivial number of these ventures are able to secure the support that allows them to turn latent entrepreneurial potential into real social and economic impact.

Table 3.2 Reported IRIS impact objectives

	Percent of sample[a]	Sample mission statement
Employment generation	33.9	'… use technology and e-learning to build career paths that connect candidates to jobs'
Income/productivity growth	27.5	'… provide innovative technological and managerial solutions to micro entrepreneurs in the milk supply chain'
Community development	24.2	'… increase citizen engagement and give citizens a greater voice in how and which government projects are funded'
Access to education	21.9	'… empower young people to be the change and serve the world'
Health improvement	19.2	'… provide healthcare for free, using smartphones, to billions of people'
Equality and empowerment	17.9	'… challenge the status quo of ability, sport and athleticism with a disability sports news network'
Agricultural productivity	16.4	'… improve the livelihood of farmers and young people by offering effective agricultural and agribusiness consultancy services'
Access to financial services	14.4	'… be the ultimate customer choice in credit finance and help customers achieve their lifetime goals'
Capacity building	14.3	'… help organizations demonstrate the positive impacts of their social programs'
Access to information	12.3	'…provide reliable computing infrastructure for the continent'
Food security	11.4	'… create sustainable means of nutrition for the vulnerable in our society by recovering food that otherwise would have been wasted'

[a]The sum of all percentages exceeds 100% because entrepreneurs are allowed to specify more than one impact objective on their EDP application surveys

Still on the topic of venture impacts, the EDP application survey asks entrepreneurs three questions about current efforts when it comes to impact measurement: 'Does your venture regularly track itself against any of the Impact Reporting Investment Standards (IRIS) impact measures? Has your venture ever taken a B Impact Assessment or Global Impact Investing Ratings System (GIIRS) Survey? and Does your venture regularly track its impacts using any other established measurement approaches?' While all of the ventures in the EDP sample have the explicit aim of generating specific social or environmental impacts, only 38 percent of them report taking efforts to measure these impacts. Roughly 14 percent report using IRIS measures and only 7 percent report using all or part of the B Impact Assessment toolkit, which is linked to the GIIRS. These latter impact assessment frameworks are used by more than 2500 certified B Corporations around the world,[16] and are considered by many to be 'the gold standard for funds that manage their portfolio's impact with the same rigor as their financial performance.'[17]

While a growing number of impact investors and other funding organizations promote the use of IRIS metrics or B Corp certification among their funded companies, most of the ventures that apply to accelerators are very young and have not yet been exposed to, or influenced by these sector expectations.[18] In support of this observation, roughly two-thirds of the entrepreneurs indicate that they are not using these specific approaches because they have never heard of them. Finally, note that roughly 28 percent of the sample reports using other impact measurement systems, surveys, indicators, platforms, or studies to document and communicate their impacts.[19]

It may be surprising, or even troubling, that over 60 percent of the impact-oriented ventures in the EDP sample do not formally track their impacts. It is also relevant for the analyses in this book because it makes it virtually impossible to evaluate impact-oriented accelerators based on their ability to influence a specific set of venture-level impact measures. Not only do the sampled ventures aspire to move a wide range of different needles (see Table 3.2), they do so without a coherent set of expectations about which measures provide the best evidence of impact. Therefore, they attract applicants who are, more often than not, unable to provide the critical preprogram measures that are required to calculate short-term and long-term changes. This issue, which is revisited in the last chapter of the book, should be kept in mind as we move through Chaps. 4 through 10.

When considering the impact-oriented ventures that apply to receive acceleration services, it is also important to recognize the other vectors of diversity that characterize the EDP sample. Not only are these ventures setting up to address different societal issues, they also come to accelerators with a range of business types and a variety of entrepreneurial backgrounds (see Table 3.3). Consider something as simple as a venture's age, which gives a rough idea of its stage of development. In the EDP sample, the ventures' ages at application—calculated as the application year minus the reported year of founding—range from virtually brand new (i.e., many founders apply during their founding years) to more than 70 years. The oldest venture to apply for acceleration services in the EDP sample had been in business for 74 years. This nonprofit describes itself as a service business working in the agriculture sector in Central America. It reported decent prior-year revenues and full-time employees, but no prior-year equity investment, loans, or grants. This venture was seeking roughly $100K of debt and equity investment over the next 12 months (but was not accepted into the program to which it applied). Notwithstanding these outliers, most of the applicants are young companies, in business for an

Table 3.3 Ventures and entrepreneurs in the EDP sample

	Full EDP sample
Venture age	Average = 2.4 years
Legal form	For-profit, 79.1%
	Nonprofit, 10.8%
	Other, 6.4%
	Undecided, 3.4%
Top five sectors	Education, 17.2%
	Agriculture, 15.3%
	Health, 12.1%
	Financial services, 9.7%
	ICT, 6.9%
Any intellectual property	42.7%
Multiple founders on team	76.8%
Average founding team age	35.0 years
Any prior founding experience	59.0%
Any prior accelerator participation	28.6%
Founding team gender	All men, 48.6%
	All women, 14.9%
	Mixed-gender, 34.8%

average of just 2.4 years. Clearly, most impact-oriented ventures are not waiting long before seeking out acceleration services.

Although the pursuit of specific societal goals was once the exclusive domain of nonprofit organizations, this is no longer the case.[20] Instead, there has been a surge of for-profit and hybrid organizations that aspire to take on social and environmental challenges while building a platform for commercial success and investor returns. This movement is evident, and arguably amplified, in the EDP sample, where less than 11 percent of the ventures are nonprofits. Instead, more than 79 percent of the ventures come to accelerators as for-profit companies, while another 6 percent apply with an 'other'—typically hybrid—legal form.[21] Overall, the impact-oriented accelerators that partner with the EDP attract a lion's share of applicants seeking to leverage the power of business to jointly create captured financial value for owners and investors, and value that is shared with a broader array of stakeholders.[22] However, the composition of nonprofit versus for-profit applicants does vary across programs. Several of the EDP partners are so clear about their focus on for-profit entrepreneurs that they attract zero nonprofit ventures into their application pools. Other programs are more agnostic about legal form and attract up to 40 percent nonprofit applications.

These typically young and mostly for-profit ventures work across a range of industry sectors. The five most prolific sectors—education, agriculture, health, financial services, and ICT—account for more than 60 percent of the sample. Chapters 9 and 10 look more closely at these sector participation figures to see how they track across emerging-markets versus high-income countries, and across male versus female founding teams.

Many of the individuals and organizations that seek to identify and support scalable impact-oriented ventures believe that the most promising candidates develop and hold proprietary intellectual property that is protected by patents, copyrights, or trademarks.[23] Consistent with this orientation, roughly 43 percent of the applicants to the programs in the EDP sample report holding some intellectual property.

Turning to the founders of these impact-oriented ventures, more than three-quarters of the EDP sample report having more than one founder on their teams. We calculate the average age of the one to three primary founders reported for each team. The average for the entire sample is roughly 35 years.[24] This is consistent with a recent study which uses a much larger sample of American companies to report that 'the average age of entrepreneurs at the time they founded their companies is 42.'[25] When it comes to impact-oriented ventures seeking acceleration, it is clearly not just a young person's game.

Regardless of age, when starting a new company, it often pays to have some prior entrepreneurial experience on the founding team.[26] For this reason, the EDP application surveys ask 'How many new organizations did each founder start before launching this venture?' Responses to this question indicate that roughly 59 percent of the ventures in the sample have founding teams with some prior for-profit or nonprofit founding experience. There might also be advantages to having founders who participated in another accelerator program before launching into this next phase of business development. Almost 29 percent of the founding teams in the sample indicate that someone participated in another accelerator at some point in the past.

Finally, there is considerable interest in the gender composition of founding teams; so much so that Chap. 10 is dedicated to the topic. For now, it is interesting to see that roughly 50 percent of the ventures in the EDP sample list only men among their top three founders. At the other extreme, less than 15 percent of the ventures list only women on their founding teams.

Chapters 1 and 2 made several references to possible differences between the impact-oriented accelerators that partner with the EDP and more traditional programs like Y Combinator. One of these differences is in the demographics of their applicant pools. According to YC Summer 2017 Stats, the average age of 2017 Y Combinator applicants is roughly 30 years, five years younger than the average for EDP applicants. Moreover, only 22 percent of the 2017 Y Combinator applicants have female founders, compared to roughly half of the EDP applicants.[27]

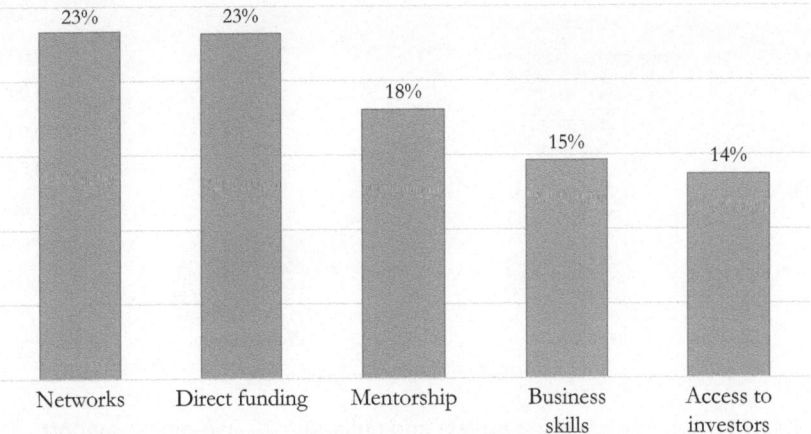

Fig. 3.3 Accelerator benefits ranked #1 by EDP applicants

Before turning attention to five of the variables that most accelerator programs try to influence, it is important to consider the benefits that impact-
oriented entrepreneurs seek when they apply to accelerators. Building from
the general belief that entrepreneur support programs aim to help entrepreneurs identify and close the various knowledge, network, and capital gaps that
stand between current potential and ultimate success, the EDP application
surveys present entrepreneurs with a list of the potential benefits that are typically associated with entrepreneurial accelerators and ask them to rank these
benefits in terms of how important they are to their venture's development
and success. Figure 3.3 shows the five accelerator benefits that are ranked first
by most of the ventures in the EDP sample. It shows an almost equivalent
interest in securing support when it comes to closing network and capital
gaps; with roughly 23 percent of the sample expressing a dominant interest in
these kinds of support. When it comes to the way that entrepreneurs hope to
address their current business challenges, the desire to develop mentorship
relationships seems to be more important than the felt need to develop specific business skills.

Figure 3.3 attests to a strong interest among impact-oriented entrepreneurs
in obtaining direct funding for their ventures, along with a modest interest in
gaining access to potential funders. This aligns with one of the stated goals of
most accelerators; that of helping promising ventures identify and close capital
gaps so that they can stabilize and then grow both operations and impacts. To
get a sense for the types and amounts of capital that accelerator program applicants are seeking, the EDP application survey—under the separate headings
of 'equity financing, debt financing and philanthropic support'—asks them,

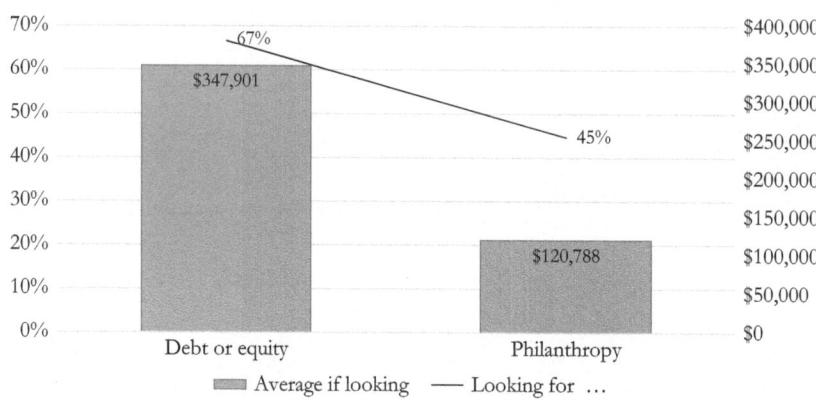

Fig. 3.4 EDP applicants seeking private and philanthropic investment support

'How much additional investment are you planning to secure for your venture in the next 12 months?' After setting aside a small number of extremely ambitious responses that fall more readily under the heading of wish lists as opposed to plans, roughly 67 percent of the entrepreneurs report specific targets for debt plus equity funding, while just under 45 percent report specific targets for philanthropic support (see Fig. 3.4).[28] Further analysis reveals that roughly 29 percent of the entrepreneurs in the sample report specific 12-month aspirations for both debt and equity financing and philanthropic support. A nontrivial number of impact-oriented entrepreneurs hope to receive both private sector and philanthropic investment as they build their businesses. For those with specific debt and equity aspirations, the average amount that is built into their 12-month plans is roughly $348,000, compared to an average of roughly $121,000 for those seeking specific levels of philanthropic support. The combination of more entrepreneurs seeking larger amounts of funding from private sources aligns with the large number of for-profit and hybrid organizations in the sample to further highlight the growing reliance on markets—in this case financial markets—among social and socially oriented entrepreneurs.

This concludes our introduction to the thousands of entrepreneurs and ventures that populate the EDP sample. While they have a number of things in common, they also vary in several important respects. They are mostly young for-profit companies that also want to generate specific societal impacts. However, their impact aspirations are diverse. They all applied to accelerator programs. However, they come with different business ideas and models and with different entrepreneurial backgrounds. They also prioritize different accelerator benefits, seeking more or less help closing knowledge, network, or capital gaps. Even when we isolate the latter aspirations, they reveal different levels of interest in securing private versus philanthropic capital injections.

The core similarities—that is, market-based, impact-oriented entrepreneurs seeking out acceleration services—underpin the main question tackled in this book: Do accelerator programs stimulate the development of promising impact-oriented ventures? However, the many differences necessitate choices about what it actually means for accelerators to systematically influence early-stage ventures. The remainder of this chapter explains and motivates our focus on the role played by accelerators when it comes to stimulating revenue, employment, and investment growth.

Focusing on Revenues, Employment, and Investment

One of the biggest challenges associated with studying accelerator effectiveness is that programs seek to accelerate different things. One constellation of factors is highlighted by the Seed Accelerator Rankings Project, which provides annual rankings of the more traditional accelerator programs. These annual rankings are based on weighted assessments of the financial valuation of portfolio companies, the number of qualified exits (either in the form of initial public offerings or acquisitions), the number of companies that raised at least $200K of outside equity, survival rates for accelerated companies, founder satisfaction scores, and the number of program alumni.[29] Another set of factors is implied by an infographic produced by the Global Accelerator Network, which comprises almost 100 (mostly traditional) accelerators working around the world. In addition to variables that track the number and gender of applicants, they report on the amount of startup funding (overall and from programs directly), whether ventures have earned any revenue, and company valuations.[30] To get a sense for the full range of variables that impact-oriented accelerators emphasize, consider Endeavor, an organization that 'works to catalyze long-term economic growth by selecting, mentoring, and accelerating the best high-impact entrepreneurs worldwide.' A quick look at Endeavor's impact dashboard shows the range of outcomes, related to human, financial, intellectual and social capital, they seek to influence as they work in several developing countries.[31]

Although accelerators have many goals, a common set of aspirations relates to advancing the commercial operations of cohort ventures. This makes sense if one thinks in terms of the underlying desire to harness the power of business and markets to deliver scalable societal impacts. Regardless of its specific impact objective, a for-profit company must generate revenues that more than cover the costs associated with delivering that impact. Therefore, a desire to scale impact typically corresponds with some growth in earned revenues. Among the outlays associated with scaling impacts are the costs of recruiting and retaining employees, especially for ventures that include employment generation among their impact objectives. This suggests another association between impact and employment growth. Finally, laying the foundation for future company and impact growth typically requires the deployment of financial resources in advance of earning revenues. While some of these funds come from founders, most growing ventures require capital injections from outside equity investors, from banks and other lenders, or from philanthropic supporters.

Clearly, these commercial and investment metrics do not ensure societal impact. However, they are typically considered to be corequisites for the development of impact-oriented ventures. And, given the highly diverse and, in many cases, unmeasured impacts, focusing on a core set of widely pursued and commonly measured commercial and investment metrics gives some sense of accelerators' effects on the commercial foundations upon which impacts are based. Therefore, this book focuses on two variables that indicate the current commercial performance of ventures; their revenues and employees. It also focuses on three forms of investment that facilitate future growth: the levels of outside equity, debt, and philanthropy. At a minimum, programs meet their acceleration goals if one or more of these variables tend to increase faster for participating ventures compared to ventures that applied to programs but were not accepted.

Several EDP application survey questions generate the prior-year revenue, employment, and investment data analyzed in this book:

- What was your venture's total earned revenue in calendar year (2012, 2013, 2014, 2015)?
- Not counting founders, on December 31 (2012, 2013, 2014, 2015), how many people worked for your venture?
- How much equity financing did your venture obtain from all outside sources in calendar year (2012, 2013, 2014, 2015)?
- How much did your venture borrow from all of these sources in calendar year (2012, 2013, 2014, 2015)?
- How much philanthropic support (e.g., seed grants, awards, or donations) did your venture receive from all outside sources in calendar year (2012, 2013, 2014, 2015)?

Table 3.4 Revenues, employment and investment, averages and correlations

Levels, overall (N = 5614)						
	Average	(1)	(2)	(3)	(4)	(5)
(1) Revenues	$47,608	1.00				
(2) Full-time employees	3.22	0.37	1.00			
(3) Outside equity	$15,453	0.08	0.07	1.00		
(4) Total debt	$7168	0.19	0.22	0.07	1.00	
(5) Philanthropic support	$13,933	0.32	0.08	0.00	0.01	1.00

Levels, participated (N = 890)						
	Average	(1)	(2)	(3)	(4)	(5)
(1) Revenues	$79,137	1.00				
(2) Full-time employees	3.37	0.39	1.00			
(3) Outside equity	$21,713	−0.01	0.04	1.00		
(4) Total debt	$14,618	0.15	0.20	0.04	1.00	
(5) Philanthropic support	$25,046	0.37	0.02	0.01	0.01	1.00

Changes (N = 2902)						
	Average	(1)	(2)	(3)	(4)	(5)
(1) Revenues	$18,800	1.00				
(2) Full-time employees	0.73	0.13	1.00			
(3) Outside equity	$7907	0.04	0.04	1.00		
(4) Total debt	$4023	0.05	0.06	−0.08	1.00	
(5) Philanthropic support	$3456	0.12	0.02	0.04	0.05	1.00

The top third of Table 3.4 shows how applicants fared on these five metrics in the year prior to application. On average, the 5614 applicants report $47,608 of earned revenue. These are used, in part, to hire an average of 3.2 full-time employees. As they work to develop their ventures, these applicants are supported by an average of $15,453 of outside equity investment in the year prior to application. These investments are deployed in tandem with an average of $7168 of prior-year borrowing and $13,933 of philanthropic support.

This brief summary makes it sound like these five variables might move in tandem with one another. However, the data suggest that the factors that move one variable typically have different effects on the others. This is evident by looking at the correlations among the five variables. While there are modest positive correlations between prior-year revenues and the number of full-time employees ($\rho = 0.37$), as well as prior-year debt ($\rho = 0.19$) and philanthropic support ($\rho = 0.32$), the correlation between prior-year revenues and the amount of outside equity is surprisingly low ($\rho = 0.08$). Aside from a modest positive correlation between full-time employees and new debt ($\rho = 0.22$), the pair-wise correlations among the other four variables are all less than $\rho = 0.10$.

Nor is it the case that accepted and rejected entrepreneurs look the same on their application surveys. Isolating the 890 entrepreneurs that were selected to

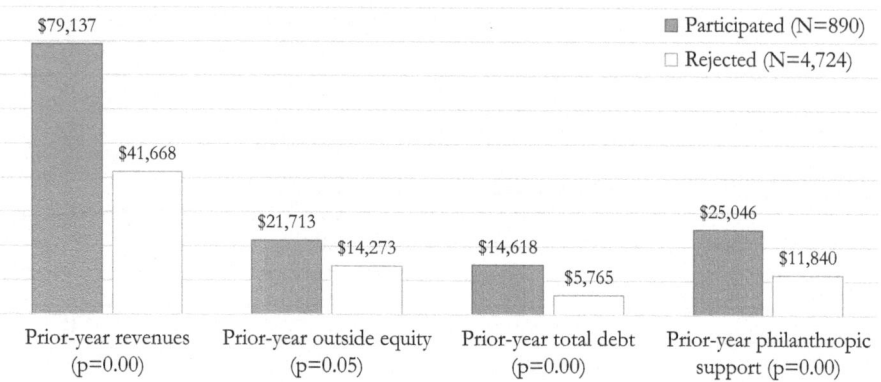

Fig. 3.5 Prior-year revenues and investment for participated and rejected ventures

participate in the various EDP accelerators, there is a clear—and understandable—bias in favor of ventures that demonstrate superior recent commercial and investment performance. It is well known that accelerators are selective by design—a topic covered in Chap. 7—and prefer to work with entrepreneurs whose ventures are more promising. Consistent with this belief, the participating ventures report an average of $37,469 more prior-year revenues than those that were rejected; a difference that is statistically significant. There are similar significant differences for the three investment variables (see Fig. 3.5). That said, the pattern of correlations among the five variables is similar in the smaller sample of participating ventures.

In the year following the close of applications for each program, participating and rejected entrepreneurs are asked these same five questions again, this time focusing on the subsequent calendar year. Responses from the application and follow-up surveys are used to calculate the year-over-year changes in earned revenues, full-time employees, and investment levels. The lower panel in Table 3.4 presents the average changes observed on the entire group of ventures whose founders responded to the first follow-up survey. The across-the-board positive average changes for the 2902 participating and rejected ventures suggest a tendency toward improvement among all ventures that are still in operation, and whose founders elect to provide follow-up information, one year later. On average, the revenues reported on follow-up surveys are $18,800 higher than those reported on application surveys. There are also modest increases in the reported number of full-time employees (+0.7) and on all three types of outside investment, with outside equity having the largest average increase (+$7907).

Before analyzing the one-year change variables, we must ensure that the entrepreneurs who provide follow-up information by responding to first-year follow-
up surveys are representative of each underlying group of applicants. To do this,
we compare the application averages for follow-up survey respondents and non-
respondents in both the participated and rejected venture sub-samples. For
example, among program participants, the average number of full-time employees reported on the applications of entrepreneurs who respond to follow-up
surveys (3.3) is slightly lower than the application average for entrepreneurs who
do not respond (3.5). This difference is not statistically significant ($p = 0.74$). The
corresponding application average for rejected entrepreneurs who complete
follow-up surveys (3.4) is slightly higher than the application average reported by
rejected entrepreneurs who do not complete follow-up surveys (3.0). Again, this
difference is not statistically significant ($p = 0.25$). In similar comparisons of
earned revenues, outside equity, debt, and philanthropy reported on application
surveys, none of the pairwise differences are significant, with p-values ranging
from 0.35 (debt, rejected applicants) to 0.93 (philanthropy, rejected applicants).
This gives us confidence that the patterns that we present, which are based on
data provided by entrepreneurs who responded to follow-up surveys, are not
obviously biased and therefore misleading.

When isolating an accelerator's ability to stimulate change, it is important
to account for the fact that all ventures in the follow-up sample grow on average. It is also important to recognize that the correlations among the five
change variables are even lower than the correlations among their corresponding levels. For example, while the correlations between earned revenues and
the other four variables range from $\rho = 0.08$ (outside equity) to $\rho = 0.37$ (full-
time employees), the correlations between one-year changes in the same variables range from $\rho = 0.04$ (outside equity) to $\rho = 0.13$ (full-time employees).
These lower correlations suggest that it is difficult for accelerators to generate
across-the-board improvements in the commercial performance of their
cohort ventures. This should be kept in mind as we transition from our
venture-level analysis in Chap. 4 to the program-level analyses reported in
Chaps. 5 through 8.

Concluding Remarks

This chapter provides a first look at the EDP data that are analyzed in this
book, explaining the motivation behind this multi-year data-collection effort
and how it grew over the 2013–2017 period. After describing the application
and follow-up surveys, and the approach to data collection, we outline the
steps taken to arrive at the final sample of entrepreneurs and ventures. This
EDP sample covers a range of impact-oriented accelerators working with a

range of different ventures. Chapters 4 through 10 will leverage this underlying diversity to provide a series of nuanced observations that relate to accelerators' effects on impact-oriented ventures. To prepare for these demonstrations, it is important to recognize the challenges associated with measuring and analyzing social and environmental performance. Because commercial performance is typically considered a co-requisite of social and environmental performance for impact-oriented ventures, we home in on five measures of revenue, employment, and investment growth to focus our assessments of accelerator program effects. Finally, we used the EDP data to show that all ventures, including rejected ventures, are growing on average, and that participating ventures tend to display stronger commercial and investment performance on their application surveys. These two observations must be kept in mind as we begin our deeper dive into potential accelerator effects.

Appendix

Appendix 1: EDP Application Survey Questions

Contact and Venture Information

- What is your first name? Last name?
- What is your phone number?
- What is your email address?
- What is your Skype username?
- What is the name of your venture?
- Currently, in which country are your venture's main operations?
- In what country is your venture headquartered?
- We are interested in the web presence of your venture. Does your venture currently have any of the following? An active website? A Facebook page? A Twitter account? A LinkedIn group or page?
- In what year was your venture founded?
- Is your venture a: Nonprofit? For-profit company? Undecided? Other?
- What primary sector is being impacted by your venture's activities?
- What are the financial goals for your venture? Cover costs? Cover costs and earn some profit?
- Do you have some specific profit margin in mind?
- What annual profit margins would you be happy achieving on average?
- Individuals can also have non-financial motives for launching new ventures. Does your venture have the explicit intent of creating social or environmental impacts?

- A mission statement is a concise message that expresses how your venture generates financial, social, and/or environmental value through its activities. Please write your current mission statement in the space below. If you do not currently have a mission statement, explain in 100 words or less how your enterprise generates financial, social, and/or environmental value.

Impacts and Metrics

- Which of the following impact objectives does your venture currently seek to address?
- What is the demographic group of the primary beneficiaries targeted by your venture's activities?
- Does your venture regularly track itself against any of the Impact Reporting Investment Standards (IRIS) impact measures?
- Has your venture ever taken a B Impact Assessment or Global Impact Investing Ratings System (GIIRS) Survey?
- Does your venture regularly track its impacts using any other established measurement approaches?

Business Model

- What is the current operational model of your venture?
- Would you say that your venture is invention-based (i.e., a company that builds upon newly created technology owned by the venture and/or its founders)?
- Whether assigned by an owner or obtained in some other way, did your venture receive any of the following during calendar year 20XX? Patents? Copyrights? Trademarks?
- How many new patents?
- How many new copyrights?
- How many new trademarks?

Venture Financing

- What was your venture's total earned revenue (do not include any philanthropic investments or donations in this amount) in calendar year 20XX?
- Profit is the business' income after all expenses and taxes have been deducted. Roughly speaking, what was your venture's profit margin (as a percentage of total investment) for calendar year 20XX?

- Not counting founders, on December 31, 20XX, how many people worked for your venture (excluding contract workers who are not on the business' official payroll)? Full-time employees? Part-time employees?
- How much, if any, did your venture pay in wages, salaries, and benefits to full-time and part-time employees in calendar year 20XX (do not include wages, salaries, and benefits to contract workers who are not on the business' official payroll)?
- In addition to these full-time and part-time employees, how many seasonal workers and volunteers did you employ during 20XX?
- How much of their own money did all of the founders put into the business (do not include any money borrowed from others or credit cards) in calendar year 20XX?
- Please indicate whether your venture has received any of the following investments from outside sources since founding: Equity (equity investment is money received in return for some portion of ownership)? Debt (not including any personal debt obtained on behalf of the business)? Philanthropy (e.g., seed grants, awards, or donations)?
- From which sources has your venture received this outside equity?
- How much equity financing did your venture obtain from all outside sources in calendar year 20XX? Since founding?
- From which sources has your venture obtained borrowed funds?
- How much did your venture borrow from all of these sources in calendar year 20XX? Since founding?
- From which sources has your venture received these donations?
- How much philanthropic support (e.g., seed grants, awards, or donations) did your venture receive from all outside sources in calendar year 20XX? Since founding?
- How much additional investment are you planning to secure for your venture in the next 12 months? Over the next 3 years? Equity financing? Debt financing? Philanthropic support?

Founders

- Please name up to three individuals who are the primary members of your venture's founding team. A founder is a person who is actively involved in the start of the venture and/or has had a financial stake in the venture from the start/early days of the venture.
- How many additional people (not listed above) are also on the founding team?

- Now, please provide the following information about each of the three founders listed above: Age? Gender? Country of Birth? Country of Current Residence? Highest Level of Education Completed?
- How many new organizations did each founder start before launching this venture? For-Profits? Nonprofits? Other Entities?
- We are interested in the career backgrounds of these founders. Please provide the following information about the two more recent paid full-time jobs held by each of the above founders before launching this venture. Organization Type? What Role? How Long? Country?

Entrepreneurial Accelerators

- The following are some of the potential benefits that are typically associated with entrepreneurial accelerators. Please rank these benefits in terms of how important they are to your venture's development and success. (1 being the most important and 7 being the least important)
- _____ Network development (e.g., with potential partners and customers)
- _____ Business skills development (e.g., finance and marketing skills)
- _____ Mentorship from business experts
- _____ Access and connections to potential investors/funders
- _____ Securing direct venture funding (e.g., grants or investments)
- _____ Gaining access to a group of like-minded entrepreneurs
- _____ Awareness and credibility (e.g., association with a recognized program, press/media exposure)
- What other potential benefits would you look for from accelerator programs that are not included in the above list?
- Has anyone on your founding team participated in any of the following accelerator programs? Which year did you attend?

Appendix 2: EDP Follow-Up Survey Questions

Venture Information

- What is your: First name? Last name?
- What is your email address?
- What is the current name of your venture?
- Has your venture changed its name in the past year?
- Currently, in which country are your venture's main operations?

- Is your venture a: Nonprofit? For-profit company? Undecided? Other?
- Whether assigned by an owner or obtained in some other way, did your venture receive any of the following during calendar year 20XX? Patents? Copyrights? Trademarks?
- How many new patents?
- How many new copyrights?
- How many new trademarks?

Venture Goals and Impacts

- What are the financial goals for your venture? Cover costs? Cover costs and earn some profit?
- Do you have some specific profit margin in mind?
- Do you have some specific profit margin in mind?
- Individuals can also have non-financial motives for launching new ventures. Does your venture currently have the explicit intent of creating social or environmental impacts?
- Which of the following impact objectives does your venture currently seek to address?
- Did your venture track itself against any of the Impact Reporting Investment Standards (IRIS) impact measures in 20XX?
- Did your venture take a B Corporation Impact Assessment or Global Impact Investing Ratings System (GIIRS) survey in 20XX?
- Did your venture track its impacts using any other established measurement approaches in 20XX?

Financials and Operations

- What was your venture's total earned revenue (do not include any philanthropic investments or donations in this amount) in calendar year 20XX?
- Profit is the business' income after all expenses and taxes have been deducted. Roughly speaking, what was your venture's profit margin (as a percentage of total investment) for calendar year 20XX?
- Not counting founders, on December 31, 20XX, how many people worked for your venture (excluding contract workers who are not on the business' official payroll)? Full-time employees? Part-time employees?
- How much, if any, did your venture pay in wages, salaries, and benefits to full-time and part-time employees in calendar year 20XX (do not include wages, salaries, and benefits to contract workers who are not on the business' official payroll)?

Venture Financing

- How much of their own money did all of the founders put into the business (do not include any money borrowed from others or credit cards) in calendar year 20XX?
- Please indicate whether your venture has received any of the following investments from outside sources since founding: Equity (equity investment is money received in return for some portion of ownership)? Debt (not including any personal debt obtained on behalf of the business)? Philanthropy (e.g., seed grants, awards, or donations)?
- From which sources has your venture received this outside equity?
- How much equity financing did your venture obtain from all outside sources in calendar year 20XX? Since founding?
- From which sources has your venture obtained borrowed funds?
- How much did your venture borrow from all of these sources in calendar year 20XX? Since founding?
- From which sources has your venture received these donations?
- How much philanthropic support (e.g., seed grants, awards, or donations) did your venture receive from all outside sources in calendar year 20XX? Since founding?
- How much additional investment are you planning to secure for your venture in the next 12 months? Over the next 3 years? Equity financing? Debt financing? Philanthropic support?

Entrepreneurial Accelerators

- In 20XX, did anyone on your founding team participate in any of the following accelerator programs?

Notes

1. Jeremy C. Short, Todd W. Moss & Tom Lumpkin. 2009. 'Research in social entrepreneurship: Past contributions and future opportunities.' *Strategic Entrepreneurship Journal*, 3(2): 161–194.
2. Randal Kempner & Peter W. Roberts. 'Aren't accelerators great? Maybe.' *WSJ Accelerators Blog* (April 2015).
3. See http://www.doingbusiness.org/data/exploretopics/entrepreneurship
4. See https://www.gemconsortium.org/data
5. See https://www.gemconsortium.org/research-papers

6. See https://www.kauffman.org/microsites/kfs

7. See https://www.kauffman.org/microsites/kfs/bibliography

8. See https://www.galidata.org/

9. William A. Sahlman. 2010. 'Endeavor: Creating a Global Movement for High-Impact Entrepreneurship.' *Harvard Business School Case #9-810-049.*

10. See http://foundationcenter.org/find-funding/990-finder

11. See http://cvcx.org/

12. GALI is made possible by its co-creators, Social Enterprise @ Goizueta at Emory University and the Aspen Network of Development Entrepreneurs, and its founding sponsors, including the U.S. Global Development Lab at the U.S. Agency for International Development, Omidyar Network, The Lemelson Foundation and the Argidius Foundation. Additional support for GALI has been provided by the Kauffman Foundation, Stichting DOEN, and Banamex.

13. IRIS is a catalog of generally accepted metrics that leading impact investors use to measure social, environmental, and financial success. See https://iris.thegiin.org/about/faq

14. EDP program partners also retain ownership of all of their application data.

15. IRIS provides a standardized list of 18 social impact objectives and seven environmental impact objectives that companies might pursue. See https://iris.thegiin.org/

16. See https://bcorporation.net/

17. See http://b-analytics.net/giirs-funds

18. A closer look at the data reveal that ventures that received philanthropic funding are more likely to measure their impacts. Ventures that measure impacts are also slightly older (3.3 years) than those that do not (2.5 years).

19. *Entrepreneurship & Acceleration Questions from the Field: Impact Measurement* (May 2016).

20. Julie Battilana, Matthew Lee, John Walker, & Cheryl Dorsey. 2012. 'In search of the hybrid ideal.' *Stanford Social Innovation Review*, Summer.

21. This relatively small share of nonprofits is more dramatic than the 41 percent nonprofit share reported for the 2017 Echoing Green applicant pool. See *A Look at 2017 For-Profit & Hybrid Applications,* Echoing Green (May 2017).

22. Filipe M. Santos. 2012. 'A positive theory of social entrepreneurship.' *Journal of Business Ethics*, 111(3): 335–351.

23. Jonathan T. Eckhardt, Scott Shane, & Frederic Delmar. 2006. 'Multistage selection and the financing of new ventures.' *Management Science*, 52 (2): 220–232.

24. For a more detailed look at the younger founding teams, see *Entrepreneurship & Acceleration Questions from the Field: Youth Entrepreneurship in Africa* (February 2015).

25. Pierre Azoulay, Benjamin Jones, J. Daniel Kim, & Javier Miranda. 2018. 'The average age of a successful startup founder Is 45.' *Harvard Business Review On-Line*, July.
26. There is an established stream of academic research that focuses on whether prior founding experience influences the performance of new ventures. See, for example, Frédéric Delmar and Scott Shane. 2006. 'Does experience matter? The effect of founding team experience on the survival and sales of newly founded ventures.' *Strategic Organization* 4(3): 215–247.
27. See https://blog.ycombinator.com/yc-summer-2017-stats/
28. The eight entrepreneurs who reported equity aspirations greater than $5,000,000 or philanthropy aspirations greater than $4,600,000 were set aside before creating Fig. 3.4.
29. See http://www.seedrankings.com/
30. See https://www.gan.co/data/2018-infographic/
31. See https://endeavor.org/impact/

4

Is Acceleration Working?

There is growing pressure around the world to support broad-based entrepreneurship as a way to unleash more of the economic and social benefits that are currently latent within businesses and markets. In response, resources are being devoted to designing and running accelerator programs that identify and support promising impact-oriented entrepreneurs. For these investments to continue, and for the invested time and money to deliver optimum results, we need more research into the effects that accelerators are having on the ventures that participate in their programs. In this respect, the few academic studies that are making their way toward scholarly journals are showing mixed results. One study of Y Combinator graduates suggests that accelerated ventures, when compared to a matched sample of similar companies, receive less investment and tend to fail faster. This suggests that accelerators help some entrepreneurs to cut their losses earlier.[1] Another study applies a mixed-methods approach to a select group of US and European accelerators and finds uneven effects. While accelerators tend to accelerate the arrival rate of important business milestones, not all programs show these positive effects.[2] Another study of acceleration in emerging markets focuses on the Start-Up Chile program. It shows that offering basic accelerator services—little more than a support grant and co-working space—does not deliver positive outcomes. However, combining basic services with more intensive entrepreneurial support leads to improved fundraising and more rapid company growth.[3] Finally, a qualitative study of an Indian accelerator shows how it provides a bridge between participating ventures and their entrepreneurial ecosystems, stimulating connections between entrepreneurs and possible mentors and investors.[4]

© The Author(s) 2019
P. W. Roberts, S. A. Lall, *Observing Acceleration*,
https://doi.org/10.1007/978-3-030-00042-4_4

These academic studies are complemented by a small number of practitioner reports that focus on acceleration in emerging markets. One report covers USAID's Partnering to Accelerate Entrepreneurship (PACE) grantees and finds that 'SGBs that receive shorter, less individualized technical assistance – such as cohort-based, time-bound incubators and accelerators – demonstrate an average revenue growth over two times and job growth over one-and-a-half times that of other SGBs.'[5] Another report focuses on accelerator programs run by TechnoServe in four Central American countries. It shows how 'carefully-designed accelerator programs can facilitate revenue growth on average.' However, it also finds 'important differences in revenue-growth performance' across the participating ventures.[6]

The analyses in this book contribute to this developing body of work by observing a broad sample of impact-oriented accelerators (see Chap. 3). In doing so, we adopt a focused notion of what it means to say that accelerator programs are working: when the short-term commercial performance of participating ventures exceeds the performance of those ventures that were rejected from the same applicant pools. First, the various observations in this book are based on a small number of variables that track the commercial performance of impact-oriented ventures. As we argued in Chap. 3, growth in earned revenues and full-time employees indicates the expanding commercial performance of early-stage ventures. Growth in investment numbers like outside equity, new borrowing, and philanthropic contributions indicates their capacity to secure the funds that will allow them to continue growing operations and impacts into the medium term.

Second, the assessments are based on one-year changes in these five variables. The main reason for this decision to focus on short-term changes is pragmatic and driven by the inability to secure the data required for longer-term analyses. The EDP was launched in 2013 and the analyses in this book are based on application and follow-up data collected before the end of 2017. This produces a limited observation window that provides a maximum of four years of follow-up data. However, the earlier years—from which more years of follow-up data are available—include fewer ventures (e.g., there were only 870 applicants in 2013) and programs (nine in 2013). Moreover, follow-up survey response rates decline moving from the first follow-up survey (roughly 50 percent of the entrepreneurs responded) to the third (roughly 30 percent responded). These two factors produce a 60 percent decline in the number of available observations between the first and second follow-up year.

Another reason for emphasizing the immediate effects of acceleration relates to the underlying construct of acceleration. As accelerators gain in popularity, it is important to remember their defining feature relative to other entrepreneur support programs like incubators. Recall from Chap. 2 that incubators tend to protect startups from their external environments, often working with them over several years. This is consistent with the underlying definition of incubation which, according to Merriam-Webster, is 'to maintain something under conditions favorable for hatching, development, or reaction.' With this developmental orientation, it makes sense for researchers to look past the immediate effects of incubation and focus on longer-term growth and survival rates.[7] On the other hand, accelerators tend to focus on intensifying market interactions within a short period. This is also consistent with the underlying definition of acceleration, which is 'the act or process of moving faster or happening more quickly.'[8] The shift in mindset moving from incubation to acceleration favors intense intervention that yields immediate changes in the trajectories of participating ventures. It therefore makes sense to expect accelerator programs to induce changes in revenue and investment flows that are evident straight away.

It is also reasonable to expect that these immediate changes translate into superior longer-term commercial performance which, in turn, supports larger social and environmental impacts. However, readers must use caution when inferring the long-term impact implications of acceleration based on the short-term commercial performance effects presented in the next few chapters. It is possible that the EDP accelerators are stimulating the short-term commercial performance of participating ventures and thus meeting the stated aims of entrepreneur acceleration, but that short-term acceleration does not deliver the longer-term benefits that program managers and funders are seeking. In the final chapter of this book, we discuss the importance of developing research strategies that also track the longer-term accelerator effects on social and environmental outcomes.

Finally, the assessments focus on the average changes experienced by groups of participating ventures relative to comparison groups of rejected ventures. Because the performance of non-selected ventures also changes over time, it is not enough to show that accelerated ventures grow their revenues, employment, or investment levels. Rather, the analysis must show that participating entrepreneurs grow these variables faster than those who apply but are not accepted into programs. When making these comparisons, we must also recognize another defining characteristic of the accelerator model. Accelerator programs start by actively building pipelines of promising entrepreneurs before selecting the most promising among them. In this respect, it is impossible to argue that the individuals who apply to accelerators represent a random sample of impact-oriented entrepreneurs. Nor is it possible to argue that the ventures that participate in the sampled programs are randomly selected from all applicants. These two facts must be kept in mind as we present baseline evidence on the effects of acceleration in the remainder of this chapter and in Chap. 5. At that point, Chaps. 6 and 7 will look more closely at the specific implications of pipeline-building efforts and entrepreneur selection.

A First Look …

Matching data reported in application surveys with data collected one year later in follow-up surveys allows us to calculate the extent to which revenues, employees, equity, debt, and philanthropy change during the year of acceleration:

- Revenue growth = $\text{revenue}_{\text{follow-up}} - \text{revenue}_{\text{application}}$
- Employment growth = $\text{FT employees}_{\text{follow-up}} - \text{FT employees}_{\text{application}}$
- Equity growth = $\text{outside equity}_{\text{follow-up}} - \text{outside equity}_{\text{application}}$
- Debt growth = $\text{new borrowing}_{\text{follow-up}} - \text{new borrowing}_{\text{application}}$
- Philanthropy growth = $\text{philanthropy}_{\text{follow-up}} - \text{philanthropy}_{\text{application}}$

The information in Table 4.1 is based on application and follow-up surveys completed by 650 entrepreneurs who participated in one of the EDP accelerators and another 2252 who applied but did not participate. Each cell in the table presents the average year-over-year change in reported revenues, full-time employees, or investment levels observed during the year in which programs are run. The first column shows the averages for participating entrepreneurs, while the second column shows the average changes among entrepreneurs who applied but were not accepted. The third column calculates the differences between these two averages to show the average accelerator effects.

The first thing to note is that all of the numbers in Table 4.1—including those in the second column—are positive. When calibrating the effects of

Table 4.1 Year-over-year growth, participated versus rejected

	Participated ($N = 650$)	Rejected ($N = 2252$)	Difference	Sig.
Average revenue growth	$22,393	$17,763	$4630	$p = 0.67$
Average employment growth	1.35	0.56	0.80	$p = 0.11$
Average equity growth	$12,048	$6711	$5336	$p = 0.29$
Average debt growth	$6820	$3215	$3605	$p = 0.21$
Average philanthropy growth	$5725	$2800	$2926	$p = 0.55$

accelerator programs, we must account for the fact that, on average, rejected entrepreneurs and ventures continue to evolve. Instead of simply applauding the positive raw change numbers for participating entrepreneurs reported in the first column, we must compare them to the hold out group of rejected entrepreneurs. In this respect, it is encouraging that every one of the reported averages for participating entrepreneurs is greater than the corresponding average for the rejected sub-sample. The differentials are greatest for outside equity investment (where the participant advantage is roughly $5300) and revenue (where the participant advantage is roughly $4600). This provides preliminary evidence that participating in accelerators has across-the-board positive effects on commercial performance.

It is important to note, however, that none of these average differences is statistically significant. Indeed, it can be challenging to find an accelerator's true impact based on simple effect averages. Consider that most of the movement in year-over-year changes in these five commercial variables takes place in the tails of the distribution, especially when it comes to the three investment variables. Table 4.2 shows that almost 80 percent of the ventures in the EDP sample report zero year-over-year changes in either outside equity or debt. In most cases, these ventures are simply shut out of the equity investment game before and after applying to accelerators. Among the remaining ventures, roughly the same percentage report one-year gains (+13 percent) and losses (+9 percent), which are both quite substantial on average. The 246 ventures with declining outside equity investment lost roughly $90,000 worth of investment on average, while the 365 ventures that grew outside equity investment experienced an average gain of almost $125,000. Similarly, more than 60 percent of the ventures report no change in philanthropic support, with the larger remainder again roughly split between those that report increases and decreases.

Table 4.2 Negative-growth, no-change, and positive-growth ventures

	Negative growth	No change	Positive growth
Revenues	N = 549 (18.9%) Average = −$98,828	N = 887 (30.6%)	N = 1466 (50.5%) Average = $74,225
Full-time employees	N = 606 (20.9%) Average = −4.33	N = 1023 (35.3%)	N = 1273 (43.9%) Average = 3.74
Outside equity	N = 246 (8.5%) Average = −$90,131	N = 2291 (79.0%)	N = 365 (12.6%) Average = $123,611
Total debt	N = 263 (9.1%) Average = −$53,050	N = 2296 (79.1%)	N = 343 (11.8%) Average = $74,711
Philanthropic support	N = 446 (15.4%) Average = −$49,122	N = 1823 (62.8%)	N = 633 (21.9%) Average = $50,453

This distributional issue is confounded by what some might call a 'faster-to-fail' motivation that accelerators activate with ventures that find themselves at or near the bottom of the pack. While some supporters of accelerators think that they should have a positive impact on every entrepreneur, most experienced practitioners know that this is a naïve aspiration. Instead, accelerators are charged with working intensely with entrepreneurs who demonstrate some promise to uncover their true potential. Then, they zero in on this group to ensure that they have ample opportunities and sufficient resources to scale their operations. When programming efforts reveal that certain ideas, ventures or teams may not have what it takes to prosper, it is acceptable to usher them toward failure, or at least counsel them to consider serious, time-consuming pivots. Accelerators should not deploy or divert valuable programmatic, social, and financial resources in the direction of less-than-promising entrepreneurial efforts. In support of this idea, one recent academic study suggests that 'accelerators help resolve uncertainty around company quality sooner such that founders can make funding and exit decisions accordingly.'[9]

Figure 4.1 reveals these differing effects at the opposite ends of the growth distributions, supporting the idea that accelerators may be implicated in both driving positive results at the top end of the distribution and negative growth outcomes at the bottom. Relative to the no-growth ventures, the percentage of positive-growth ventures in Table 4.2 that also participated in accelerator programs is relatively high across all five variables, especially for debt (29 percent versus 20 percent), equity (29 percent versus 20 percent), and philanthropy (27 percent versus 21 percent). However, the same is true for the

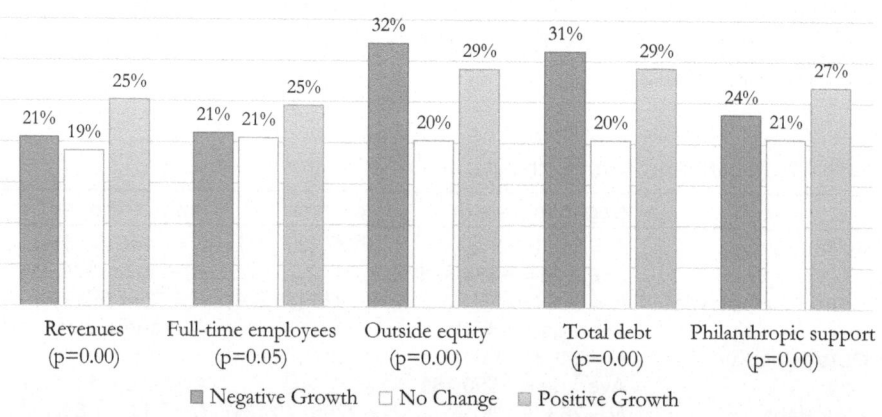

Fig. 4.1 Accelerator participation and negative-, no-, and positive-growth ventures

negative-growth ventures, where the percentage of accelerator program participants is also higher across the board, and especially for debt (32 percent) and equity (31 percent).

Because these opposing effects are statistically significant, the 'faster-to-fail' caveat must be kept in mind as we interpret the average effects reported in the remainder of the book. It is also important that researchers develop more nuanced ways to isolate the complex effects that acceleration has on the commercial performance of participating ventures.

Focus on Top-Growing Ventures

Given these opposing effects, it is instructive to look more closely at the top end of each distribution to appreciate whether and where accelerators contribute to extreme high-growth outcomes, those that arguably will have the greatest future impact. We identify the top 50 one-year growth outcomes for each of the five variables. Consistent with the low correlations among these five variables, the group of applicants that landed in the top 50 for revenue, employee, equity, debt, or philanthropy growth includes 218 ventures (see Table 4.3). None of the ventures in the EDP sample appear in either four or five of these top-50 lists, and only two appear in three lists. One of these latter two applicants reached the top 50 in the revenue, employee, and debt growth categories. It is a five-year-old for-profit venture that works in the health sector in Mexico. The other reached the top 50 in the employee, equity, and debt growth categories. It is a one-year-old for-profit venture working in the agriculture sector in India.

Table 4.3 Isolating the top-50 growth outcomes

	In any top-50 list (N = 218)	Not in any top-50 list (N = 2684)	Sig.
Average revenue growth	$266,232	−$1297	p = 0.00
Average employment growth	6.95	0.23	p = 0.00
Average equity growth	$134,254	−$2355	p = 0.00
Average debt growth	$65,933	−$1006	p = 0.00
Average philanthropy growth	$81,923	−$2917	p = 0.00
Percent participated	36.7%	21.2%	p = 0.00
	(N = 80)	(N = 138)	
Participated only:			
Average revenue growth	$170,554	$321,697	p = 0.04
Average employment growth	4.98	8.10	p = 0.13
Average equity growth	$137,113	$132,596	p = 0.91
Average debt growth	$60,801	$68,908	p = 0.77
Average philanthropy growth	$84,500	$77,476	p = 0.86

Both companies were founded by all-male teams with some prior entrepreneurial experience and some proprietary intellectual property. Neither were selected to participate in the programs to which they applied.

Comparing these 218 companies to the much larger sub-sample that landed outside any of the five top-50 lists illustrates how the development of early-stage ventures is close to a winners-take-all endeavor. For instance, while the 218 top-growth companies reported an average one-year revenue growth of more than $250,000, the other 2684 ventures reported declining revenues on average. These stark differences are evident across all of the five variables under consideration.

The 'Percent participated' row of Table 4.3 shows that roughly 37 percent of the applicants that participated in an EDP accelerator made it into the roster of top-50 growth companies, compared to only 21 percent of the rejected ventures. This difference, which is significant, suggests that, at the margin, accelerators usher their cohort ventures into the upper echelons of company growth outcomes.

Accounting for Different Starting Points

Chapter 3 showed that accelerators have a tendency to select entrepreneurs and ventures with more reported revenues, employment, and investment. This makes sense if acceleration services are more valuable when applied to ventures that are already in preferable positions. This begs the question of whether, and to what extent, the observed effects of acceleration are simple artifacts of these more attractive pre-acceleration positions. To provide some insights, we jointly estimate a series of simple regression equations that relate follow-up levels of revenues, employees, and investment to their corresponding levels reported in application surveys, and on a variable that indicates program participation.[10] To extrapolate from any program-specific effects on accelerator outcomes, these equations also include a series of fixed-program effects.

Table 4.4 shows that there are positive and significant carry-over effects from the application into the follow-up data. For example, roughly 56 percent of prior-year revenues carry over into the follow-up year, suggesting that each dollar of revenue reported on applications translates into 56 additional cents the next year. Because the ventures accepted for participation tend to come in with higher levels of revenues, employees, and investment, their follow-up performance will also be higher, regardless of whether they participated in an accelerator. However, these prior-year performance effects do not eliminate the observed effects of acceleration. After controlling for prior-year

Table 4.4 Simple regression equations that control for prior-year performance

	Follow-up revenues	Follow-up FT employees	Follow-up equity	Follow-up debt	Follow-up philanthropy
Application revenues	0.56**	–	–	–	–
Application FT employees	–	0.36**	–	–	–
Application equity	–	–	0.58**	–	–
Application debt	–	–	–	0.42**	–
Application philanthropy	–	–	–	–	0.52**
Participated	$25,536*	1.42**	$12,218*	$10,143**	$11,774**
Fixed program effects	Yes	Yes	Yes	Yes	Yes
N	2902	2902	2902	2902	2902
'R-squared'	0.43	0.37	0.34	0.14	0.38

Estimated using a seemingly-unrelated regression model. $**p < 0.01$, $*p < 0.05$

performance, and for any effects that are specific to particular programs, the effects of acceleration are positive, large, and significant across the board. On average, accelerator participation corresponds with more than $25,000 of additional revenues that support the hiring of 1.4 more full-time employees. Participating ventures also have access to almost $35,000 more combined equity, debt, and philanthropic investment.

In the end, these various observations support the same conclusion. Participation in accelerator programs tends to be associated with superior commercial performance during the year in which the program operates.

Decomposing the Average Acceleration Effects

Just because overall average effects are positive does not mean that acceleration has the same effects on all kinds of ventures. Table 4.5 sets the stage for two deeper dives reported in Chaps. 9 and 10 by showing how accelerator 'growth bumps' vary across performance indicators and across different venture types. Accelerator growth bumps are defined as:

- Revenue growth bump = revenue growth$_{participated}$ − revenue growth$_{rejected}$
- Employment growth bump = employment growth$_{participated}$ − employment growth$_{rejected}$

Table 4.5 Accelerator bumps across different types of ventures

	Revenue growth bump	Employment growth bump	Equity growth bump	Debt growth bump	Philanthropy growth bump
Overall	$4630	0.80	$5336	$3605	$2925
Nonprofits	−$5433	0.61	−$68	−$6054	$15,546
Education sector	−$22,988	1.81	$26,292	−$10,233	$29,739
Agriculture sector	$26,668	0.74	−$12,424	$3681	−$5382
Health sector	−$11,453	−0.55	$14,214	$3603	$10,054
Financial services sector	$16,303	0.24	$1241	$14,252	−$9704
ICT sector	$69,161	0.23	$16,130	$5667	$3882
Any intellectual property	−$11,332	0.94	$12,457	$6479	−$30
Multiple founders on team	$4807	0.84	$6218	$505	$917
Prior founding experience	−$6104	0.96	$11,526	$7131	−$2286
Prior acceleration experience	$13,205	2.27	$7859	$13,647	$13,444

- Equity growth bump = equity growth$_{participated}$ − equity growth$_{rejected}$
- Debt growth bump = debt growth$_{participated}$ − debt growth$_{rejected}$
- Philanthropy growth bump = philanthropy growth$_{participated}$ − philanthropy growth$_{rejected}$

The first thing that Table 4.5 shows is that nonprofits derive fewer benefits from acceleration. While the majority of the ventures in the EDP sample operate as for-profit companies, roughly 11 percent are nonprofits. It seems that participating nonprofits benefit from acceleration in only one performance domain: increased philanthropic support (+$15,546 compared to rejected nonprofits). At the other extreme, they actually experience lower revenue, equity, and debt growth on average than their rejected counterparts. Given the general emphasis on for-profit ventures by most accelerators, and the absence of any programs that exclusively focus on nonprofits, this observation is sensible. However, it also raises questions that warrant further study. Is the accelerator model inherently better-suited to support for-profit ventures? If so, are there similar or different interventions for those entrepreneurs who want to deliver market-based benefits using the nonprofit organizational form? It is also important to ask whether accelerators that work with mixed cohorts of nonprofit and for-profit ventures produce different outcomes over-all than those that focus on just one organizational type?

More thinking is also required when it comes to the different patterns of accelerator effects across sectors. Accelerated ventures in the education sector seem to be driving the positive employment bump (+1.8 compared to +0.8 in the overall sample), and they seem to be doing this with a relatively large bump in outside equity investment and philanthropic support. These invest-ment bumps come with a decline in earned revenues. Health sector ventures seem to experience a similar pattern, but one that is more muted and without the short-term bumps to employment. These patterns seem consistent with the standard venture capital model of venture development where immediate injections of capital allow entrepreneurs to pause their selling efforts to focus on prototype and business model development. Acceleration in the agricul-ture sector produces larger bumps in earned revenue, but lower bumps—actually negative—in outside equity and philanthropic investment. This seems to be more of a 'sing-for-your support' model where ventures learn that outside investment might be harder to come by as they focus on earning the funds that will be required for future growth. There is a similar pattern in the financial services sector, but these ventures seem to be receiving an above-average bump in borrowed funds. This constellation might be a reflection of the established pattern of support for the global microfinance movement, which relies on large pools of loan funds to grow their own lending opera-tions. Finally, ICT ventures are off the charts when it comes to their revenue bump. This corresponds with above-average equity investment and, to a lesser extent, debt bumps. However, these funding bumps do not translate into larger bumps in full-time employment, suggesting that the immediate injec-tion of new funding is being spent elsewhere.

Another constellation of effects that (predictably) aligns the observed accel-erator bumps with typical venture capital-type expectations is seen among the ventures that report having proprietary intellectual property; that is, patents, trademarks, and copyrights. Here, there is a negative earned revenue bump and relatively high outside equity and debt bumps. It seems that accelerators are helping these kinds of ventures defer their need to earn revenues by help-ing them attract the investment that funds the development of innovative prototypes. The same can be said for ventures whose founders report having prior entrepreneurial experience. Past research consistently finds that external equity, debt, and philanthropic investors consider prior entrepreneurial expe-rience as one sign of credibility for a founding team.[11] This helps the experi-enced founding teams attract external investment on the basis of their past record of success, instead of current revenue growth.

The final row of Table 4.5 addresses the implications of serial acceleration. Some commentators are critical of the practice of serial acceleration, suggesting that it creates a pattern of dependence among entrepreneurs who become adept at communicating a permanent state of promise to accelerator selection committees. At the same time, valuable acceleration services are being diverted from other entrepreneurs who might otherwise benefit. With these concerns in mind, the practice of going through multiple accelerators is not uncommon, as was shown in Chap. 3. Some of the program managers that we interviewed were not critical of this pattern. As entrepreneurs 'do the rounds' at different programs, they build larger and stronger networks while raising the profile of their ventures. In support of this latter position, the EDP data suggest that ventures whose founders report prior accelerator experience on their application surveys experience greater accelerator growth bumps across the board. These effects suggest an accumulative impact of acceleration that gives rise to new and more intriguing questions about how accelerators produce their effects.

Finally, when it comes to operating in high-income countries versus emerging markets, there are larger-than-average bumps for equity investment and debt among ventures that work in high-income countries. However, these ventures experience dramatically lower-than-average increases in revenues and employees. These important differences are explored in Chap. 9. And, contrary to some optimistic beliefs about the ability of accelerators to level the gender playing field, the lion's share of the observed accelerator bumps is experienced by ventures with all-male founding teams. The two exceptions are the modest advantages for teams with women when it comes to employment growth and philanthropic investment. These differences are explored in Chap. 10.

The final observation in this chapter anticipates a transition to the program-level analyses presented in Chaps. 5 through 8. The 78 programs in the EDP sample produce a wide range of acceleration effects, on average (see Table 4.6). In the middle of the program-level distribution, average program outcomes are quite ordinary. For instance, participating ventures in the median program experienced an average of just over $13,000 in revenue growth in the year in

Table 4.6 Average growth in key variables by program, participated ventures only

	Minimum program	Median program	Maximum program
Change in revenues	−$334,447	$13,206	$263,613
Change in FT employees	−2.20	0.00	14.50
Change in outside equity	−$77,000	$0	$222,800
Change in total debt	−$112,996	$0	$200,000
Change in philanthropic support	−$134,824	$536	$128,200

which their program operated. However, the gap between the top program (+$263,613) and the bottom program (−$334,447) is dramatic. Similar patterns of substantial program-level disparities are observed for the average employee and investment outcomes as well. This wide range of program-level outcomes prompts us to look past the positive average effects of acceleration and begin to probe the program-level differences that might be associated with superior accelerator performance.

Concluding Remarks

The observations in this chapter offer an overall endorsement of the accelerator model. On average, accelerated ventures display greater one-year growth in revenues, employment, and investment than rejected ventures. These effects are more impressive after accounting for the fact that accelerator participation is also associated with declining growth outcomes among the (arguably) less promising ventures that participate in accelerator programs. Focusing on the top end of these growth distributions, accelerated ventures are far more likely to be among the top ventures, the ones that are outpacing the others by huge margins. Finally, positive average accelerator effects remain evident after accounting for prior-year performance, suggesting that the better performance of participating ventures is not a simple extrapolation of recent commercial and investment successes.

The observations at the end of this chapter also point to considerable variability in these effects across ventures. There are differences among the non-profit ventures, those with proprietary intellectual property, and those whose founders have prior entrepreneurial experience. We also see considerable variability from program to program. This cautions against treating accelerators as simple black boxes. The observations in the next several chapters heed this caution by disaggregating accelerator work into three primary domains to learn more about how decisions related to pipeline-building, entrepreneur selection, and program design influence accelerators' ability to drive new funding into their cohort ventures.

Looking Ahead: A Closer Look at Accelerator Programs
So far, data from GALI and the EDP have been used to paint a broad picture of the global accelerator landscape, before asking the general question of whether accelerators have identifiable effects on the development of impact-oriented ventures. According to venture-level data compiled by the EDP between 2013 and 2017, on average, both participating and rejected ventures

improved their commercial performance during the year after they applied to accelerators. Follow-up revenues, full-time employment, outside equity investment, debt, and philanthropic support all trend upward for the ventures in the sample. The fact that rejected entrepreneurs are able to make progress on these various commercial dimensions raises the bar for what it means for an accelerator to claim that it is having an effect on early-stage ventures. Acceleration is only evident when the performance changes for participating ventures are better than those observed for non-participating, or rejected, ventures. In this respect, it is encouraging that the growth results for participating ventures tend to be higher than those observed among rejected entrepreneurs.

However, just because the effects of acceleration are positive overall does not mean that the effects are similar for entrepreneurs working in every region around the world, or that acceleration is equally powerful for different kinds of entrepreneurs. The final two chapters take up these issues by examining acceleration effects among ventures operating in emerging markets (Chap. 9) and ventures founded by women entrepreneurs (Chap. 10). Nor do the results in Chap. 4 mean that every program is equally adept at accelerating venture performance. In the next part of the book, we shift attention to the program level in order to show that some accelerator programs are better than others when it comes to accelerating the flow of financial resources into participating ventures (Chap. 5). This exploration continues as we examine which programmatic choices related to pipeline building (Chap. 6) and entrepreneur selection (Chap. 7) seem to influence the ability to accelerate these funding flows. Then, Chap. 8 looks at several specific interventions, like curriculum usage and mentorship program design, to determine whether they correlate with success when it comes to attracting financial resources from customers, investors, lenders, and donors.

Notes

1. Sandy Yu. 2016. How Do Accelerators Impact the Performance of High-Technology Ventures? Working paper.
2. Susan L. Cohen, Christopher B. Bingham & Benjamin L. Hallen. 2018. 'The role of accelerator designs in mitigating bounded Rationality in new ventures.' *Administrative Science Quarterly*, forthcoming.
3. Juanita Gonzalez-Uribe & Michael Leatherbee. 2017. 'The effects of business accelerators on venture performance: Evidence from Start-Up Chile.' *The Review of Financial Studies*, 31(4): 1566–1603.

4. Ketan, J. Goswami, Robert Mitchell & Suresh Bhagavatula. 2018. 'Accelerator expertise: Understanding the intermediary role of accelerators in the development of the Bangalore entrepreneurial ecosystem.' *Strategic Entrepreneurship Journal,* 12(1): 117–150.

5. See *Accelerating Entrepreneurs: Insights from USAID's Support of Intermediaries.* United States Agency for International Development.

6. *Accelerating Revenue Growth for SGBs in Central America: Lessons Learned from Ten Technoserve Cohorts.*

7. Alejandro S. Amezcua, Matthew G. Grimes, Steven W. Bradley & Johan Wiklund. 2013. 'Organizational sponsorship and founding environments: A contingency view on the survival of business-incubated firms, 1994–2007.' *Academy of Management Journal,* 56(6): 1628–1654.

8. See https://www.merriam-webster.com/

9. Sandy Yu. 2016. How Do Accelerators Impact the Performance of High-Technology Ventures? Working paper.

10. Seemingly-unrelated regression is an efficient method for examining systems of equations in which the dependent variable differs across equations, but the errors terms are correlated. See Arnold Zellner. 1962. 'An efficient method of estimating seemingly unrelated regressions and tests for aggregation bias.' *Journal of the American Statistical Association,* 57(298): 348–368.

11. Paul Robson, Charles Akuetteh, Ian Stone, Paul Westhead & Mike Wright. 2013 'Credit-rationing and entrepreneurial experience: Evidence from a resource deficit context.' *Entrepreneurship & Regional Development,* 25 (5–6): 349–370; Eli Gimmon & Jonathan Levie. 2010. 'Founder's human capital, external investment, and the survival of new high-technology ventures.' *Research Policy,* 39 (9): 1214–1226; M. Scarlata & L. Alemany. 2010. 'Deal structuring in philanthropic venture capital investments: Financing instrument, valuation and covenants.' *Journal of Business Ethics,* 95(2): 121–145.

5

Driving the Net Flow of Funds

The analyses in Chap. 4 address the general question of whether accelerators have identifiable effects on variables that correlate with the development of early-stage ventures; namely, revenues, employment, and investment. These observations add to the slowly accumulating evidence of the positive effects of acceleration coming from other studies. However, this general support for accelerators does not mean that their effects are even across programs. Consider the 2016 GALI report that compared four high-performing Village Capital programs to four lower-performing programs. The former group includes a program where participants experienced a one-year average equity investment bump (i.e., an increase relative to rejected applicants) of more than $110,000, while the latter group includes a program where the average equity growth for participants was almost $170,000 lower than the corresponding average for rejected ventures. A similar pattern appears in another study that provides 'evidence that certain sampled accelerators both aid and accelerate the development of new ventures … [while] some accelerators had no effect or even negatively affected some outcomes.'[1]

Because accelerators demonstrate variable efficacy, it is important to recognize the different domains of accelerator work, and then look more closely at the program choices within each of these domains to see which correspond with superior outcomes for entrepreneurs, and superior value for money for the accelerator program funders.[2]

© The Author(s) 2019
P. W. Roberts, S. A. Lall, *Observing Acceleration*,
https://doi.org/10.1007/978-3-030-00042-4_5

The NFF

It should be obvious by now that accelerators work in a range of sectors and regions with a range of ventures and founding teams trying to move the needle on a range of venture-level outcomes. In this complicated context, it can be difficult to gain clarity on the cause-and-effect relationships that produce positive accelerator outcomes. To develop a solid foundation for what should become a more robust stream of research, we presents a structured look at the various accelerator program design choices that influence one important variable: the NFF into participating ventures.

Early-stage ventures must have financial resources to stabilize and grow. These funds come through a finite number of channels: they can be earned (i.e., revenues); they can come through investment (i.e., outside equity); they can be borrowed (i.e., new debt); and they can be donated (i.e., philanthropic support). The next several chapters focus on the NFF, a variable that measures the average total increase in financial resources for participating ventures compared to their rejected counterparts. This NFF variable, which integrates four of the variables analyzed in Chap. 4, is calculated by first subtracting the revenue, equity, debt, and philanthropy numbers reported in application surveys from the corresponding numbers reported in follow-up surveys. Then, for each program, we compute the average one-year changes for participating ventures minus the average one-year changes for those that applied but did not participate:

- Net revenue growth = average revenue growth$_{participated}$ − average revenue growth$_{rejected}$
- Net equity growth = average equity growth$_{participated}$ − average equity growth$_{rejected}$
- Net debt growth = average debt growth$_{participated}$ − average debt growth$_{rejected}$
- Net philanthropy growth = average philanthropy growth$_{participated}$ − average philanthropy growth$_{rejected}$

The NFF variable is the sum of these four differentials. It represents the net flow of incremental funding that a program stimulates into a typical participating venture during the acceleration year:

- Net flow of funds (NFF) = net revenue growth + net equity growth + net debt growth + net philanthropy growth

It is important to recognize what is gained and sacrificed by examining a single indicator of an accelerator's ability to drive new funding into participating ventures. Averaging venture-level outcomes two times—first across entrepreneurs and ventures and then across different funding flows—creates a simplified context that allows us to relate program-level variables to a single indicator of accelerator effectiveness. However, it also means that we must be circumspect when interpreting patterns that are revealed in the data. After all, we cannot be certain that an interesting program-level effect is not the result of some venture or entrepreneur differences that have been suppressed. Also, averaging across four change variables that are virtually uncorrelated—remember Tables 3.3 and 3.4 in Chap. 3—allows the researcher to be agnostic about which specific flow is driving the overall flow-of-funds. However, it is possible (and even likely) that some of the program choices that influence net revenue growth might be inconsistent with the choices that influence, for example, net equity growth. We address this latter issue throughout this chapter and in Chaps. 6 through 8 in a series of comments about high-performing programs whose dominant funding impact is on revenue growth versus those whose dominant impact is on equity investment growth.

A Smaller Sample of Programs

The current analyses cover 52 of the EDP accelerators from the venture-level sample analyzed in Chaps. 3 and 4. All of these programs provide a sufficient number of data points to calculate program-level average changes in revenues, outside equity, new debt, and philanthropy for both participating and rejected ventures. They also provide reliable information on their program-manager surveys (see below). Table 5.1 shows that roughly half of these 52 programs were run in North America. Most of the remaining programs were run in Latin America & Caribbean (10 programs), Sub-Saharan Africa (9 programs), and South Asia (5 programs).

Across the 52 programs, the average growth in the total flow of funds for rejected entrepreneurs is $25,337 (see Table 5.2). This means that the total of

Table 5.1 The program-level sample

	Programs	Applicants	Participated, with follow-up data	Rejected, with follow-up data
Programs run in:				
North America (United States and Canada)	27	1757	237	695
Latin America and Caribbean	10	1093	134	363
Sub-Saharan Africa	9	1212	119	554
South Asia	5	375	30	114
East Asia and Pacific	1	26	6	7
Total	52	4463	526	1733

earned (revenues), invested (equity), borrowed (debt), and donated (philanthropy) funds reported on the first follow-up surveys is roughly $25,000 higher than the corresponding average reported on the application surveys of rejected applicants. The next four rows of Table 5.2 show that most of these new funds came from increased revenues and outside equity investment. This across-the-board average improvement among non-accelerated applicants sets the bar for ventures that participate in programs. On average, participants in the sampled programs experienced an overall funding increase of $56,223, which is more than double the average reported among the rejected ventures. Therefore, we may surmise that accelerators are responsible for an average NFF of more than $30,000 for each of the ventures that they work with; or $56,226 minus $25,337. The largest NFF component is net equity growth. Compared to the average growth reported by rejected ventures, accelerator participants attracted more than $15,000 of incremental equity investment.

While these averages are impressive, they mask a wide range in NFF outcomes across programs. Figure 5.1 shows the minimum, maximum, and average NFF for the programs in the sample, along with the corresponding ranges for each

Table 5.2 The NFF and its four components

	Average one-year change for participated ventures	Average one-year change for rejected ventures	Sig.
Total flow of funds	$56,223	$25,337	$p = 0.10$
Revenue growth	$16,081	$10,061	$p = 0.65$
Equity growth	$23,387	$7870	$p = 0.09$
Debt growth	$8300	$3249	$p = 0.34$
Philanthropy growth	$8455	$4197	$p = 0.46$

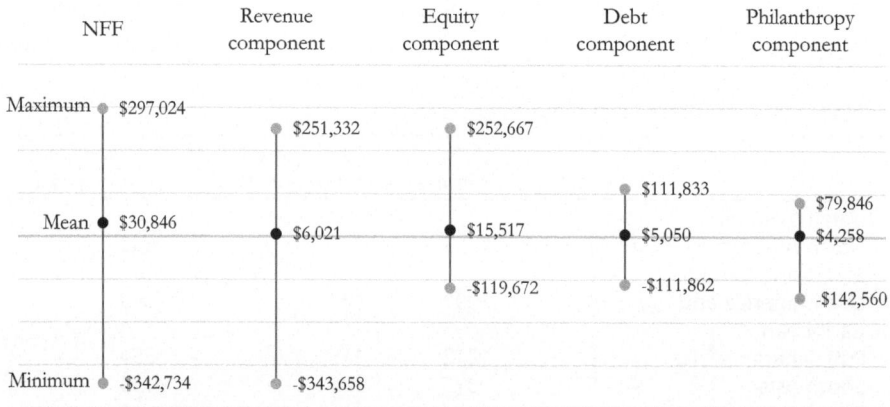

Fig. 5.1 The range of NFF and its four components

NFF component. This considerable variability—particularly when it comes to net revenue and net equity growth—suggests that the optimistic averages reported in Table 5.2 mask very different outcomes achieved by individual programs.

The Four Components of the NFF Variable

Although four NFF components combine to determine the NFF into participating ventures, they are not highly correlated (see Table 5.3). In fact, the pairwise correlations are often close to zero or even negative. The one exception is the correlation between net revenue and net philanthropy growth which is correlated at $\rho = 0.17$. Table 5.3 also shows that the component with the highest correlation with overall NFF is net revenue growth ($\rho = 0.80$), while the lowest correlation is with net debt growth ($\rho = 0.24$). This suggests that accelerators' efforts that improve short-term revenue growth also tend to have positive effects on the other three funding flows. The opposite is true for efforts that improve the levels of borrowed funds.

This decomposition suggests that the work of getting promising early-stage ventures on a path toward financial stability and growth takes different trajectories, and that accelerators may have to adopt different approaches when it comes to driving incremental funding into their ventures. Interviews with program managers suggest that many accelerators explicitly aim to catalyze equity investment, with programming focused on investment readiness and connections to equity investors. However, these interviews also indicate that this focus on equity is not a universal, or the only goal of accelerators. Program managers take into consideration that:

- entrepreneurs must show revenue growth to attract investment. As one program manager said, 'our curriculum is based around investment readiness. But if you don't have the customer piece – the recurring revenue – then you won't get to Series A financing. So even though we're focused on equity financing, revenues are required to obtain it.'

Table 5.3 Correlations among the four NFF components

	(1)	(2)	(3)	(4)	(5)
(1) Net flow of funds	1.00				
(2) Net revenue growth	0.80	1.00			
(3) Net equity growth	0.40	−0.03	1.00		
(4) Net debt growth	0.24	−0.03	−0.11	1.00	
(5) Net philanthropy growth	0.42	0.17	−0.06	0.08	1.00

- equity investments are not always needed or desired. 'We discovered that it is good to learn from companies how much money they want to raise. But it's also good for them to learn whether they really need investment. Entrepreneurs oftentimes think that success equates with investment, but sometimes it's actually a bad outcome for them.'
- accelerators' first priority is often to learn what it takes to move each business forward: 'The reason our program worked was that it was very customized. Our ventures go through a deep diagnosis phase – what do they need, and what do they think they need that they don't?'

In light of these qualitative insights, we take another look at the interplay among the components that make up the NFF variable. We start by organizing the sample based on which of the four funding components makes the largest contribution to NFF (see Table 5.4). For roughly one-third of the programs, the largest contribution to NFF comes through net revenue growth. Another one-third of the programs see the largest gains coming through net equity growth. The final third of the programs drive NFF mainly through improvements in debt or philanthropy. The programs that are dominated by net revenue growth produce the greatest average NFF because participating ventures experience substantially higher revenue gains alongside somewhat higher growth in equity and philanthropy. The 17 programs whose largest NFF component is net equity growth combine substantial equity investment gains with modest gains for net debt growth, but also net declines in revenues and philanthropy. At the other extreme, the six programs whose strongest contribution comes through increased borrowings see modest gains in that component that are swamped by net declines in revenues, equity, and philanthropy.

Table 5.4 The NFF by dominant component

	Programs	NFF	Net revenue growth	Net equity growth	Net debt growth	Net philanthropy growth
Net revenue growth dominates	19	$93,424	$85,562	$1666	−$1104	$7300
Net equity growth dominates	17	$40,156	−$18,611	$65,773	$6141	−$13,146
Net debt growth dominates	6	−$103,563	−$108,912	−$28,910	$41,545	−$7287
Net philanthropy growth dominates	10	−$23,232	−$34,275	−$16,944	−$7007	$34,994

Separating High-NFF and Low-NFF Programs

Figure 5.1 showed that the positive overall NFF average masks considerable variability across programs, where the NFF ranges from +$297,024 to −$342,734. This suggests that accelerators can have substantial positive effects on the flow of funds into participating ventures, but they can also be associated with negative effects. Given these discrepancies, it is important to learn more about the program choices that correspond with favorable NFF outcomes.

Because of the relatively small number of programs in the sample and the presence of outliers, we decided to split the sample based on programs whose average NFF is greater than the corresponding cost per venture of running their programs. In the EDP program surveys (see below), program managers are asked, 'To the nearest $10,000, what is the total financial cost associated with running this program? Please include all living stipends paid to participating entrepreneurs, but do not include any financial investments that you expect to make into the ventures themselves.' Dividing this dollar figure by the number of participating ventures provides an estimate of the per-venture cost of running the program. Tagging programs whose overall NFF is greater than this cost threshold identifies those that more than cover their costs by driving more incremental funding into ventures than the funds spent on running the program.

In most of the programs in the sample, the NFF exceeds the reported per-venture cost. For these accelerators, $1 spent on programming translates into more than $1 of incremental funding—earned, invested, borrowed or donated—for participating ventures. Figure 5.2 shows that these 33 high-NFF accelerators return an average NFF that exceeds $97,000. This funding advantage comes from almost $107,000 of new funds flowing into each participating venture, compared to less than $10,000 for each venture that was rejected from the same applicant pools. The second panel of Fig. 5.2 shows how most of this improved NFF comes from stimulating revenue growth and additional outside equity investment.

The 19 programs that did not cover their operating costs had an average NFF of −$85,263. This relatively poor funding effect resulted because each participating venture experienced a roughly $30,000 decline in its total flow of funds, while each corresponding rejected venture saw total funds increase by more than $50,000 on average. The majority of this NFF deficit came from diminished net revenue growth and lower outside equity investment growth.

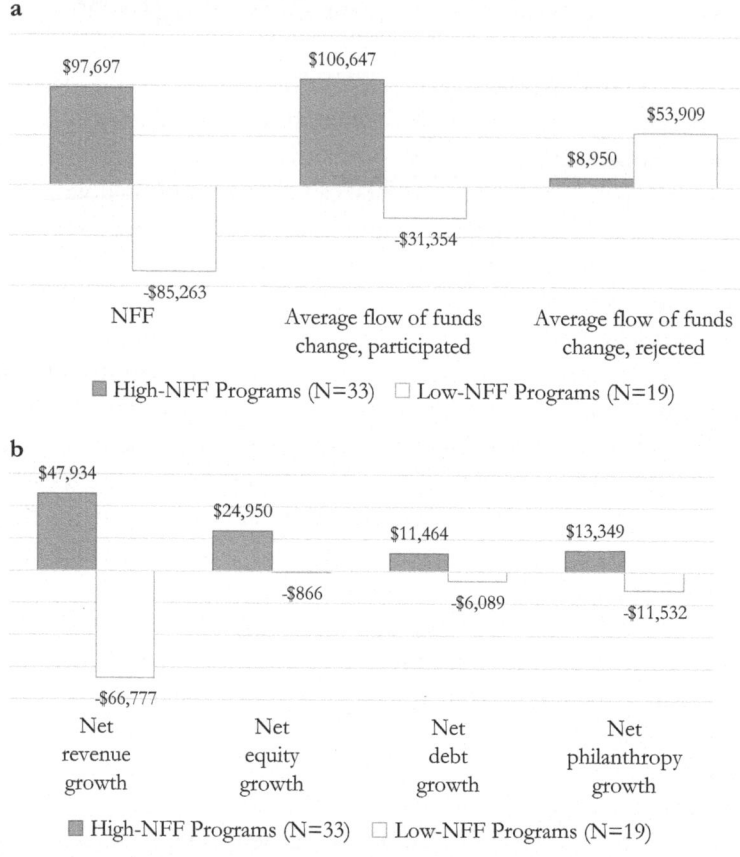

Fig. 5.2 **(a)** Average NFF and NFF for high-NFF and low-NFF programs **(b)** Average NFF and NFF components for high-NFF and low-NFF programs

Unpacking the Accelerator Model

On average, impact-oriented accelerators are stimulating positive flows of funds into participating ventures. However, they do so with varying degrees of effectiveness. From this baseline of evidence, we can begin to address more specific questions about which accelerator program choices tend to correspond with superior NFF outcomes. This more nuanced research requires a concise framework for thinking about how accelerators do their work.

One of the outputs from the 2016 GALI report is a typology that categorizes the various domains of accelerator work.[3] The first accelerator program to partner with the EDP was Village Capital. To get a better handle on the full

While it is important to track the flows of funds into impact-oriented ventures, it is also important to consider other indicators of enterprise development. One obvious candidate is employment growth, because this is another tangible growth metric and because employment creation is an important impact objective for many ventures, programs, and funders. While it is reasonable to expect that stimulating full-time employment growth might take longer than revenue or investment growth, we see that high-NFF programs also demonstrate greater net increases in the number of full-time employees (see Fig. 5.3).

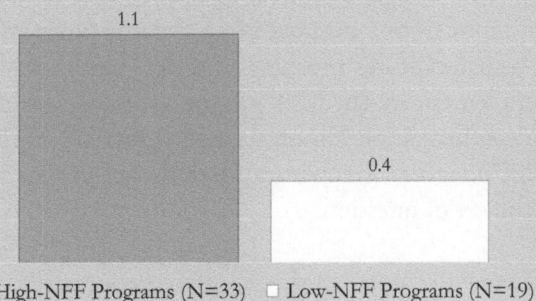

Fig. 5.3 One year changes in full-time employees for high-NFF and low-NFF programs

range of factors that might account for performance differences across its various programs, we assembled a small group of Village Capital personnel with first-hand experience with those programs and presented them with a series of program performance differences. We asked each of them to brainstorm all of the possible reasons why we might be seeing these performance differences. The specific instructions were: 'For each of the three contrasts presented below, please think for a moment and then fill in the blanks to suggest all plausible reasons why there may be differences between the programs that had positive impacts on cohorts and those that had negative impacts. You do not have to believe every one of your listed reasons. We would like to be exhaustive in our development of possible explanations. However, when you are finished, please indicate which of the listed explanations you think are most plausible.' This brainstorming exercise generated a list of more than 100 potential factors that might be implicated in accelerator program performance differences. With these in hand, a research team organized and consolidated the various factors into a concise typology of categories and sub-categories; one that is consistent with the limited academic literature on accelerators.[4] The major categories revealed by these Village Capital informants include pipeline development, entrepreneur selection, and program design, which include activities that address the knowledge, network, and capital gaps faced by participating entrepreneurs. After making choices about which ventures, regions, sectors, and impact areas to target, accelerators spend considerable time and effort building pipelines of applicants, selecting the most promising entrepreneurs, and then designing and offering programming that closes the knowledge, network, and capital gaps that are identified by entrepreneurs, mentors, and investors.

This typology led to the development of a program-level survey—developed with additional input from a number of accelerator program managers working with EDP—that captures meaningful differences in how accelerators are designed and implemented. The EDP program surveys were developed to provide comparable information about a range of variables within each of the categories. It includes the following questions (an Appendix to this chapter houses the full set of questions):

- General: Where will (most of) this program be located?
- Pipeline-building: Does this program have an explicit sector focus?
- Entrepreneur selection: Roughly how many individuals formally participate in selecting ventures into this program? Roughly what percentage of these selectors are female?
- Programming: Does this program have a structured curriculum that is distributed to participants in written or electronic form? Will this program feature pitch nights or demo days that connect participants to potential investors?

This survey was introduced into the EDP in January of 2016, including a wave of retrospective surveys that targeted managers of programs that launched before 2016.

A First Look at the NFF Drivers

After considering numerous factors, we focus on a group of variables that are often mentioned in commentaries about accelerator effectiveness, variables that produce surprising effects, and variables whose effects warrant further scrutiny. The next three chapters describe the most interesting observations related to pipeline-building (Chap. 6), entrepreneur selection (Chap. 7), and accelerator programming (Chap. 8). As a precursor to these analyses, we examined several of the general factors that were raised by the Village Capital informants.

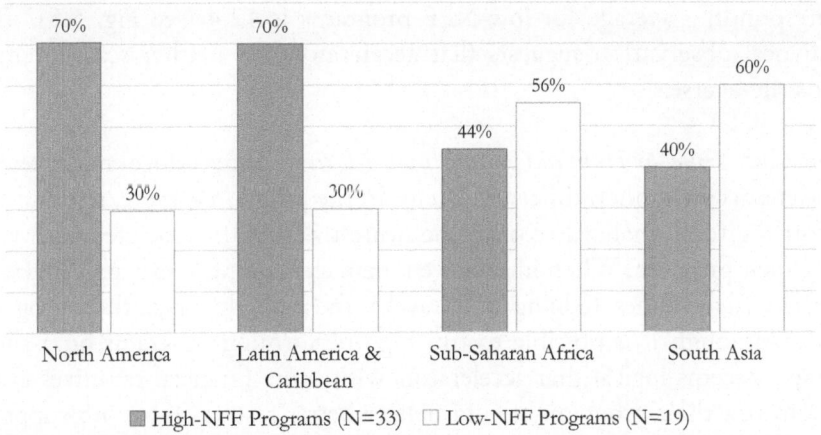

Fig. 5.4   World Bank regions for high-NFF and low-NFF programs

Does Program Location Matter? Given the current fascination with how eco-systems influence entrepreneurial outcomes, it is possible that the more suc-cessful accelerators are those that run in more established ecosystems. After all, they are often described as essential parts of strong entrepreneurial ecosys-tems, like those found in Silicon Valley, Berlin, and London.[5] The EDP pro-gram surveys identify the country or region in which each program operates. Figure 5.4 shows that roughly 70 percent of the 27 accelerators run in North America are high-NFF programs. While this seems to imply that accelerators are more successful in high-income countries, there is a similar percentage of high-NFF programs among the 10 Latin America & the Caribbean programs (70 percent). In the two smaller groups of programs run in South Asia and Sub-Saharan Africa, there are more low-NFF programs than high-NFF pro-grams. The fact that two of three emerging-market regions have a lower percentage of high-NFF programs suggests an association between region and accelerator performance. However, the stronger performance in a third emerging-market region (i.e., Latin America and the Caribbean) makes this assertion tenuous.

Does Cohort Size Matter? There are clearly challenges associated with run-ning programs with larger cohorts of promising entrepreneurs and ventures. At the same time, there are possible benefits associated with having connec-tions to a larger number of high-potential colleagues. Consistent with this latter belief—although the difference is not statistically significant—the average cohort size for high-NFF programs is 14.5 ventures, while the corresponding average for low-NFF programs is 12.4 (see Fig. 5.5). This equivocal observation suggests that accelerators are neither scale-oriented nor scale-averse.

Does Cost, Time, or Human Capital Input Matter? Three critical resources for accelerators are money, time, and talent. In the program surveys, respondents report the total financial cost (to the nearest $10,000) associated with running their program. When interviewed, managers point to expenses like salaries, as well as venues, lodging, and travel as the main drivers of these program costs. Although it is possible to run high-performing programs on a shoestring, it seems logical that accelerators with more financial resources available to run their programs should deliver better results. Table 5.5 supports this notion by showing that high-NFF programs are more expensive to run on average. However, given their slightly larger average cohort sizes (see Fig. 5.5), they actually spend less per venture on average—a difference of about $6000.

Program managers are also asked to report the duration of their program and the number of individuals deployed on selection committees and in mentor pools. Average program duration is similar among the high-NFF and

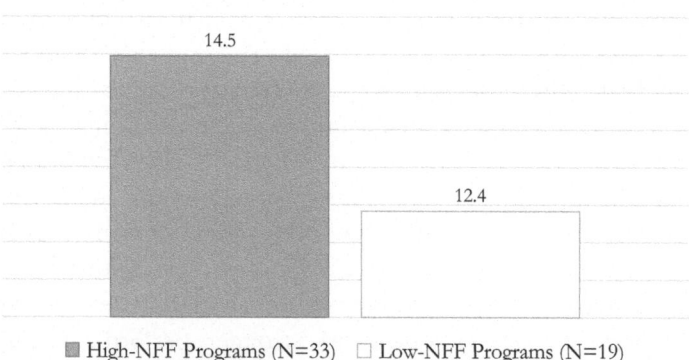

■ High-NFF Programs (N=33)   ☐ Low-NFF Programs (N=19)

Fig. 5.5 Average cohort size for high-NFF versus low-NFF programs

Table 5.5 Cost, duration, and human capital inputs for high-NFF versus low-NFF programs

	Program cost	Cost per venture	Duration	Individuals involved
High-NFF programs	$208,257	$15,544	3.3 months	104
Low-NFF programs	$193,783	$22,030	3.7 months	111
Sig.	$p = 0.80$	$p = 0.24$	$p = 0.64$	$p = 0.80$

low-NFF programs, centering on roughly 3.5 months. The total number of people deployed as selectors and mentors is also very similar across the two groups, averaging slightly more than 100 people.

Do the Emphasized Program Benefits Matter? Accelerators are set up to offer different experiences and therefore benefits to their entrepreneurs. Some programs focus on skill-building, while others emphasize connections to investors and customers. Still others emphasize their ability to invest directly in the ventures that they support. In this latter respect, we asked several program managers about the relative emphasis on providing investment for participating ventures. A typical response was, 'Most of our entrepreneurs would rank access to investment a high [priority] when they joined. But, after their first workshop, they start to realize that it's not just about investment-readiness. The program is delivering on other components that are more relevant and that serve as stepping stones to get to investment.' This more broad-based orientation is picked up in the program surveys, which ask managers to rank their programs' emphasis on different accelerator benefits. Figure 5.6 shows little in the way of significant differences across the two groups of programs when it comes to the benefits that are given the highest priority. Compared to low-NFF programs, high-NFF programs actually place less emphasis on providing funding directly to their entrepreneurs. However, this small sample result—only six programs in the entire sample list this benefit as their top priority—is at odds with an observation made later in Chap. 8, which suggests that programs that make these direct investments actually have a higher average NFF.

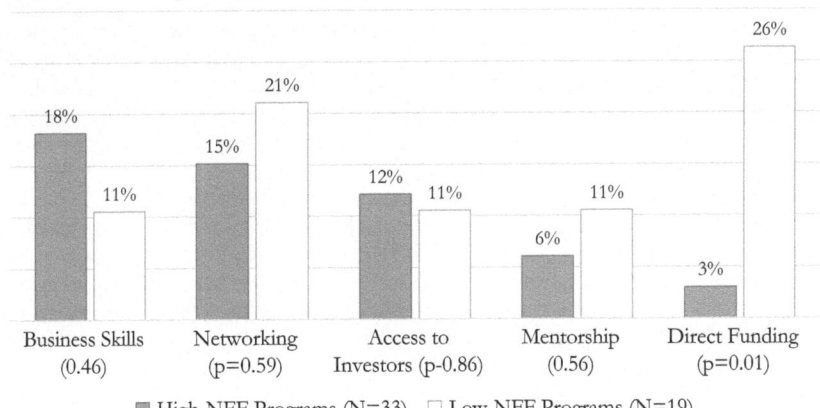

Fig. 5.6 Accelerator benefits ranked #1 by high-NFF versus low-NFF programs

Although it is convenient to place all high-NFF programs into the same bucket, a closer look shows that the majority of them (17 programs) are most effective at stimulating net revenue growth. In other words, their dominant NFF component (see Table 5.4) is net revenue growth. A smaller group (10 programs) is better at stimulating the flow of outside equity investment. The few remaining high-NFF programs are best at stimulating philanthropic support (5 programs) or new debt (1 program). The average NFF across these four groups of high-performing programs ranges from $105,232 (where net revenue growth dominates) and $112,064 (where net equity growth dominates) to $58,766 (where net philanthropy growth dominates) and $20,581 (where net debt growth dominates). These observations suggest that the two most promising pathways for high-NFF programs relate to stimulating net revenue and net equity growth.

Interviews with program managers reveal that while some successful accelerators have an a priori focus on driving either equity investment or revenue growth, others take a more adaptive approach, working with each entrepreneur to understand what is most relevant for them. A program manager from one Latin American accelerator that was quite good at driving revenue growth explains that 'we discovered in 2016 that it is good to define with companies how much money they want to raise in terms of investment, but it's also good for them to learn if they don't need investment ... We focus on understanding what their pain point is, and if it can be solved with the investment we try to achieve that, but otherwise, we don't.'

To learn more about the factors that might distinguish a successful revenue-driven model from a successful equity-driven model, we will present and discuss salient differences between the 17 high-NFF programs where net revenue growth dominates and the 10 programs where net equity growth dominates. For instance, roughly 80 percent of the high-NFF (equity) programs operate in North America, compared to only 35 percent of the high-NFF (revenue) programs. Accelerators in regions with less-developed investor communities acknowledge the importance of outside investment, but cite the paucity of local investors as a strong barrier. One program manager from an East African accelerator wants a 'strong focus on trying to drive investment into the ventures, but that's a component that I admit we don't have the right model for yet... Ideally, we would love to have more angels on board, but the market doesn't provide them.'

High-NFF (equity) programs also deploy an average of roughly 125 selectors and mentors, compared to roughly 85 for the high-NFF (revenue) programs. Moreover, roughly 30 percent of the high-NFF (equity) programs report the number one benefit that they provide entrepreneurs relates to networking, compared to less than 6 percent of the high-NFF (revenue) programs. We return to these observations in Chaps. 6 through 8. For now, we simply note that the two most common pathways to developing a high-NFF program differ in terms of their social capital orientation. Those that succeed by driving equity growth tend to focus more on networking, recruit more people into their programs, and succeed where existing business networks are more developed.

Concluding Remarks

This chapter introduces a program-level variable called the net flow of funds (NFF). This variable captures the extent to which accelerators drive incremental funding—earned, invested, borrowed, and donated—into their ventures. An examination of the EDP data reveals that the average NFF for programs in the sample is positive. On average, programs are accelerating the flow of funding into impact-oriented ventures. However, there is considerable variance across programs. At the end of the day, 19 of the 52 programs in the sample did not stimulate enough incremental funding to justify their program costs.

A decomposition of the NFF variable reveals that it is challenging to push all four funding components forward at the same time. Instead, most of the high-NFF programs in the sample accelerate the growth of earned revenues or outside equity investment. Fewer programs make it into the upper echelons by focusing on borrowing or philanthropic contributions.

Although the NFF is not the only measure of accelerator effectiveness, it does allow for focused assessments of the efficacy of various aspects of accelerator program design. For instance, we are able to see how accelerators that drive more funding to their entrepreneurs actually spend less per venture on their programming. We also see that average cohort sizes are slightly larger for the high-NFF programs. This introduction to high-NFF versus low-NFF accelerators sets the stage for a series of assessments of specific choices that accelerators make when designing their programs; choices related to pipeline-building, entrepreneur selection, and programming.

Appendix: EDP Program Survey

General

- What is the official name of this program?
- What is this program's expected start date? End date?
- Roughly how many participants do you plan to accept into this program?
- Where will (most of) this program be located? City? Province or state? Country?
- Is this program formally run and co-branded with any other organizations? If Yes, please provide the name and describe the role of up to three of your formal partners.

Pipeline Development

- When do you expect program applications to Open? Close?
- Roughly how many applicants do you expect for this program?
- Does this program have an explicit geographic focus?
- Does this program have an explicit sector focus?
- Does this program have an explicit impact area focus?
- Does this program have an explicit focus on Idea-stage ventures? Prototype-stage ventures? Post-revenue ventures? Growth-stage ventures?
- Does this program explicitly encourage or give preference to Women? Youth? Minorities or typically excluded groups?
- What are the primary sources for applicants into this program? Established entrepreneurial networks? Referrals from other entrepreneurs or program alumni (i.e., word of mouth)? Direct and indirect referrals from other accelerator programs? Business plan competitions? Microfinance institutions? Universities? Corporate partners? Chambers of Commerce? Outbound marketing materials?

Selection

- Roughly how many individuals formally participate in selecting ventures into this program?
- Roughly what percentage of these selectors are female?
- Will any of the following types of individuals participate in the selection process: Experienced investors? Experienced business practitioners? Experienced entrepreneurs? Program alumni? University or college professors? Foundation or donor employees?
- What are selectors asked to emphasize as they make their selection decisions? Quality or promise of the idea? Founding team? Enterprise?
- Are any of the following steps incorporated into the selection process: In-person or telephone interviews? Pitches? Group-based exercises? Tests?

Program Structure

- The following are some of the potential benefits that are typically associated with accelerators. Please rank these benefits in terms of the emphasis that they receive in this program: Network development? Business skills development? Mentorship from business experts? Access and connections to potential investors/funders? Securing direct venture funding? Gaining access to a group of like-minded entrepreneurs?

- Roughly how much emphasis is placed on each of the following topic areas: Accounting? Business plan development? Finance? Human relations? Legal? Marketing? Networking? Organization Structure and design? Presentation and communication skills?
- Who is responsible for delivering these materials: Dedicated program staff? University or college professors? Consultants? Experienced business practitioners? Experienced entrepreneurs? Program alumni?
- Does this program have a structured curriculum that is distributed to participants in written or electronic form?
- In 100 words or less, describe what additional resources or services that program participants have access to. Mentors are people who serve as guides and advisors to participating entrepreneurs. Roughly how many individuals will formally participate as mentors in this program?
- Roughly what percentage of these mentors will be female?
- Will any of the following types of individuals participate as mentors: Experienced investors? Experienced business practitioners? Experienced entrepreneurs? Program alumni? University or college professors?
- Will this program provide guaranteed capital investment for some or all program participants; either directly or through a related funding arm?
- To the nearest $10K, roughly how much financial capital has been pre-committed?
- How many program participants are guaranteed to receive funding from or through this program?
- Do these guaranteed investments come in the form of: Equity? Debt? Grants?
- Are there ways that qualifying program participants might receive investments directly from this program?
- Will this program feature pitch nights or demo days that connect participants to potential investors? (Y/N)

Follow-Up

- Will this program offer any post-program services to participants?
- What services will you offer after this program is completed?
- For how long will you offer these post-program services to program participants?
- How often will you collect data from participating ventures after this program is completed?

Notes

1. Susan L. Cohen, Christopher B. Bingham & Benjamin L. Hallen. 2018. 'The role of accelerator designs in mitigating bounded Rationality in new ventures.' *Administrative Science Quarterly*, forthcoming.
2. This chapter relies heavily on materials originally written with Abigayle Davidson and Genevieve Edens for a report entitled *Accelerating the Flow of Funds into Early-Stage Ventures: An Initial Look at Program Differences and Design Choices*.
3. *What's Working in Startup Acceleration: Insights from Fifteen Village Capital Programs*. The Aspen Institute.
4. C. Scott Dempwolf, Jennifer Auer & Michelle D'Ippolito. 2014. *Innovation Accelerators: Defining Characteristics among Startup Assistance Organizations*. Small Business Administration; Susan Cohen. 2013. 'What do accelerators do? Insights from incubators and angels.' *Innovations*, 8 (3–4): 19–25.
5. Ross Brown & Colin Mason. 2017. 'Looking inside the spiky bits: a critical review and conceptualisation of entrepreneurial ecosystems.' *Small Business Economics*, 49 (1): 11–30.

6

Building Application Pipelines

To work with high-potential cohorts of entrepreneurs and ventures, accelerators must first attract promising entrepreneurs into their applicant pools. This involves a considerable amount of structured effort in the months leading up to each program; spreading the word so that the best entrepreneurs present themselves for consideration. Reviews of program websites and interviews with program managers unearth a number of specific outreach activities that are designed to attract entrepreneurs. Program managers from the Unreasonable Institute in East Africa rely on personal and organizational networks to generate referrals. Bluebox Ventures conducts extensive online recruiting across Latin America, while hosting a number of different roadshow events. Others, like Semento Negocios, work with other entrepreneur support programs (especially those working with ventures at different development stages) and ecosystem stakeholders to identify entrepreneurs for their own programs.

When considering how these pipeline-building efforts are implicated in the success of accelerators, it is important to consider two things: (1) which specific programmatic choices correspond with superior NFF outcomes; and (2) do the number and quality of applicants also influence these NFF outcomes? We begin by focusing on the latter question: Are high-NFF and low-NFF programs differentiated by the numbers of ventures in their application pools or by the recent funding performance of these applicants?

Does Applicant Pool Size Matter? While it is arguably a recent phenomenon, one widely accepted indicator of the quality of colleges and universities is something known as 'selectivity'.[1] Better schools are those that attract a larger

© The Author(s) 2019
P. W. Roberts, S. A. Lall, *Observing Acceleration*,
https://doi.org/10.1007/978-3-030-00042-4_6

number of applicants and then reject a higher percentage of them. With a simple transfer of this logic, it becomes plausible to assume that the accelerators with larger numbers of applicants also get to consider the best entrepreneurs, which lead to enhanced program experiences and superior program performance.[2] This logic is reinforced by the fact that the best-known accelerators, like Y Combinator and Techstars, attract thousands of applicants to their programs, and have acceptance rates between 1 and 3 percent.[3] In 2018, Echoing Green, a prominent impact-oriented entrepreneur support program, received 2419 applications from entrepreneurs working in 155 countries.[4] While applicant pool size might be an indicator of the demand for, and therefore perceived quality of accelerator programs, many caution against relying on it as a measure of actual quality, especially when thinking beyond the most established programs. Whereas higher numbers of applicants may result from extensive outreach or marketing efforts, there is no guarantee that these efforts will attract high-potential applicants. Nor should acceptance rates be considered clean measures of program quality, since accelerators often make acceptance decisions conditioned on the availability of funds or other factors.[5] In support of these concerns, a 2016 GALI report found that the higher-performing Village Capital programs actually had smaller applicant pools.[6]

We find no meaningful differences in the NFF across programs with larger and smaller applicant pools. The accelerators in the EDP sample received an average of almost 86 applicants each. Across all programs, the simple correlation between the number of applicants and the NFF variable is $\rho = 0.04$. Moreover, as shown in Fig. 6.1, the high-NFF programs logged roughly 84 applicants on average, compared to 89 applicants for the low-NFF programs. Regardless of the current approach that program managers are using to

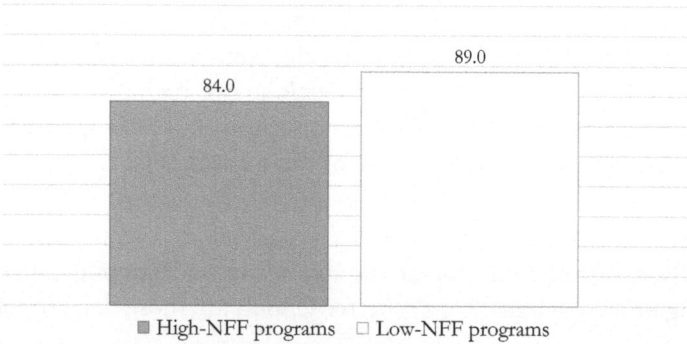

Fig. 6.1 Average number of applicants for high-NFF versus low-NFF programs

develop their applicant pools, efforts that simply pump up the numbers do not lead to more effective programs.

Do Readily Observable Indicators of Performance Matter? While it is not a strict numbers game, it still makes sense that superior NFF outcomes will come from higher-quality cohorts which, by extension, come from programs that attract better applicants. A simple strategy for attracting entrepreneurs who will bring in more funding next year is to recruit those that are already well on their way. According to this cherry-picking logic, the application pools of high-NFF programs should contain ventures that are already doing well in terms of the financial flows reported on their applications. We revisited the application data from the high-NFF and low-NFF programs and calculated the total funds—earned revenues plus outside equity, debt and philanthropy— reported for the year prior to application. Figure 6.2 reveals large differences between the two groups. However, applicants to the high-NFF programs report lower prior-year funding levels on average, with the biggest deficit found in their lower reported revenues. Instead of leaning in the direction of ventures that have already gained substantial traction, high-NFF programs seem to be able to find genuine diamonds in the rough. The question becomes 'how?'

These two observations indicate that building application pipelines that support positive accelerator outcomes is neither a simple numbers game nor a straightforward cherry-picking exercise. To move past these simple-but-ineffective approaches, we examine the different decisions that program managers make when looking to recruit entrepreneurs, including applicant

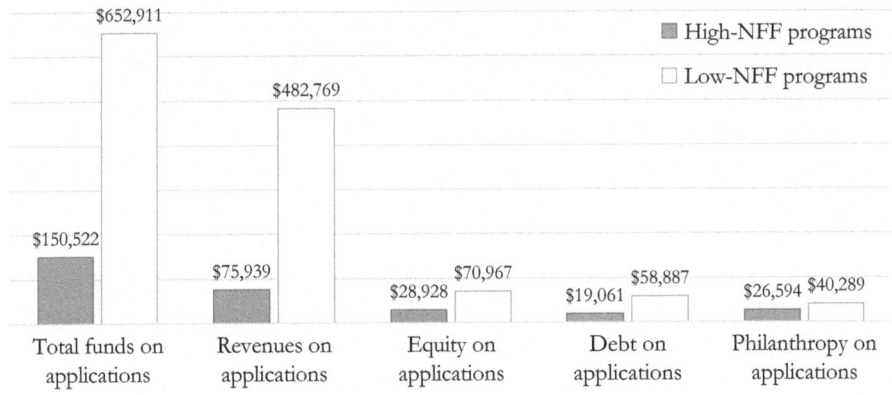

Fig. 6.2 Average flow of funds in the prior year for high-NFF versus low-NFF programs

sources, regional, sector and impact area focus, and venture stage focus. We then address the important issue of inclusion, and whether accelerators that prioritize marginalized entrepreneurs perform better or worse than those that are more agnostic.

Where Do High-NFF Programs Look for Applicants? Conversations with accelerator program managers reveal a number of different places to find promising impact-oriented entrepreneurs. To glean more systematic information about these applicant sources, the EDP program surveys ask: 'What are the primary sources for applicants into this program? Established entrepreneurial networks? Referrals from other entrepreneurs and program alumni (i.e., word of mouth)? Direct and indirect referrals from other accelerator programs? Business plan competitions? Microfinance institutions? Universities? Corporate partners? Chambers of Commerce? Outbound marketing materials?' The responses indicate that few of the EDP accelerators rely on business plan competitions or searches within universities, and none of them rely on microfinance institutions or searches through local chambers of commerce. However, 41 of these programs rely on more than one source, with 31 programs tapping three different sources. The most prolific combination has programs sourcing through their own entrepreneurial networks, using word of mouth referrals, and accepting referrals from other accelerator programs. Comparing the two groups of accelerators reveals that high-NFF programs tap significantly ($p < 0.03$) more applicant sources than their low-performing counterparts; an average of 2.5 relative to 1.8.

Looking at the specific sources, Fig. 6.3 reveals that the only significant difference relates to the reliance on established networks. More than 75 percent of the high-NFF programs rely on their own networks, compared to just 40 percent of the low-NFF programs. This difference might reflect the fact that certain programs are more established. Programs like the Unreasonable Institute and Village Capital have well-developed identities among impact-oriented entrepreneurs, having worked with hundreds of them in the past, along with scores of investors, donors, and mentors. As more programs build out their brands and connections, they might also increase their reliance on their own networks. In the meantime, we may conclude that high-NFF programs tap a wider range of recruiting channels that are built around the networks that they already have in place.

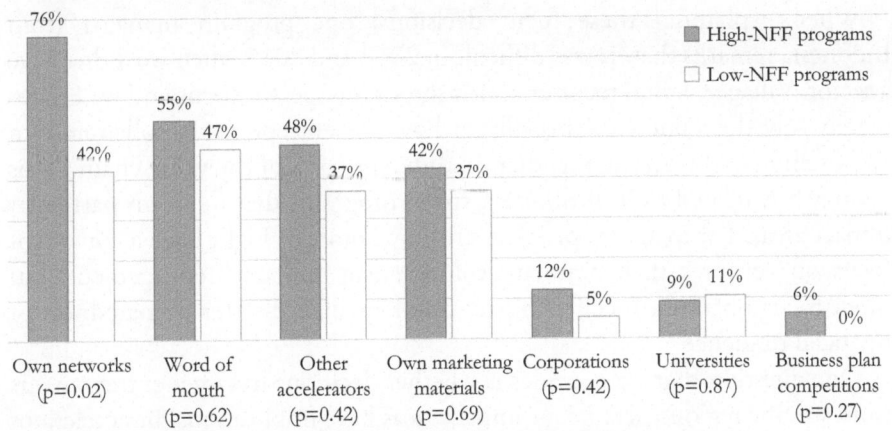

Fig. 6.3 Source of applicants for high-NFF versus low-NFF programs

What Are the Implications of Focusing Program Domains? The EDP works with a range of different accelerators. A few of them will consider applicants working anywhere in the world. Other programs not only focus on particular regions but also target a geographically diverse set of entrepreneurs. For example, the United States African Development Foundation's (USADF) Young African Leaders Initiative (YALI) Accelerator receives applicants from ventures operating in 40 African countries, while Agora Partnerships looks for promising entrepreneurs across Latin America. Another group targets fewer countries within a more bounded region. GrowthAfrica, a Nairobi-based program, targets entrepreneurs working in four East African countries. A larger and more focused group targets entrepreneurs from specific countries. This includes Brazil Lab (Brazil), Kinara (Indonesia), Invest 2 Innovate (Pakistan), and Startup Lab Mexico (Mexico). In the latter case, Startup Lab Mexico looks for entrepreneurs working in a variety of sectors. However, while their sector and impact orientation is broad, they offer programs in three Mexican cities—San Luis Potosí, Villahermosa, and Guadalupe. Finally, the sample includes a handful of programs, like Startup NY, that focus on a specific subnational region, in this case, entrepreneurs from the state of New York.

Programs can also elect to be focused on other dimensions, like sector or impact orientation. As the number of active accelerators expands, some programs are differentiating themselves by focusing on specific sectors. For example, while GrowthAfrica considers applicants from across the board, they have a stated preference for certain high-impact sectors like agriculture, education, healthcare, and renewable energy. In addition to targeting specific countries or regions, many Village Capital programs also focus on specific high-impact sectors, like healthcare and financial services.

When explaining these focus decisions, one program manager from Indonesia remarks that 'it was difficult in 2014 and 2015 when we didn't have a sector. Village Capital recommended the sector-specific focus and we immediately saw the value … especially in how the entrepreneurs collaborate in cross-selling and working together on different parts of the value chain.' This approach is related to, but different from, programs that focus on particular impact areas. For instance, programs run by Points of Light have a consistent focus on ventures that stimulate volunteerism and civic engagement, but often focus on more specific impact domains, like disaster preparedness or financial resilience.

One question that we consider is whether decisions to target entrepreneurs from specific regions, sectors, or impact areas have implications for accelerator effectiveness. Those without a specific focus are free to attract a larger and more diverse pool of entrepreneurs. This can be an important factor in less-developed ecosystems, where accelerators may find it difficult to develop cohorts due to a perceived lack of qualified applicants. This issue is raised by one program manager, who suggests that 'if you take Kenya, which is the larger market of the three we're in now, there would only be three viable sectors where we could get enough qualified candidates to run programs with themes – agribusiness and IT/mobile, and maybe green tech. Even more difficult outside Kenya (maybe just agribusiness is the only vertical with enough entrepreneurs to run a program).' Another issue relates to intra-cohort dynamics. The more domain-agnostic programs might be better at avoiding direct competition among cohort entrepreneurs. As one program manager in Kenya explains, 'people are always afraid of competition too – if we have a cohort with businesses that are too similar, the peer-to-peer component will be shut down.' This same manager goes on to introduce one of the opportunity costs of running a more generalist program: 'The downside is that we're then not able to be a sector specialist.' More focused programs can tailor offerings to a more homogenous group of entrepreneurs and ventures.[7] When entrepreneurs are doing similar things in similar areas, capacity development can focus on the particulars of one domain, while social-capital building can home in on a tighter group of supporters. As one program manager operating a health-focused accelerator remarks, 'five years ago, we had a decent network but it was sector agnostic, so as we've focused more on sectors (we have) been able to grow. We now have a much stronger network that aligns in the sectors in which we work.'

We rely on responses to three program-level questions to probe the implications of pipeline focus for accelerator program effectiveness: 'Does this program have an explicit geographic focus? Does this program have an explicit sector focus? Does this program have an explicit impact area focus?' Responses indicate that 19 programs have an explicit geographic focus. This does not necessarily mean that the other programs do not end up with geographically concentrated applicant pools. It simply means that they are open to considering applicants from any geographic locale. There are 25 programs that report having an explicit sector focus and 29 programs that target entrepreneurs working in specific impact areas. Pooling responses to these three questions reveals 36 programs that impose some kind of focus restriction on their applicant pools.

Consistent with the opposing costs and benefits mentioned above, the high-NFF and low-NFF programs do not display massive differences when it comes to placing focus restrictions on their programs (see Fig. 6.4). However, there is some evidence against geographic, sector, and impact restrictions. Overall, a higher percentage (roughly 79 percent) of the low-NFF programs impose at least one focus restriction, compared to roughly 64 percent of the high-NFF programs. The largest individual difference relates to geography, where a significantly higher percentage of the low-NFF programs report having geographic preferences.

This provides some evidence that impact-oriented accelerators are better able to drive funds into participating ventures when they adopt a less-constrained approach to pipeline-building. High-NFF programs are less likely to articulate specific preferences for geographies, sectors, or impact areas. While the differences are not large, this supports the idea that it can be hard to attract a sufficient number of promising applicants when focusing on specific domains. It also corroborates the espoused benefits of having a diversity of perspectives built into impact-oriented accelerators. As one manager remarks, 'we believe that if social problems are inter-connected, solutions should be inter-connected. Collaborations across sectors are things we love to see, either within or between

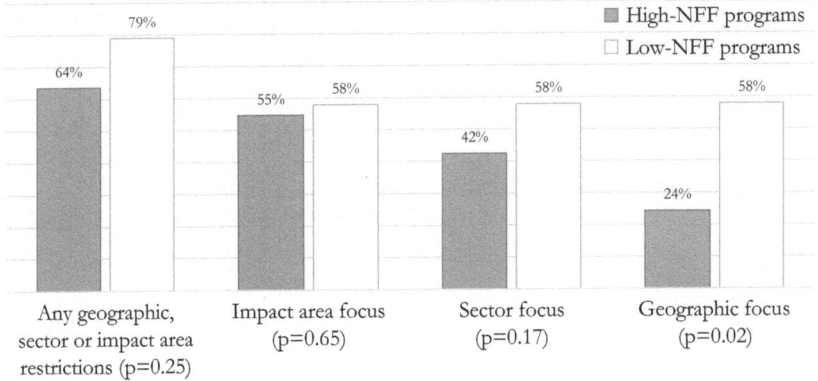

Fig. 6.4 Program focus for high-NFF versus low-NFF programs

cohorts. That's what's made us have an agnostic program. They need to see, for example, that education in rural Mexico might be failing because of lack of nutrition. We are working now on them being at the same stage – e.g., at least having a certain amount of revenue or employees – but in terms of impact, we like to mix them.'

Does It Make Sense to Focus on Ventures at Similar Stages of Development? The latter point made by this program manager points to another dimension that might focus on pipeline-building activities: the targeted ventures' stage of development. Accelerators generally prefer to work with entrepreneurs that are at similar stages in the entrepreneurial process.[8] As one manager stresses, 'if there's a spectrum of needs/sophistication, that can be more difficult. We try to minimize how different the ventures are in terms of stage.' While these stages are not always easy to define, and might vary depending on the sector or on the status of the local ecosystem, the EDP leveraged its discussions with accelerator program managers to adopt a simple set of stages that make sense for most of them. In the program surveys, managers are asked whether their recruitment has an explicit focus on any of the following stages of venture development:

- idea stage (do not yet have a working prototype or customers)
- prototype stage (have a working prototype but do not yet have earned revenue)
- post-revenue stage (have customers and functioning revenue models, but not yet cash-flow positive)
- growth stage (operating at scale and are typically cash-flow positive)

Table 6.1 shows that the majority of the programs in the EDP sample target ventures at the prototype or post-revenue stage, with a smaller number

Table 6.1 Venture stage targeted for high-NFF versus low-NFF programs

	Stages targeted	Idea stage	Prototype stage	Post-revenue stage	Growth stage
Programs targeting ...	n/a	9 programs	34 programs	38 programs	13 programs
High-NFF programs	1.82	12.1%	69.7%	78.8%	21.2%
Low-NFF programs	1.79	26.3%	57.9%	63.2%	31.6%
Sig.	$p = 0.93$	$p = 0.19$	$p = 0.39$	$p = 0.22$	$p = 0.41$

focusing on earlier idea-stage or later growth-stage ventures. This is not surprising given the stated objective of many accelerators; that of working with scalable ventures in order to expedite their growth. It is also corroborated by the manager quoted above, who goes on to say that 'there usually tends to be a couple of outliers on the early stage that we see significant promise in – maybe they're in pilot stage – but most of the pack is the same, with maybe one or two that are further along'. Looking across the two groups of programs shows that high-NFF programs are even more likely to target ventures in the prototype or post-revenue stage, while the low-NFF programs are somewhat more likely to target the earlier and later-stage ventures. It seems that the more successful accelerators are more faithfully targeting entrepreneurs whose ventures are in their most promising developmental stages.

Are There Costs Associated with Targeting Marginalized Entrepreneurs? Despite the widespread characterization of entrepreneurship as a means for economic development, there remain significant gaps in the engagement of, and support for women and minorities.[9] Because of these troubling inequities, a growing number of accelerators specifically target entrepreneurs from these underserved demographics. Some explicitly seek to populate their pipelines with women and minority entrepreneurs. For example, SheEO targets women-led ventures working in North America, Asia-Pacific, or Latin America.[10] This allows impact-oriented ventures that are run by women to join cohorts of similar entrepreneurs and receive mentoring and financial support in a tailored program. In a similar vein, Kinara Indonesia only accepts ventures with at least one female founder in order to be more inclusive. The Equitable Entrepreneurship program is an initiative from the Idea Foundry that supports immigrant and minority entrepreneurs in the Pittsburgh region. The program emphasizes region-wide opportunities while providing three months of personalized business development support and up to $10,000 in loan capital.

Other programs do not focus explicitly on marginalized groups, but seek to ensure that their pipelines are appropriately diverse. Several managers of impact-oriented programs explain how they seek out entrepreneurs that have direct experiences with focal problems or constituents, and make efforts to reach out to these underrepresented entrepreneurs. One US-based program manager explains how 'we have historically had 50 percent or more of our ventures with female cofounders, but we honestly haven't had that focus… our team is mindful and presents strong voices for women and minorities, but we just select quality entrepreneurs.' Village Capital's programs in India, for example, actively invest in this kind of diversity. Many entrepreneurs and ideas are overlooked when recruitment defaults to the major cities, such as Delhi and Bangalore. As such, their team actively recruits in smaller cities and purposefully looks beyond traditional pedigree markers (e.g., schooling levels) to find entrepreneurs that have direct experiences with the problems they are solving. They describe these efforts in the following way: 'To recruit in other cities/regions, we research in advance, set up meetings and plan events in smaller towns. Or we find local partners that have their ears to the ground.' GrowthAfrica also prioritizes the smaller cities, but knows that finding a gender-diverse pipeline of entrepreneurs outside of capital cities, or even in certain countries, is challenging. Reflecting on these efforts to be more inclusive, one manager says that, 'maybe it's because we have more of a focus, but (our) last cohort in Kenya was (our) first cohort with more women than men. We're doing fairly well in Ethiopia as well – 30 percent in first cohort. Zambia is also looking good, and in Uganda, even though hailed as highest female entrepreneur country, we've had challenges.'

As more accelerators directly or indirectly target entrepreneurs who are over-looked by traditional support programs, we must ask whether these efforts help or hurt accelerator program performance. In this respect, the EDP data provide some evidence that focusing on women or minorities actually correlates with an improvement in a program's ability to drive funding into participating ventures. Figure 6.5 shows that higher percentages of programs in the high-NFF group prioritize women and minority entrepreneurs. Program managers are not surprised by this pattern, pointing to the high motivation levels of under-

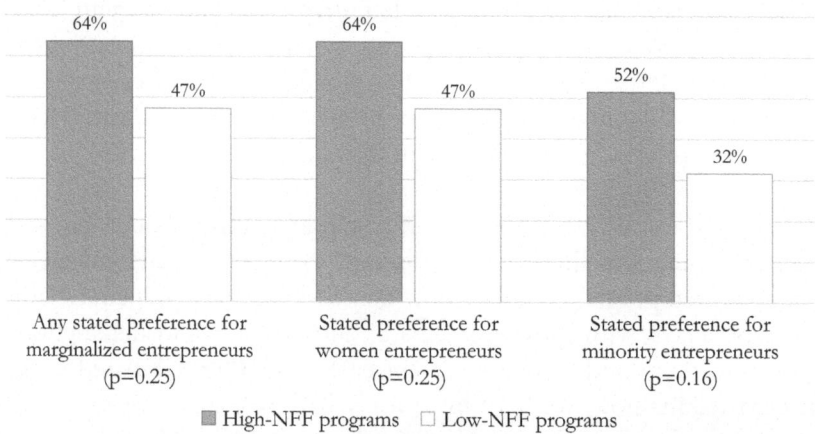

Fig. 6.5 Preference for women and minority applicants for high-NFF versus low-NFF programs

represented entrepreneurs. They also believe that having overcome considerable structural barriers in the past is a signal of their potential for future success. As one program manager from Indonesia remarks, 'our hypothesis is that they actually have potential to scale up their business but they just weren't given an opportunity, so they are under-valued when they indeed have potential to increase their value. Once they are given (an) opportunity, they treasure it and give it more effort to prove themselves. This is the one shot they're given and they don't want to waste it.'

A closer look at the EDP application data indicate that programs with a stated preference for women actually have a lower percentage of applicants with at least one female founder (see Table 6.2). However, they have a similar percentage of women in their cohorts, which suggests a slightly higher acceptance rate for teams with women founders. As one program manager from Mexico states, 'we don't conduct communications that are specific to women or minorities, but when we make the decision, we try to have cohorts that are 50-50 in terms of gender participation.' Feedback from another program manager in Mexico suggests that accelerators need to focus less on women being on founding teams and more on creating re-gendered contexts in which women entrepreneurs can thrive. However, as we show in Chap. 10, these same programs do not recruit more women as selectors or mentors. This begs the question of what specific program choices and outcomes change when programs express a preference for women (and minority) entrepreneurs.

Table 6.2 A closer look at gender in high-NFF versus low-NFF programs

	% women in applicant pool	% women selectors	% women in cohort	% women mentors
Preference for women ($N = 33$)	44.0	42.9	43.7	32.7
No preference for women ($N = 19$)	49.1	42.2	46.3	37.3
Sig.	$p = 0.35$	$p = 0.90$	$p = 0.70$	$p = 0.38$

Most people believe that it is laudable to focus on entrepreneurs who are otherwise overlooked or stigmatized. Others fear that doing so might come at the expense of the commercial success of a program or its ventures. It is therefore encouraging that programs reporting a preference for women and minority entrepreneurs are more likely to be among the high-NFF programs. While we do not yet know how or why this happens, this optimistic observation should motivate program supporters to continue working on this important goal of facilitating more inclusive entrepreneurship.

Chapter 5 initiated a closer look at the program-level factors that tend to drive high-NFF outcomes through enhanced revenue performance versus improved outside equity growth. Continuing along this line of inquiry, we see that high-NFF (equity) programs tap significantly ($p = 0.05$) more application sources (2.9 on average) than the high-NFF (revenues) programs (2.1 sources on average). The equity-dominant programs are also more likely to articulate a sector focus, 60 percent compared to 29 percent. This difference is close to significant ($p = 0.12$). A similar pattern applies to impact-area focus, although the difference is not as pronounced. On average, 70 percent of the accelerators where equity growth dominates are impact-focused, compared to 47 percent of the programs where revenue growth dominates. For accelerators that seek to drive incremental funding through net equity growth, there is some justification for building focus into the program. There is also justification for steering clear of ventures that are already in their growth stage of development. None of the ten high-NFF (equity) programs target this growth stage, compared to 41 percent of the high-NFF (revenues) programs. Finally, although differences when it comes to articulating preferences for women or minority entrepreneurs are not significant ($p = 0.26$), it is interesting to see that 80 percent of the high-NFF (equity) programs express a preference for women or minority entrepreneurs, compared to 59 percent of the revenue-dominant programs. This might suggest that it is more straightforward to convince equity investors than potential customers of the value inherent in minority-led ventures.

Concluding Remarks

Several of the observations in this chapter speak to those who are interested in how application pipelines are managed by high-NFF programs. Simplistic tactics that pump up application numbers or look for low-hanging fruit are not effective. In this latter respect, although there is a large difference in the prior-year flow of funds between the two groups of programs, these flows are actually lower in the high-NFF programs. When it comes to the more nuanced work of recruiting applicants, high-NFF programs leverage a wider range of sources that build from their own connections while relying on word-of-mouth referrals from alumni, entrepreneurs, and even other accelerators. While tapping this wider range of sources, the high-NFF programs are more disciplined when it comes to targeted venture stages. Most of the programs in the EDP sample target ventures that are at the prototype or post-revenue stage, which makes sense given that this is where potential investors and supporters expect the greatest potential for future growth. The high-NFF programs are even more wary of straying toward ventures that are either too early or more established. Nevertheless, they are not correspondingly focused when it comes to geographic, sector, or impact area focus. Despite the popular view that more focused accelerators should outperform their peers, preliminary evidence tilts in the opposite direction. The exception is programs that focus on marginalized entrepreneurs. Consistent with their underlying impact orientation, the EDP accelerators that articulate preferences for women or minority entrepreneurs are doing well when it comes to driving incremental funding into their participating ventures.

Notes

1. Willard Dix. 2016. *Don't Use College Selectivity as a Measure of Quality*. Forbes.
2. Lawrence A. Plummer, Thomas H. Allison, & Brian L. Connelly. 2016. 'Better together? Signaling interactions in new venture pursuit of initial external capital.' *Academy of Management Journal*, 59(5): 1585–1604.
3. Laurens Vandeweghe & Jyun-Ying (Trent) Fu. 2018. 'Business accelerator governance.' *Accelerators: Successful Venture Creation and Growth*.
4. *The Data: 2018 Echoing Green Fellowship Applicants*. Echoing Green (April 2018).
5. Michael Leatherbee & Juanita Gonzalez-Uribe. 2018. 'Key performance indicators' in *Accelerators: Successful Venture Creation and Growth*.
6. *What's Working in Startup Acceleration: Insights from Fifteen Village Capital Programs*. The Aspen Institute.
7. Saurabh Lall, Lily Bowles, & Ross Baird. 2013. 'Bridging the pioneer gap: The role of accelerators in launching high-impact enterprises.' *Innovations*, 8 (3–4): 105–137.
8. Michael Leatherbee & Juanita Gonzalez-Uribe. 2018. 'Key performance indicators' in *Accelerators: Successful Venture Creation and Growth*.
9. *2014 Women's Report. Global Entrepreneurship Monitor*, Babson College (2015); Charles Y. Murnieks, J. Michael Haynie, Robert E. Wiltbank & Troy Harting. 2011. 'I like how you think: Similarity as an interaction bias in the investor–entrepreneur dyad.' *Journal of Management Studies*, 48(7): 1533–1561.
10. See https://sheeo.world/

7

A Closer Look at Entrepreneur Selection

Accelerators aspire to fill a very specific role in entrepreneurial ecosystems; that of accelerating the performance of promising ventures; not every promising venture, but those whose promise is not obvious to the other individuals and organizations that might otherwise support them. To play this role effectively, one of the main elements of effective accelerators is their ability to select the right entrepreneurs. As such, most program managers expend a lot of thought and effort on multi-step selection processes.[1] In this way, they differ from other support programs that are open to anyone who can pay their fees (e.g., co-working spaces) or those that are generally less selective (e.g., training courses offered by community colleges or local economic development organizations). In fact, the most prominent accelerators are notoriously selective. Y Combinator accepts approximately 3 percent of its applicants, while Techstars has an acceptance rate of roughly 1 percent.[2] While acceptance rates are not this low for accelerators that are more impact-oriented, they still accept a relatively small percentage of their applicants. For instance, GALI survey data suggest that emerging-market accelerators have acceptance rates of roughly 11 percent.[3]

To provide context for the observations in this chapter, we probed the websites of 16 accelerators that are in the EDP sample. These searches reveal publicly-espoused preferences and selection criteria, as well as descriptions of ideal applicants. This information was supplemented by conversations with a number of accelerator program managers during a dedicated session at the ANDE Annual Conference in 2015. This background research reveals several of the factors that accelerators claim to prioritize when selecting entrepreneurs, including objective

© The Author(s) 2019
P. W. Roberts, S. A. Lall, *Observing Acceleration*,
https://doi.org/10.1007/978-3-030-00042-4_7

criteria (e.g., does the venture have positive revenues, own intellectual property, or have a technical founder) and criteria that require more subjective assessments (e.g., do the entrepreneurs have passion or tenacity). The overarching goal of these selection processes is to ensure that certain standards are met (e.g., having at least one full-time founder or some evidence of customer traction), before looking for the less-obvious indicators of the potential inherent in the founding team, the underlying business idea, or the venture itself.

To reach the decisions that finalize the cohorts for their programs, accelerators employ a complex set of screening criteria and selection practices, while deploying a variety of selectors. Their selection criteria typically include a mix of objective variables (e.g., earned revenues, hired employees, and prior investment levels) and intangible factors (e.g., evidence of resilience, perseverance, or leadership). For instance, Village Capital tries to select for-profit ventures with measurable social or environmental impacts, and with proof of genuine customer interest. More specifically, they prefer ventures with track records of earned revenue and expectations of predictable future revenues. They should also be seeking between $50,000 and $500,000 in startup capital. Their selectors assess applicants based on a proprietary framework that is broken into eight main categories—vision, impact, team, business model, potential capture, and potential for exit. Additionally, they favor ventures with at least one full-time founder, knowing that starting a scalable impact-oriented company is not something that can be done on a part-time basis. The accelerators operated by the Unreasonable Institute employ a multi-stage selection process that takes roughly three months. Through this lengthy process, selectors are looking to recruit for-profit or nonprofit ventures with evidence of customer interest and sustainable revenue streams. They prioritize multi-founder over single-founder teams and value teams with some prior founding experience. In addition to these objective criteria, applicants are also assessed based on qualitative criteria, like tenacity, entrepreneurial spirit, and founding team cohesion. The process starts with a review of the written application, which covers factors related to the market, intended social impacts, the business model, and team credentials. Entrepreneurs who proceed to the next stage participate in phone or Skype interviews, followed by a site visit and then a second interview.

The underlying goal of these selection efforts is to home in on entrepreneurs and ventures that have genuine potential to succeed and scale. However, because the financial and non-financial resources required to run accelerator programs are valuable and scarce, it is important to direct them toward projects whose potential is not already obvious. After all, what is the point of accelerating something that is already traveling at its maximum velocity? This is especially true for impact-oriented programs that rely on government and philanthropic funding.

These funders are not simply looking for a share of the future earnings of already-promising ventures. They want their accelerators to identify and work with early-stage ventures whose future impacts will not be realized without this support. This aspiration is evident in a documented debate among Endeavor selectors, when one panelist asserts that 'I agree that Javna will be wildly success but I'm not sure they really need Endeavor to succeed.'[4] In this respect, the more specific goal of impact-oriented accelerator selectors is to find promising entrepreneurs whose potential will be honed and then revealed during the program.

It can be difficult to walk this fine line of finding promising entrepreneurs and ventures whose potential is currently hidden. When reduced to its essence, the challenge is to find founding teams that cannot currently generate sufficient customer or investor interest, but that will, with the right interventions, appeal to these supporters in as little as 15 weeks. As such, it is important to examine the things that high-NFF accelerators do to ensure they are working with the most promising entrepreneurs who will also gain the most benefit from their programing efforts. Continuing the focus on the NFF variable, this chapter presents a series of observations that show whether the two groups of high-NFF and low-NFF programs differ in the size and composition of their selection committees, in their deployment of specific selection practices, or in the criteria that selectors prioritize when making their decisions.

Before getting into these specific practices and priorities, it is useful to revisit the most obvious hypothesis—high-NFF accelerators are simply more selective. Given the perception of quality attached to selectivity and acceptance rates (see Chap. 5), many people naturally expect the better-performing programs to also be more selective. However, high-NFF programs are not more selective. They accept roughly 16 percent of their applicants, compared to roughly 19 percent for the low-NFF programs. These basic acceptance rates are not definitive predictors of accelerator program quality because there are too many other factors that determine applicant pool size and program cohort size, the two variables that combine to produce the acceptance rate variable.

The Size and Composition of Selection Committees

Accelerator program selectors are required to evaluate a large number of applicants based on a range of criteria, many of which are subtle. Therefore, the size and composition of selection committees might influence the efficacy of the selection panels, and subsequently the effectiveness of the accelerator program itself. While a thorough review of the academic literature that pertains to

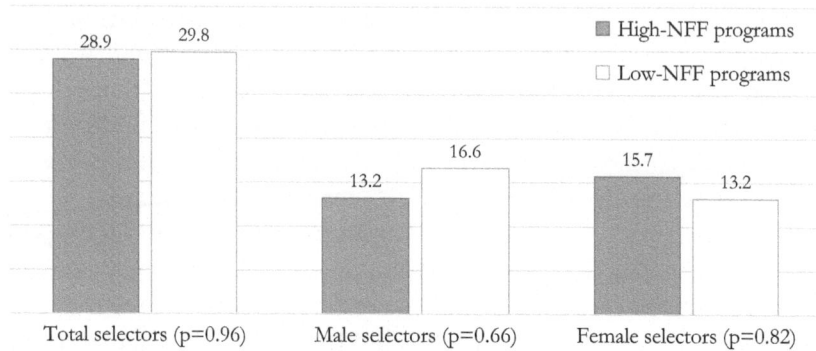

Fig. 7.1 Number and gender of selectors for high-NFF versus low-NFF programs

team size and demography is beyond the scope of this chapter, the primary tradeoffs can be summarized as follows. Larger and more diverse teams have more resources available to process information, and more perspectives to offer when it comes to interpreting that information. This tends to produce better decisions. However, larger numbers and more diversity also make group processes more challenging. This tends to work against group effectiveness.[5] Figure 7.1 suggests an almost perfect tradeoff between these benefits and costs when it comes to the size of selection committees. On average, the number of selectors working for high-NFF and low-NFF programs are almost identical. Moreover, while high-NFF programs have a slightly higher share of women selectors, these differences are not particularly large.

This latter observation leads to another question of professional background diversity. Several different professions, and therefore perspectives, tend to be included on selection committees. Table 7.1 shows that selectors most often include investors, business practitioners, entrepreneurs, program alumni, and representatives from donor organizations. However, there is no significant difference in selector diversity between the high-NFF and low-NFF programs. The former group of selection committees house an average of slightly more than three different professional backgrounds, while the latter houses slightly less. Nor do the specifics of team composition differ much between the high-NFF and low-NFF programs. The most salient difference is the moderately greater tendency to deploy program alumni among the high-NFF programs; roughly 33 percent of their committees include alumni relative to just 16 percent of the low-NFF programs. When accelerators have stimulated successful entrepreneurs in previous cohorts, it makes some sense to leverage their perspectives by engaging them as selectors for subsequent cohorts.

Table 7.1 The background diversity of selectors used by high-NFF versus low-NFF programs

	Groups used	Investors	Business practitioners	Entrepreneurs	Program alumni	Donor representatives
Programs using …	n/a	37	35	26	14	23
High-NFF programs	3.03	72.7%	63.6%	48.5%	33.3%	45.5%
Low-NFF programs	2.84	68.4%	73.7%	52.6%	15.8%	42.1%
Sig.	$p = 0.71$	$p = 0.74$	$p = 0.46$	$p = 0.77$	$p = 0.17$	$p = 0.82$

What About Process and Criteria?

We now turn our attention to the various steps that these selectors follow, and the criteria they invoke as they work through these various steps.

Does It Pay to Have More Steps in the Selection Process? Accelerators tend to develop extensive selection processes that involve combinations of written applications, interviews, group exercises, tests, and even pitches. These latter steps are designed to look past the basic written application data in order to glean additional insights about entrepreneurs, ideas, and ventures. For example, Echoing Green requires an online application with accompanying team resumes and recommendation letters, as well as a competitive analysis of similar organizations. It also recommends that applicants submit minute-long video pitches of their ventures; something that explains the basic idea while showing their own personality, energy, and passion for their work. They advise applicants to develop video pitches that are authentic and jargon-free, and that also inspire action. Other accelerators have similarly nuanced selection processes. GrowthAfrica follows a multi-stage process of reviewing written applications to develop shortlists for each program. Each shortlisted candidate then has an in-person interview, followed by additional due diligence.

To calibrate the effects of these many possible steps, the EDP program surveys ask 'Are any of the following steps incorporated into the selection process: In-person or telephone interviews? Pitches? Group-based exercises? Tests?'. Table 7.2 shows that the majority of the accelerators in the sample make use of interviews.[6] The salience and importance of interviews are validated in conversations with accelerator program managers, as well as information posted on their program websites. Given the many ways that interviews can be conducted at varying cost and convenience points (e.g., in-person, video, or telephone), they represent a flexible way to assess

Table 7.2 Selection steps taken by high-NFF versus low-NFF programs

	Steps taken	Interviews	Pitches	Group exercises	Tests	Other
Programs using ...	n/a	45	11	3	2	2
High-NFF programs	1.36	90.9%	18.2%	9.1%	3.0%	15.2
Low-NFF programs	1.37	78.9%	26.3%	0.0%	5.3%	26.3
Sig.	$p = 0.99$	$p = 0.22$	$p = 0.48$	$p = 0.18$	$p = 0.69$	$p = 0.33$

entrepreneurs on some of the more qualitative criteria. Roughly one-third of the programs in the sample also require pitches. In the investment world, these carefully crafted speeches allow entrepreneurs to convince potential investors that their businesses or business ideas are worthy of consideration.[7] Although some accelerators are moving these pitch moments into their selection processes, there is no evidence that they are associated with better program performance. Finally, only two accelerators in the EDP sample have formal testing as part of their selection process, and only three employ some form of group exercise.

In the end, discriminating high-NFF and low-NFF programs is difficult because there are few differences in the adoption of the various steps. Because most programs deploy written applications, interviews, plus one other step, the count data from the EDP have a difficult time identifying best practices. However, as we continue to observe entrepreneur selection processes across a growing range of accelerators, we may see some innovations that correlate with program performance. For example, Village Capital recently partnered with a psychometric testing company to identify possible founding team characteristics that might be associated with future success.

Is It Best to Focus on the Team, the Idea, or the Enterprise? A common debate in conversations with accelerator program managers and selectors is whether to focus on the quality of the founding team, the underlying business idea, or the actual enterprise. While a number of nuanced issues are subsumed under these three criteria, it is useful to see how accelerators weigh these three general factors, and whether the different weights correspond with different program outcomes. Many program managers will tell you that they prioritize the founding team and its accumulated experience. As one program manager from Indonesia explains, 'the main criteria is the founder, so we invite only companies with at least one full-time cofounder, and put higher priority to companies with founders who have prior professional experience in the same sector, so it's both the commitment of the founders and their prior experience.' This founding team orientation includes intangible factors like fit and coachability. This same Indonesian program manager continues by saying that 'we look for culture-fit. Even beyond pedigree, we look for – are you coachable? Do you have character?' This founding team focus is well-established in the entrepreneurial finance literature, where many investors emphasize bets that are placed on 'jockeys' (i.e., entrepreneurs) over those made on 'horses' (i.e., ideas and enterprises).[8] After all, early-stage entrepreneurs are often encouraged to pivot—or even change business ideas entirely—during their early years. While these pivots morph the idea and venture under consideration, they do not change the individuals responsible for making the key decisions. The focus on teams is also understandable given the paucity of hard information about the other two criteria. The experiences and credentials that entrepreneurs bring to the table are anchored in the recent past, and are therefore observable. However, the promise of a business idea or a nascent enterprise will only be revealed in the future.

Although the decision to emphasize the quality of the founding team is both common and understandable, others believe that the combination of a sound idea or enterprise plus a solid team is critical to success during and after the accelerator program experience. It is not uncommon to hear that 'ideas can be incredible, but if you don't have a solid business model and the team isn't equipped to do it, it's a non-starter.'

The EDP program surveys ask program managers, 'What were selectors asked to emphasize when they made their selection decisions?' Respondents are asked to weight the importance of the quality of the founding team, the business idea, and the enterprise itself; with the three weights summing to 100 total points. Surprisingly, Fig. 7.2 shows that the enterprise is considered to be the most important selection criteria by the majority of the EDP program managers. However, there are no meaningful differences between the high-NFF and low-NFF programs when it comes to reported selection emphases. The high-NFF programs do place greater emphasis on the enterprise and the idea relative to the founding team. However, the differences are not significant. While our many conversations suggest that the primary consideration should be the quality of the founding team, a more balanced picture emerges from the EDP program data. It turns out that taking the time to

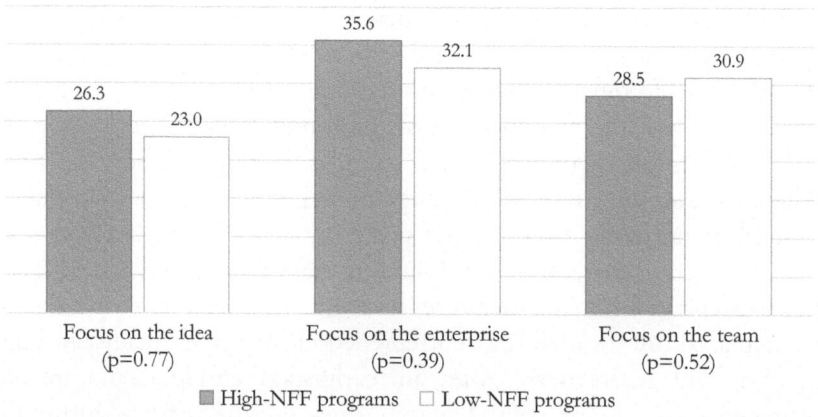

Fig. 7.2 Selector emphasis by high-NFF and low-NFF programs

assess the quality of an idea or a nascent enterprise can be (at the margin) productive. As one US-based program manager explains, 'the business is usually where we do our deepest grilling – unit economics, plan for scale, will it work?' Another one says, 'first and foremost the business must be viable and investable, with potential to scale.'

We close out this chapter by continuing our look at the factors that support high-NFF programs where equity growth dominates compared to those where revenue growth dominates. First, it makes sense that almost all of the high-NFF programs where equity growth dominates include investors on their selection committees. Roughly 90 percent of them report using investors, compared to just 59 percent of programs where revenue growth dominates. This difference is marginally significant ($p = 0.09$). The high-NFF (equity) programs also deploy more selectors on their panels; roughly 43 compared to 21. Although this difference is not significant ($p = 0.21$), the larger number of selectors provides another indication that driving equity growth depends more on the number and range of connections that are generated for participating entrepreneurs. Finally, it is interesting that none of the high-NFF (equity) programs employ pitches as one of their selection steps. This compares to roughly 35 percent of the high-NFF (revenue) programs; a difference that is significant ($p = 0.03$). This small-sample observation seems odd given that pitch events have become a core component of the accelerator model when it comes to exposing entrepreneurs to potential equity investors (see Chap. 8).

Concluding Remarks

This chapter starts by stressing the importance of understanding entrepreneur selection. For different—and some might say opposing—reasons, unpacking selection practices and effects matters to accelerator program managers, and to researchers and program funders. On the one hand, virtually every accelerator program manager knows that program success depends on the ability to identify and select the most promising entrepreneurs and ventures. It is simply too hard, and too expensive, to get 'blood from stones' or 'silk from sow's ears.' On the other hand, those who want to calibrate the true effects of acceleration on participating ventures are convinced that this desire to select the most promising entrepreneurs and ventures confounds estimates of true program performance.[9] These opposing interests in entrepreneur selection present a real dilemma. As selectors become better at their jobs, the more promising cohorts that they assemble become bigger targets for criticisms of cherry-picking; concerns that the real 'treatment effect' of accelerator programming will be masked by the 'selection effect' of highly-effective selectors.

For the former group of program managers, it is troubling that we do not find many obvious design factors that systematically correlate with better program outcomes. There is no evidence that high-NFF accelerators are more selective. Nor do we find meaningful differences in the size or composition of their selection committees. Both high-NFF and low-NFF programs place similar levels of importance on the quality of the founding team, the idea, and the enterprise. While these observations may help program managers understand which practices are not implicated in overall accelerator performance, it would be more useful to provide more positive insights. We suspect that our failure to find specific successful selection practices relates to the fact that accelerator program selection is currently more art than science. Remember that the real challenge for these selection committees is to find promising entrepreneurs that other supporters do not currently recognize as promising. Almost by definition, this belies formulaic approaches that might be picked up by quantitative research.

For this reason, we implore other researchers, especially those with skills in qualitative analysis, to take a closer look at these two groups of high-NFF and low-NFF ventures to divine the subtle factors that allow high-performing accelerators to identify and work with more promising entrepreneurs and ventures. In the meantime, the growing group of 'randomistas'[10]—those who think that the only valid way to assess accelerator performance is to randomly allocate entrepreneurs to programs—can take some solace in the fact that we currently know very little about the blueprints that lead to successful entrepreneurial selection.

Instead of simply controlling for selection, we should be asking 'would the estimated effects of acceleration have happened anyway?' In an ongoing research project with Li-Wei Chen, we are developing a complex model of accelerator selection decisions using a combination of qualitative insights and computer-aided modeling. This work recognizes that many of the selection steps and criteria used by accelerators are also available to other supporters and investors. These efforts reveal a generic, or readily-observable promise. For example, any interested stakeholder can determine, and then process, the implications of having prior-year revenues and investment, or indicators of a founder's credentials, like education levels or prior entrepreneurial experience. The project also recognizes that some accelerators are better (and different) than others when it comes to uncovering and interpreting softer cues that are not obvious to those who are not looking as closely, or not looking through the same lens. If we believe that accelerators are having effects on the ventures that they support, and if we believe that their selection work is a critical contributor to these effects, then we must distinguish between the two elements of selection: one is generic and one that can only be gleaned through an accelerator's unique processes and heuristics. As we continue this study of EDP accelerators and ventures, these observations should help us better understand this important domain of accelerator work.

Notes

1. Michael Leatherbee & Juanita Gonzalez-Uribe. 2018. 'Selection issues.' *Accelerators: Successful Venture Creation and Growth.*
2. Laurens Vandeweghe & Jyun-Ying (Trent) Fu. 2018. 'Business accelerator governance.' *Accelerators: Successful Venture Creation and Growth.*
3. See https://www.galidata.org/accelerators
4. William A. Sahlman. 2010. 'Endeavor: Creating a Global Movement for High-Impact Entrepreneurship.' *Harvard Business School Case #9-810-049.*
5. Katherine Phillips & Charles A. O'Reilly. 1998. 'Demography and diversity in organizations: A review of 40 years of research.' *In Research in Organizational Behavior.* JAI Press.
6. Clearly, all of the programs in the EDP sample also build written applications into their selection processes. This is the only way to get applicants to complete the EDP application surveys.
7. See https://www.investopedia.com/terms/e/elevatorpitch.asp
8. Steven N. Kaplan, Berk A. Sensoy, & Per Strömberg. 2009. 'Should investors bet on the jockey or the horse? Evidence from the evolution of firms from early business plans to public companies.' *The Journal of Finance*, 64(1): 75–115.
9. Nicky Khaki. *Ease Off on the Accelerators: Why GALI's Latest Study on Accelerator Programs May Be Overstating Their Impact.* NextBillion (July 2018).
10. Andrew Leigh. 2018. *Randomistas: How Radical Researchers Are Changing Our World.* Yale University Press.

8

Programming to Close Knowledge, Network, and Capital Gaps

After accelerators complete the hard work of developing application pools and the complicated work of selecting promising entrepreneurs from those pools, their attention turns to executing programs. To see how this is not a straightforward undertaking, just remember the five main categories of benefits that entrepreneurs seek when applying to accelerators (first presented in Fig. 3.3). To support the entrepreneurs in their cohorts, accelerators offer programming that develops general and specific business skills, typically with active support from experienced mentors. They also help develop entrepreneurial networks, making sure to cultivate connections to different supporters, including potential investors. As knowledge and network gaps are identified and closed, accelerators also ensure that the most promising entrepreneurs get the funding needed to stabilize and grow their ventures. All of these tasks are hard and every one of them is important.

Many impact-oriented entrepreneurs specialize in the means-ends linkages that pertain to their specific impact objectives. They are doctors, teachers, or development professionals. They are well versed in the technologies that underpin the FinTech, EdTech, HealthTech, or renewable energy movements. However, their specialties are rarely in traditional business domains. Therefore, founding teams are often lacking when it comes to the basic—and some might say boring—business functions. Accelerators present critical educational opportunities in training sessions and workshops that focus on hard skills like accounting and finance, as well as softer skills related to organization and communication. Often, these lessons are delivered by accelerator staff members. Other times, programs bring in external speakers and facilitators.

© The Author(s) 2019
P. W. Roberts, S. A. Lall, *Observing Acceleration*,
https://doi.org/10.1007/978-3-030-00042-4_8

At all times, speed and practicality are the primary considerations. Accelerators are not business schools and entrepreneurs are not MBA students. The goal is to provide enough educational insights so that entrepreneurs can identify their next critical challenges and take immediate steps to begin closing those gaps. This is why mentorship is thought to be so important. Studies of prominent accelerators stress the importance of mentorship to the accelerator model, where they serve as critical-but-neutral advisors to entrepreneurs.[1] The advice they provide is a critical conduit through which abstract business concepts are translated into concrete action plans.

Another thing that accelerator program managers will tell you is that context is every bit as important as content and delivery. As one program manager remarks, 'our current incarnation is framed around how entrepreneurs talk to each other and investors … less of program facilitators lecturing to entrepreneurs and more facilitation of independent thought, and then interactions between entrepreneurs and mentors. Maybe 20 percent of the time is a facilitator from our team or a sector expert imparting some sort of new framework or talking about a specific subject area. 50 percent is either self-reflection or peer interaction, the remaining 30 percent of the time is spent with external mentors.' At the heart of the accelerator model is the engagement of cohorts, making peer-to-peer learning an essential part of their design. Entrepreneurs go through programs in groups of (typically) 8 to 15, and how they engage with these peers—all of whom were selected because of the quality of their ideas and founding teams—can be instrumental to their accelerator experience. Therefore, program managers think carefully about how much time entrepreneurs should spend working alone, with mentors, or with their peers.

Finally, stimulating access to seed and growth capital—typically, but not always, in the form of outside equity investment—is always mentioned as one of the critical accelerator program benefits.[2] Some accelerators address this need by making direct investments into some or all of their entrepreneurs. Almost all of them convene gatherings that facilitate connections with potential investors. The most common of these gatherings is a pitch or demo day at the end of the program. Here, entrepreneurs present their ventures to an audience of potential investors, along with media and other ecosystem stakeholders, who are invited because of their latent interest in the ventures that are matriculating from the program.

When it comes to program design, the impact-oriented accelerators in the EDP sample share many of the same features as their counterparts working in more developed ecosystems. Village Capital uses a structured curriculum, which has evolved since 2011 with their accumulating experiences and is delivered during three four-day workshops. Because raising external investment is one of their key success metrics, these workshops include modules that help entrepreneurs develop the hard and soft skills required for successful fundraising. The programs culminate in an important feature of the Village Capital model. Every entrepreneur in each cohort rates each of their peers at the end of the program, with the top entrepreneurs becoming eligible for (typically) $50,000 in equity or convertible debt funding from the program itself. Because the Unreasonable Institute emphasizes mentoring, it engages strong mentors who are not directly investing or partnering with participating ventures but can make introductions and stimulate relationships with potential investors and supporters. GrowthAfrica emphasizes business planning and leadership. Endeavor works with local business leaders to advise and inspire their high-growth entrepreneurs. Programs run by the USADF and Points of Light directly invest in some of their ventures, providing funding in the form of grants, debt, or equity.

While there are similarities across these and other impact-oriented programs, we must also recognize how accelerators prioritize and design their various program elements. By observing differences across the EDP accelerators, we begin to unlock the black box of their programming and provide some guidance to managers about which choices seem to correlate with better program outcomes.

Closing Knowledge and Network Gaps

An obvious first place to look for programmatic effects on accelerator performance is within the curriculum that is presented to entrepreneurs. However, it is equally important to recognize the fact that both content and delivery might also matter. To structure our observations related to curriculum, content, and delivery, we focus on several of the program survey questions: Is the program built around a structured curriculum? What topic areas are emphasized in the programming? Who is recruited to deliver this content? And, how do the entrepreneurs spend their time as they digest and implement new ideas?

What Is the Effect of Having a Structured Curriculum? For those who liken the education that is offered in top business schools to the programming offered in accelerators, a structured curriculum is critical. It is also important for programs that want to replicate their successes because a well-honed curriculum can move from one program to the next. On the EDP program surveys, managers are asked, 'Does this program have a structured curriculum that is distributed to participants in written or electronic form?' Based on responses to this question, there is no indication that using a structured curriculum sets the high-NFF programs apart from their peers (see Fig. 8.1).

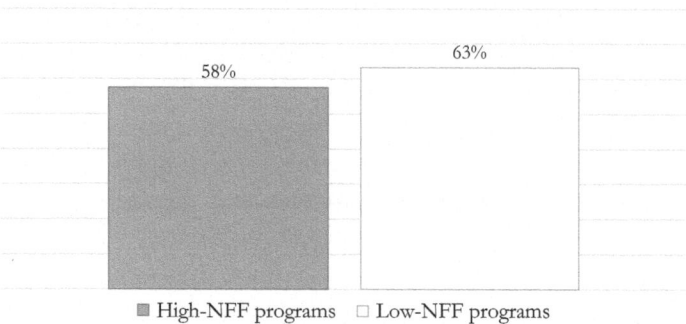

Fig. 8.1 Use of a structured curriculum among high-NFF and low-NFF programs

Nearly 60 percent of the accelerators in the sample report having a structured curriculum. There is a somewhat lower level of structured curriculum usage among the high-NFF programs, although this difference is not significant.

Conversations with program managers shed some light on this equivocal observation. Many of them view the curriculum as something to be assessed regularly and tweaked as needed. They know that a curriculum's effectiveness depends in part on the ventures that are selected and that content must be adjusted to meet the specific needs of each cohort. One US-based program manager explains that 'each program does NOT have the same curriculum. Each program is structured – it always has a set schedule and structure, and it just changes from program to program.' An Indonesian accelerator uses a curriculum with 'the flexibility to adjust the structure to the participants' needs and wants.' In addition to flexibility, continuous improvement is a recurring theme in these conversations, with an East African program manager noting that 'our curriculum is one of the things we strive to continuously develop – there is a set curriculum, or methodology, that we spent quite some resources on, and we think it's part of what we want to continue building on and make even stronger.'

Do the Top Programs Emphasize Certain Topic Areas? Having a curriculum is one thing. What the program actually covers is another question. Whether or not they make use of a structured curriculum, accelerators can place different emphasis on different topic areas. Several stress the importance of business plan development. Others focus on network development. Still others home in on financial planning and accounting fundamentals because this is where their entrepreneurs need the most support. According to one manager, 'a lot of entrepreneurs were assisted with financials and forecasting and (we) believe this to be one of the biggest value-adds. This was also one of the weakest points for those coming into the program.'

Table 8.1 Topics covered and emphasized in high-NFF versus low-NFF programs

	High-NFF programs	Low-NFF programs	Sig.
Number of topics covered	6.0	5.4	$p = 0.36$
Networking	18.3	14.2	$p = 0.15$
Accounting and finance	17.9	18.7	$p = 0.77$
Business process development	14.9	14.3	$p = 0.87$
Communication skills	13.2	12.0	$p = 0.63$
Human resources and legal	9.7	9.2	$p = 0.78$
Organization design	8.2	9.1	$p = 0.66$
Marketing	6.1	6.8	$p = 0.68$

To provide insights about the implications of different topical choices, we examine the responses to the question: 'Roughly how much emphasis is placed on each of the following topic areas?' After combining accounting and finance into a single topic, and human resources and legal into another, Table 8.1 shows how program managers report their coverage across seven different topic areas. The majority of the sample (42 programs) report covering six or seven of these topics. This leaves little scope for differences in topical breadth. However, the bottom rows of Table 8.1 give an idea of how the different areas are prioritized. They indicate that high-NFF programs place somewhat more emphasis on softer skills like networking. While these insignificant differences might speak to the direction that accelerators might go as they refine their program content, managers should be wary of understating the importance of accounting and finance, and business development skills. Consistent with the above comments from experienced program managers, there is a continuous interplay between the types and needs of entrepreneurs selected into cohorts and the content covered in programs. It makes sense that the skills and credentials that are favored by program selectors described in Chap. 7 (e.g., college degrees, prior entrepreneurial experience, and prior CEO or executive director experience) bring more of the basic business skills into the more successful programs. Since most accelerators adapt their programming to fit each cohort, this might lead to a reduced emphasis on business skills, but not a reduced need for these skills among entrepreneurs.

Who Should Deliver the Materials? Accelerators engage a range of individuals to deliver their materials, including their own staff (44 programs), experienced business practitioners (32 programs), experienced entrepreneurs (28 programs), and hired consultants (25 programs). However, there is no evidence that a program's ability to drive new funding to its entrepreneurs is related to the type of individuals doing the teaching.[3]

How Is the Time Spent? Because the 'what' (i.e., curriculum and topics) and the 'who' (i.e., content deliverers) have little effect on typical program performance, we turn our attention to questions of 'with whom' and 'where.' When deciding how and where the entrepreneurs will spend their time, many programs use workshop models that combine in-person and remote sessions. Entrepreneurs receive in-person support in short spurts and then return to their homes and businesses to put their new insights to work. Several interviews and conversations reveal how programs are always iterating the amount of time that entrepreneurs spend in each mode, looking to create experiences where entrepreneurs are able to unplug from their typical day-to-day activities to focus on generating new ideas, while also plugging back in to quickly apply valuable new insights.

The EDP program surveys ask managers to estimate how much time entrepreneurs spend working with their cohorts (on-site or remotely) and working alone (on-site or remotely). The responses suggest that high-NFF programs spend roughly 74 percent of their program time on-site, compared with 66 percent of the time for the low-NFF programs (see Fig. 8.2). At the same time, entrepreneurs in high-NFF programs spend 42 percent of their time engaged with their cohort, compared with just 29 percent of the time in low-NFF programs. This latter difference is significant ($p = 0.04$). These two higher-engagement differences mean that entrepreneurs in high-NFF programs also spend significantly ($p = 0.06$) less of their accelerator time off-site and working alone: 13 percent compared with 24 percent. These patterns highlight the importance of cohort dynamics for the accelerator model. Entrepreneurs who are engaged in their program and working alongside peers appear to derive more benefits from the experience than those who spend more time working remotely and alone.

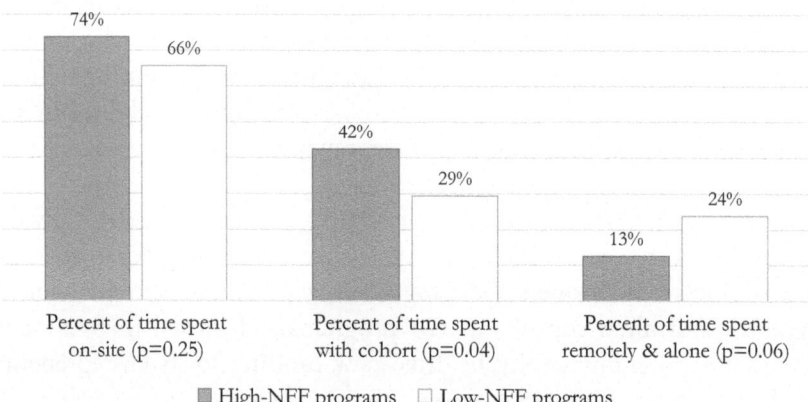

Fig. 8.2 How participants spend their time in high-NFF versus low-NFF programs

Learning more about cohort dynamics requires a closer look at the qualitative aspects of an entrepreneur's experience. In 2016, we engaged several EDP programs in order to speak with some of their entrepreneurs and mentors: 31 individuals from high-performing programs and 32 from low-performing programs. Among other things, they were asked to list three adjectives that best describe cohort dynamics—including how entrepreneurs work together and get along with one another—and to provide examples to explain these adjectives. Although the adjectives used to describe cohort dynamics were largely positive among both groups of programs, there were some minor differences. Participants in high-performing programs describe entrepreneurs as mutually supportive with an emphasis on shared opportunities. They use adjectives like 'collaborative,' 'productive,' and 'sincere' and share examples like 'everyone took comments and feedback well and used them to improve' or 'it was a great environment to put it all on the table; a very transparent environment that nurtured a sense of sharing and vulnerability.' This suggests that entrepreneurs in high-performing cohorts focus more on partnerships and peer-to-peer involvement. Entrepreneurs in high-performing programs also tend to mention that their peers are open to giving and receiving feedback, noting how 'people took accountability for feedback and were thoughtful and pointed about that feedback.' They also describe a collegial atmosphere among peers, who are 'open about growth areas of the business, challenges etc. ... everyone was offering solutions.' Importantly, the high-performing cohorts build up a strong sense of trust and community. One person remarks that 'suggestions were followed immediately by offers to assist in executing said suggestion,' while another mentions that an entrepreneur from another company had joined their board of advisors.

Low-performing cohorts seem to place more emphasis on innovation and creativity when describing their peers. Adjectives like 'innovative,' 'passionate,' and 'knowledgeable' are common, as are examples such as 'entrepreneurs all wanted to change the world – always high intensity' and 'people knew their sector and shared (their) perspectives on how to sell to specific targets.' They present fewer adjectives related to trust and community, and more that relate to competition. This suggests that cohorts in low-performing programs may be more individualistic and self-reliant.

From these discussions, it appears that networking and collaboration are more predominant among the high-performing programs, while individual innovation and acumen are more evident in the low-performing programs. However, because individuals from low-performing programs did not describe their cohorts as not collaborative, these observations should be considered preliminary rather than definitive.

What Roles Do Mentors Play?

One of the key support mechanisms that accelerators provide is access to mentors.[4] Chapters 3 and 5 showed how mentorship is one of the key benefits sought by entrepreneurs (see Fig. 3.3) and, to a lesser extent, provided by accelerators (see Fig. 5.6). Mentors share their knowledge and experiences, provide advice on recurring challenges, suggest potential strategies for growth, and expose mentees to their own networks.[5] They often have extensive experience in the relevant sectors, as successful entrepreneurs, investors, or managers.

Given the espoused importance of mentorship for accelerators, one might imagine that programs with more mentors or those where entrepreneurs spend more time with their mentors would perform better. However, the high-NFF programs in the sample recruit an average of 55 mentors each, while the low-NFF programs work with roughly 59 mentors. This difference is both insignificant ($p = 0.78$) and in the wrong direction. When it comes to mentor counts, one program manager explains that the 'number of mentors is a lot more calculated than people think. Mentors are busy people, and we want to make sure we utilize them, especially if they're flying out for the program. We try to have a small enough roster of mentors so that they feel utilized and meaningful, but a big enough roster so they can address all the needs on the table.' Nor do entrepreneurs in the high-NFF programs spend more of their time working with mentors. They allocate roughly 31 percent of entrepreneur's time to mentor interactions, compared with roughly 34 percent for the low-NFF programs. Once again, this insignificant ($p = 0.59$) difference is not in the expected direction (see Table 8.2).

Like many aspects of accelerator work, the simplest numbers do not account for any systematic performance differences across programs. However, when we look at the composition of mentor pools, some interesting differences begin to emerge (see Fig. 8.3). High-NFF programs are significantly more likely to recruit investors as mentors: 88 percent of them compared with 66 percent of the low-NFF programs. There are similar positive differentials associated with using business practitioners and entrepreneurs as mentors. It is interesting to see this positive effect for using entrepreneurs against the

Table 8.2 Time spent with mentors in high-NFF versus low-NFF programs

	On-site with mentors	Remote with mentors
High-NFF programs	23.9%	7.3%
Low-NFF programs	25.3%	8.3%
Sig.	$p = 0.78$	$p = 0.74$

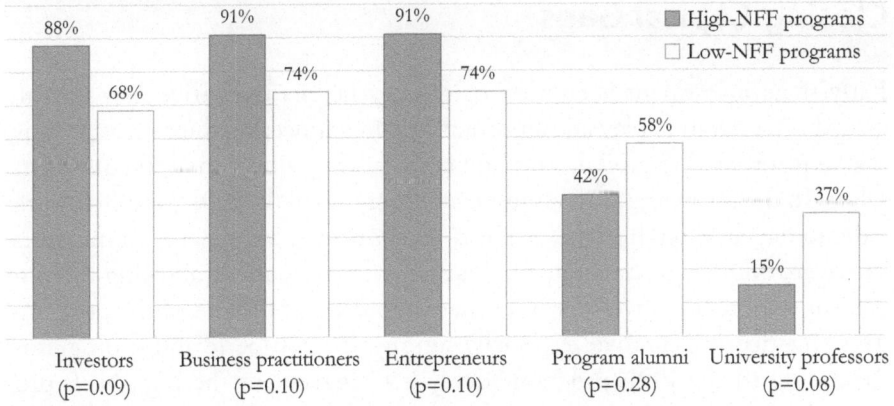

Fig. 8.3 Mentor backgrounds for high-NFF versus low-NFF programs

negative, albeit insignificant (p = 0.28), effect for using program alumni. The only group of mentors that is significantly (p = 0.08) associated with negative NFF outcomes is university professors. This probably reflects the pace and practicality of learning in accelerator models, two things that might make insights from university professors less relevant.

Selecting and recruiting mentors based on professional backgrounds is only one of the tactics deployed by successful accelerators. Intangible factors, such as mentor quality, commitment, and fit, are also critical drivers of successful mentorship programs. Here, program managers stress that 'mentorship abilities of experts vary considerably' and 'relevant expertise does not necessarily translate into an ability to impart that knowledge to others.' They also note that 'effective matchmaking takes careful consideration and clearly impacts how effective a mentor will be.' As one US-based program manager explains, 'we vet all of our mentors pretty significantly, and we make sure they're good mentors. There are a lot of really smart people who don't know how to help others (those that are good at what they do without knowing how to explain why). We try to make sure these high-performing people are actually good mentors (don't just focus on their own accomplishments). We have a mentor recommendations and expectations guide. We keep it informal, but vet them and check for culture fit.' Another East-African program manager says that 'mentors are not picked based on being in the same industry, but based on personal skills/expertise. They are more meant to work as a coach/buddy rather than as a technical expert. There is always someone who can be a listening ear/friend when times are tough. It's someone who will keep the entrepreneur on target, some supervision in terms of what commitments have been made and what keeps those commitments on track.' These qualitative insights point to the need for more fine-grained analyses of mentoring within accelerator programs.

Closing Capital Gaps

Early-stage investment is another of the key factors that drive new venture growth. Accelerators play an important role in connecting their most promising ventures to this capital, in many cases making direct investments themselves. In the former respect, almost every program in the EDP sample features a demo day, or a pitch night, as a way to connect entrepreneurs to investors. These are events that celebrate graduating entrepreneurs by allowing them to present to potential investors and other supporters at the end of the program. This practice is pervasive, especially among the top-performing programs. According to the EDP program surveys, 97 percent of the high-NFF programs have demo days or pitch nights, compared with 75 percent of the low-NFF programs. This difference is significant ($p = 0.03$).

In recent years, the institutionalized practice of hosting pitch events is coming under scrutiny because it may work against marginalized entrepreneurs. Pitching tends to favor confident speakers who match the preconceptions of audience members. In most cases, this means white men over women and minority entrepreneurs. One recent study finds that the same business plan pitched by a man received considerably more interest compared with when it was pitched in the same way by a woman.[6] This bias is problematic for impact-oriented accelerators that aspire to, among other things, level the playing field for different entrepreneurs working on different business ideas. As such, accelerators like Village Capital and New Ventures are questioning the value of their pitch events and are looking for ways to encourage investors to make decisions based on more in-depth and less biased entrepreneur interactions. Ross Baird notes that 'for entrepreneurs who don't pitch well – or who don't fit investors' mental image of a successful entrepreneur – Demo Days may hurt more than they help.' Taking this idea seriously, Village Capital is moving away from pitch events in order to facilitate more one-on-one conversations with investors. This works better for most entrepreneurs because 'it flips the power dynamic: Instead of standing onstage, racing through slides and being peppered with hardball questions, the entrepreneur and investor are sitting at the same table, the entrepreneur is leading the meeting and they are talking through the business as equals.'[7] This movement away from pitch events is relatively recent. In its wake, we will see accelerators experimenting with different ways to facilitate investor engagement. It remains to be seen which of these new approaches will take hold and what their effects on the NFF will be.

Does It Help to Make Direct Investments into Participating Ventures? There is more variability in the programs' commitment to making direct investments in participating ventures. Among the 52 programs in the sample, 37 (or roughly 70 percent) guarantee investment funds for some or all of their cohort members. These investments come in the form of equity, loans, and grants. The percentage of accelerators that guarantee investment is only somewhat greater among the high-NFF programs (76 percent) than the low-NFF programs (63 percent). However, the average NFF for the programs that guarantee at least some investment is considerably higher: positive $48,490 compared to negative $12,674.

Because the direct investments made by accelerators show up in the investment numbers reported by accelerated ventures on their follow-up surveys, it might seem unsurprising that programs that provide these direct investments have a higher average NFF. However, when we subtract the average per-participant investment reported by accelerators from the overall average NFF, there are still higher net funding flows for the cohorts whose programs provided direct investment: roughly $31,000 compared with the same negative $12,674. Table 8.3 shows that this direct investment also corresponds with higher net revenue growth. The average net revenue growth for programs that make direct investments is more than $26,000 greater. These differences seem sensible to program managers, who suggest that the direct investments made by accelerators can be fairly inconsequential in terms of their monetary contributions, but can stimulate progress on the part of entrepreneurs while helping to catalyze follow-on investments. As one program manager suggests, 'the direct investment we provide is very small after the program, but if they improve their business they can tap into a more sizable investment (this is AFTER the program) ... most people see the funding from an accelerator as a sign that their business is working.'

Table 8.3 NFF before and after accounting for direct investments

	Average NFF	Average NFF (excluding program investment)	Average net revenue growth
Provides direct investment	$48,490	$31,449	$13,685
Does not provide direct investment	-$12,674	-$12,674	-$12,884
Sig.	$p = 0.11$	$p = 0.24$	$p = 0.37$

Concluding Remarks

Effective accelerator programming is complicated, context sensitive, and tailored to the strengths and weaknesses of the different cohorts. As such, many of the broad quantitative observations—related to the use of a structured curriculum, the topics covered during a program, or the professional backgrounds of the people delivering content—are not systematically different across high-NFF and low-NFF programs. Nor do simple quantitative descriptors of mentorship programs—like the number of mentors or the time spent with them—distinguish high-NFF programs from their lower-performing counterparts.

Looking underneath these broad parameters, we are reminded that the cohort-based approach is at the heart of the accelerator model. As such, programs in which the entrepreneurs spend more time working onsite and working with other entrepreneurs tend to outperform those in which entrepreneurs spend more time working alone and remotely. Extending this observation, there are some qualitative differences in participants' perceptions of cohort dynamics, with high-performing programs developing cultures of engagement, collaboration, and trust. At the same time, the raw mentor numbers seem to be less important than the specific backgrounds of those mentors. Programs that are able to recruit investors and entrepreneurs as mentors tend to deliver better NFF results. This opens the door to another set of qualitative observations about the softer mentor attributes that contribute to better mentorship programs and better accelerator outcomes.

When the programs are done, there is some evidence that those making direct investments into at least some of their ventures experience better NFF outcomes. However, this does not mean that the sole, or even the primary, vehicle for the increased flows of funding is the investment itself. Rather, these investments build confidence in the founding team while serving as signals of underlying quality to other potential supporters. This translates into even more outside investment and greater revenue growth.

Finally, the observations about pitch events and demo-days are interesting because they suggest a tension between their current efficacy and the underlying mission of impact-oriented accelerators. While pitch events seem to connect entrepreneurs to promising supporters and therefore improve the NFF into ventures, they might also exacerbate problems faced by women and minority entrepreneurs. As some accelerators test alternatives to their demo days, it is important that we keep watching and learning from their experiments.

Overview of Program-Level Observations

This part of the book concludes by summarizing the most important and actionable observations from Chaps. 5, 6, 7, and from this chapter, those related to accelerator pipelines, entrepreneur selection, and accelerator programming:

Debt and Philanthropy Should Take a Backseat Very few high-NFF accelerators have net debt growth or net philanthropy growth as their dominant components (see Table 5.4 and Fig. 5.2). Moreover, programs where either of these components dominates do not do well when it comes to the overall flow of funds. This dim outlook on driving new debt is corroborated in conversations with experts, where increasing debt financing does not appear to be a high priority for accelerator program managers. The observation in respect of philanthropy is a bit more controversial, as many protagonists have come to see grant support as a critical surrogate for the angel investments that are hard to come by in many regions and sectors.[8]

Supporting Marginalized Entrepreneurs Can Be Good Business Although most people think that it is a good idea to focus on entrepreneurs who are otherwise overlooked or stigmatized, many fear that doing so comes at the expense of the success of the program and its ventures. It is therefore encouraging that programs reporting a preference for women and minority entrepreneurs are more likely to be among the high-NFF programs.

Money Isn't Everything, But It Helps When it comes to the operating costs of accelerators, high-NFF programs actually spend less per venture on average. They also tend to de-emphasize the benefits of making direct investment in their participants and are no more likely than their low-NFF counterparts to make these direct investments. However, programs that invest directly in their entrepreneurs have a much higher average NFF, even after removing their direct investment dollars from the equation. These direct investments also seem to stimulate net revenue growth.

There Are No Clear Numbers for Developing Successful Mentorship Programs We find no significant differences between high-NFF and low-NFF programs in the quantitative elements of their mentorship programs. However, there is some quantitative and qualitative evidence that selecting the right mentors with the right professional backgrounds (i.e., investors and entrepreneurs) correlates with improved program performance.

Among the high-NFF programs that are driving either net revenue growth or net equity growth, we can flag the following as important issues for further deliberation: (1) Driving net equity growth is consistent with a focused approach. High-NFF programs that drive more equity growth are more likely to specialize in their pipeline building and their selection of entrepreneurs: 60 percent have a specific sector focus (compared with 33 percent of revenue drivers), 80 percent prefer to work with women (compared with 59 percent), and 60 percent prefer to work with minorities (compared with 47 percent). (2) Net equity growth is tied more closely to relationships and social capital. High-NFF programs that drive more equity growth tend to focus on the personal aspects of relationships: They are more likely to select their cohorts based on the quality of the founding team, emphasize networking as a primary accelerator benefit, and prioritize in-person mentoring sessions over those that take place remotely. (3) To stimulate net revenue growth, look for more developed ventures and focus on skills. High-NFF programs that drive more revenue growth tend to emphasize business skill development and are more likely to target ventures that are more mature.

Looking Ahead: A Closer Look at Marginalized Places and People

Chapter 3 used GALI survey data to show how accelerator programs are springing up around the world to support entrepreneurs whose ventures want to generate specific social or environmental impacts. Then, Chap. 4 analyzed venture-level data from the EDP to show that accelerators are having noticeable effects on the commercial and investment performance of the ventures that they engage. To probe these overall accelerator effects more deeply, Chaps. 5, 6, 7, and this chapter integrated program-level data from the EDP to break down the operations of the sampled accelerators and analyze the choices made when building application pipelines, selecting entrepreneurs, and then working to close their various knowledge, network, and capital gaps. We motivated these various analyses by stressing the importance of encouraging early-stage ventures that seek to generate and scale various social and environmental impacts. If we take seriously the idea that world needs more market-based solutions to problems related to poverty, inequality, and environmental degradation, then we must find ways to identify and support the most promising impact-oriented entrepreneurs so they can stabilize and grow their new ventures.

The final part of this book extends this core motivation to consider two more domains in which current entrepreneurial support processes are faltering, and thus two additional problems that accelerators are being called upon to address. The first relates to place. It is well known that some, but not all, countries perform well when it comes to allowing promising entrepreneurs to build companies. For instance, Germany, Japan, and the United States were recently ranked as the three most entrepreneurial countries, while 'countries from Africa and Latin America dominate the bottom group.'[9] Although specific cause-and-effect relationships are debated, people living in these latter entrepreneurial dead spaces clearly miss out when it comes to the many benefits—including better jobs and incomes, and better products and services—that emerge when promising entrepreneurs are allowed to turn promising ideas into viable companies at rates that are similar to those observed in countries like Germany, Japan, and the United States. We saw in Chap. 2 that a large number of accelerators aspire to stimulate and support high-growth ventures in emerging markets like those found in Africa and Latin America. Chapter 9 revisits the venture-level data from the EDP to determine whether the observations and effects presented in Chap. 4 are consistent across ventures that operate in high-income countries and emerging markets.

A second major shortcoming when it comes to entrepreneurial support processes relates to people. It is also well known that the chances of achieving entrepreneurial success are impaired for minorities and women. In his review article, Timothy Bates wrote that 'minorities seeking to create viable business ventures have traditionally faced higher barriers than whites as they sought to exploit market opportunities, raise financing, and penetrate mainstream networks.'[10] In her recent overview of the gender gap in entrepreneurship, Sarah Kaplan noted that 'as tough as it is for talented women to climb the corporate ladder as compared to men, female entrepreneurs may have it even harder.'[11] The most-respected voices on the topic of inclusive entrepreneurship believe that the challenges for under-represented entrepreneurs stem less from the quality of their ideas and efforts and more from the way that individuals and organizations in the broader ecosystem calibrate and respond to their underlying potential. Given their capacity to recognize entrepreneurial potential and then close the various knowledge, network, and capital gaps that arise in underdeveloped ecosystems, several commentators believe that accelerators are well placed to address the incremental challenges faced by marginalized entrepreneurs. Chapter 10 tackles the second of these two critical biases by focusing on the gender composition of the founding teams in the EDP sample. This final chapter re-examines the EDP data to carefully articulate the specific challenges that women founders face when raising the investment funds required to stabilize and scale their businesses. The chapter closes by documenting the extent to which accelerators are addressing these gender-specific challenges.

Notes

1. Susan L. Cohen, Christopher B. Bingham, & Benjamin L. Hallen. 2018. 'The role of accelerator designs in mitigating bounded Rationality in new ventures.' *Administrative Science Quarterly*, forthcoming; Ronit Yitshaki & Israel Drori. 2018. 'Understanding mentorship.' *Accelerators: Successful Venture Creation and Growth*.
2. Susan Cohen & Yael Hochberg. 2014 Accelerating Startups: The Seed Accelerator Phenomenon. Working paper.
3. As an aside, the program survey responses indicate little use of university professors (six programs) and alumni (nine programs), even though many accelerators claim affiliations with universities and boast of their talented alumni network.
4. C. Scott Dempwolf, Jennifer Auer, & Michelle D'Ippolito. 2014. *Innovation Accelerators: Defining Characteristics among Startup Assistance Organizations.* Small Business Administration.
5. Ronit Yitshaki & Israel Drori. 2018. 'Understanding mentorship.' *Accelerators: Successful Venture Creation and Growth*.
6. Alison Wood Brooks, Laura Huang, Sarah Wood Kearney, & Fiona E. Murray. 2014. 'Investors prefer entrepreneurial ventures pitched by attractive men.' *Proceedings of the National Academy of Sciences*, 111(12): 4427–4431.
7. Ross Baird. Why this investor is ditching Demo Days. *TechCrunch* (March 2017).
8. Catherine Cheney. 2018. How Blended Capital Can Help Entrepreneurs Make It Through the Missing Middle. *Devex* (January 2018).
9. Entrepreneurship: Innovation flourishes in these countries where enterprising citizens have a startup mentality. *U.S. News and World Report*, 2018.
10. Timothy Bates. 2011. 'Minority entrepreneurship.' *Foundations and Trends in Entrepreneurship*, 7 (3–4).
11. Sarah Kaplan. 2017. 'Tackling the gender gap in entrepreneurship.' *INSEAD Knowledge* (February 2017).

9

Acceleration in Emerging Markets

When thinking about the entrepreneurs and ventures that aspire to create major impacts, it is important to look past the well-publicized startup stories and consider ventures like Sehat Kahani in Pakistan. Sehat Kahani aspires to 'democratize healthcare by building an all-female health provider network to deliver quality healthcare solutions using telehealth.' Looking to the future, the founders are planning to create more than 100 e-health centers in underserved communities across Pakistan by the end of 2020.[1] In Rwanda, SafeMotos is an Uber-style ride-hailing platform designed for motorcycle taxis. According to its website, SafeMotos works on several UN sustainable development goals (SDGs), including building a safer taxi experience (SDG 11), developing a local technology industry (SDG 9), increasing taxi drivers' economic productivity through technology (SDG 8), and enabling women to become taxi drivers (SDG 5). With over 150 drivers and 200,000 registered trips, SafeMotos was recently ranked by Fast Company Magazine as Africa's seventh most innovative company.[2]

It is also important to consider the role that accelerators play in the development of these emerging-market ventures. The two founders of Sehat Kahani participated in the i2i accelerator (2015 and 2017), the Telenor Velocity accelerator (2016), and the SPRING accelerator (2017). The founders of SafeMotos also had important experiences applying to and participating in accelerators: 'When SafeMotos co-founders Nash and Peter Kariuki found out they didn't get into Tigo's Think Accelerator, they weren't disappointed. Instead, they decided to work even harder in developing their smartphone application which will make Motos safer and more convenient for customers. Their good work was rewarded when an Irish startup accelerator called Carma

© The Author(s) 2019
P. W. Roberts, S. A. Lall, *Observing Acceleration*,
https://doi.org/10.1007/978-3-030-00042-4_9

AXLR8R heard about the SafeMotos concept. After a lengthy vetting process, Carma invested into SafeMotos and has given them a position in their accelerator where they will be collaborating with a talented product development team, benefiting from a global mentorship network and gaining access to additional investment opportunities.'[3]

Many people believe that the impact-oriented ventures that work in countries like Pakistan and Rwanda are exponentially important. Just like the ventures started in North America and Western Europe, they offer the promise of scalable solutions to social and environmental challenges. At the same time, they offer incremental economic opportunities for entrepreneurs and potential employees in places that struggle to develop a fair share of normal economic activity. Identifying more of these promising ventures, and then smoothing their pathways to growth is seen as one way to create viable alternatives to more traditional employment-based livelihoods.[4]

This imperative to double down on entrepreneurs who launch impact-oriented ventures in places where development challenges are greatest has led to many broad-based efforts to identify and support promising ventures in emerging markets. The Global Entrepreneurship Congress, now in its 11th year, 'brings together thousands of delegates from more than 170 countries to discuss economic and policy challenges around growing entrepreneurial ecosystems.'[5] Meanwhile, the World Bank's infoDev program oversees 'a global network of business incubators and innovation hubs for climate technology, agribusiness, and digital entrepreneurs.'[6] Another example is the USAID's Partnering to Accelerate Entrepreneurship initiative, which works to 'catalyze private-sector investment into early-stage enterprises and identify innovative models or approaches that help entrepreneurs bridge the pioneer gap – thus unlocking the potential of thousands of promising enterprises around the world.'[7]

These efforts recognize the importance of accelerator programs when it comes to supporting promising entrepreneurs who lack the support that more developed ecosystems tend to provide. This has led to a proliferation of accelerators that focus on emerging markets. In fact, roughly two-thirds of the organizations identified by GALI's Global Accelerator Survey run accelerators in emerging markets.[8] The blueprints used to design these programs often adopt elements from the more-famous programs in the United States and Europe.[9] The problem with simple replication, however, is that emerging-market entrepreneurs, ventures, and ecosystems are quite different. Therefore, the same kind of program run in different country contexts might produce very different results: 'As the impact accelerator market matures, there is increasing recognition that a one-size-fits-all approach is not effective. Market dynamics are highly unique in different industries or geographies, and thus it is most useful to give enterprises lessons and resources that are directly related to their specific niche.'[10]

Because of this heightened need and these greater challenges, it is critical to understand the effects that accelerators are having on ventures that operate in emerging markets. Building from the baseline analyses presented in Chap. 4, this chapter asks a pair of related questions: (1) Are the impact-oriented entrepreneurs from emerging markets different from those working in high-income countries? and (2) Do entrepreneurs working in emerging markets receive the same benefits from participating in accelerator programs?[11] Answers to these questions will go a long way toward informing program managers whether and where they can generalize accelerator models from places like Boston and Silicon Valley, and where they need to consider modifications to the basic model.

Emerging Markets Versus High-Income Countries

The analyses in this chapter require an acceptable way to distinguish ventures working in emerging markets from those working in more developed countries. To help with this task, the EDP application surveys ask, 'Currently, in which country are your venture's main operations?' The ten most prolific countries in the EDP sample are the United States (1628), Mexico (642), Kenya (597), India (539), Uganda (338), Nigeria (218), Nicaragua (177), Colombia (119), Canada (118), South Africa (98), and Tanzania (98). With this information in hand, the EDP organizes operating countries according to the 2015 World Bank country classifications.[12] In this classification, high-income economies (e.g., the United States) are those with 'a Gross National Income (GNI) per capita of $12,736 or more.' Emerging markets comprise the other two country groups, including low-income economies (e.g., Kenya), with a GNI per capita of $1045 or less; and middle-income economies (e.g., Mexico and India), with a GNI per capita between $1045 and $12,736. Table 9.1 gives some indication of how these country categories differ from one another, with an emphasis on the contours created within the EDP sample.

This World Bank classification places 1908 of the ventures in the EDP sample in high-income countries and 3698 in emerging markets.[13] The EDP programs with the most high-income-country applicants are run by Village Capital and Points of Light. Middle-income country entrepreneurs are most likely to apply to programs run by Village Capital and the Unreasonable Institute. Finally, the greatest number of low-income country ventures are found in the applicant pools of programs run by USADF and GrowthAfrica.

Table 9.1 World Bank country categories

	High-income countries	Emerging markets	
	High-income economies	Middle-income economies	Low-income economies
GNI per capita (2014)	$12,736+	$1045–$12,736	<$1045
Ventures (in EDP sample)	$N = 1908$	$N = 2338$	$N = 1360$
Top country (in EDP sample)	United States	Mexico	Kenya
Top programs (in EDP sample)	Village Capital Points of Light	Village Capital Unreasonable Institute	USADF GrowthAfrica
World Bank regions			
North America	1746 ventures	0 ventures	
Sub-Saharan Africa	0 ventures	1797 ventures	
Latin America & Caribbean	43 ventures	1247 ventures	
South Asia	0 ventures	566 ventures	

Before launching into a presentation of the idiosyncrasies associated with starting and accelerating ventures in emerging markets, it is important to recognize that entrepreneurs do not always apply to accelerators run in their home countries. In fact, Table 9.2 shows that entrepreneurs whose ventures operate in emerging markets are considerably more likely to apply to accelerators run in other countries. While almost all of the high-income-country ventures in the EDP sample apply to accelerators run in their home countries, roughly 43 percent of the emerging-market ventures are attracted to accelerators whose main programming is offered in other countries. In most cases, the accelerators attracting applicants from other emerging-market countries are African or Latin American programs designed to support ventures working across a region, rather than within a specific country. One USADF program attracted nearly 200 young entrepreneurs from 30 African countries by offering technical assistance to grassroots ventures. The Village Capital Fintech Africa program attracted more than 100 entrepreneurs from Kenya, Nigeria, South Africa, Ghana, Uganda, Rwanda, and Tanzania who wanted to grow businesses that address financial health concerns. A third program, I3 LATAM, supported social enterprises that work to create solutions that meet the needs of low-income people across Latin America. Finally, a smaller number of emerging-market entrepreneurs apply to accelerators based in the United States. One prominent example is Unreasonable Institute, Boulder (now called Uncharted). This global program attracted entrepreneurs from around the globe who are building companies that tackle big societal problems.

Table 9.2 Where do entrepreneurs apply?

	Programs run in the same country	Programs run in a different country	Different-country program regional focus
Emerging-market applicants	N = 2095 (56.7%)	N = 1603 (43.4%)	Sub-Saharan Africa (N = 624) Latin America & Caribbean (N – 398) United States of America (N = 280)
High-income-country applicants	N = 1750 (91.7%)	N = 158 (8.3%)	

When thinking about the different ways to support impact-oriented entrepreneurs and ventures, it is important to consider the implications of being accelerated in a different country. After all, the goal of accelerators is to, one way or another, address the challenges that promising entrepreneurs face in less-than-perfect ecosystems. When this surrogating and patching work takes place in another country, it might have implications—good or bad—for the effectiveness of the programming. There is also information in the fact that virtually all of the different-country acceleration is observed among emerging-market applicants. This suggests that while there many challenges within their local ecosystems, there are not enough local options to meet the demand for high-quality support programming. To assess whether emerging-market entrepreneurs that go elsewhere for acceleration services are different and whether they experience different effects of acceleration, we divide the EDP sample into three groups: emerging-market ventures that apply to programs run in their country of operations (i.e., same country), emerging-market ventures that apply to programs run in other countries (i.e., different country), and high-income-country ventures.

As we reflect on the promise of emerging-market entrepreneurs and ventures, the general challenges they face in their ecosystems, and the overall effectiveness of emerging-market accelerator programming, we should not allow the meta-picture of two forests obscure the many tree-to-tree differences. As one sector expert notes in the 2015 GALI report, 'many of the findings that you generalize across all high-income countries and all emerging markets are actually very context-specific. Depending on the specifics of the local ecosystem, accelerator program managers and entrepreneurs will face different challenges ... it is important not to downplay the effects of subtle ecosystem differences, and the different roles that accelerators will play.' Another expert suggests that 'this report is very helpful, but the next step will be to dig in to the difference within countries, or within regions. In the United States, 78 percent of venture capital goes to just three states – New York, California and Massachusetts. In the Global South, there are a lot of nuances as well between countries and within countries.' We foreshadow these critical country-level analyses in an Appendix to this chapter.

Table 9.3 Reported IRIS impact objectives across three groups

	Emerging markets, same-country program (N = 2095)	Emerging markets, different-country program (N = 1603)	High-income countries (N = 1908)	Sig.
Employment generation	38.4%	38.8%	24.8%	$p = 0.00$
Income/productivity growth	30.2%	29.8%	22.4%	$p = 0.00$
Community development	19.9%	26.0%	27.4%	$p = 0.00$
Access to education	19.8%	19.6%	26.3%	$p = 0.00$
Health improvement	17.9%	15.0%	24.3%	$p = 0.00$
Equality and empowerment	13.8%	15.8%	24.0%	$p = 0.00$
Agricultural productivity	17.6%	19.1%	12.7%	$p = 0.00$
Access to financial services	14.2%	14.7%	14.5%	$p = 0.93$
Capacity building	14.0%	18.8%	11.0%	$p = 0.00$
Access to information	12.3%	13.7%	11.4%	$p = 0.12$
Food security	10.3%	11.7%	12.2%	$p = 0.16$

To get a sense for their different impact aspirations, it is instructive to examine the impact objectives among ventures that work in emerging markets (see Table 9.3). In three of the major impact areas, there are no meaningful differences. The goal of providing access to financial services is almost identically-distributed across the three groups of ventures. There are similar small differences when it comes to providing access to information and supporting food security. However, this is not to say that these goals are pursued in the same manner across the board. For example, Wise Banyan is a financial services venture in the United States with the goal of making investing accessible to a wider group of people. The company offers a suite of free investment advisory services to customers while also offering paid services. Companies like Lipisha and Kopo Kopo focus on mobile money applications in Kenya and Sierra Leone. These ventures provide a suite of services that allow small businesses to accept mobile payments. In India, the crowdfunding platform Milaap offers fundraising services to various charities, educational institutions, and disaster relief efforts. These examples highlight the range of approaches that are taken by ventures with similar impact objectives working in economies that are at different stages of development.

For the two most common impact objectives in the EDP sample—employment generation and supporting income and productivity growth—

the incidence is significantly higher among the two groups of ventures that operate in emerging markets. Both of these objectives are particularly salient in emerging economies where the lack of employment options and low wages, combined with job and wage uncertainty, keep too many people in moderate-to-extreme poverty. Small and growing businesses create new jobs while placing specific emphasis on higher-quality and more reliable jobs for poorer segments of the population.[14] For example, LabourNet provides skilling interventions to workers in the informal sector in India, helping to improve their employment and earnings potential.

Other more common impact areas for emerging-market ventures are agricultural productivity and capacity building. On the other hand, ventures in emerging markets are significantly less likely to focus on community development, access to education, health improvement, and equality and empowerment. In the case of community development, the diminished interest is only evident among emerging-market ventures that seek acceleration in their home countries. Finally, there is a somewhat non-intuitive pattern for ventures that work on agricultural productivity and capacity building. The lowest interest in these two objectives is understandably found among the high-income-country ventures, while the highest is surprisingly found among emerging-market entrepreneurs who seek acceleration services in other countries.

What Do Experts Think About Emerging-Market Ventures?

When thinking about how accelerators might stimulate the growth of emerging-market ventures that aspire to generate these kinds of impacts, it is important to have a clear point of view about how conditions in emerging markets differ from those in high-income economies. To establish this context, we engaged a panel of experts to brainstorm ideas about why accelerators in emerging markets might work and perform differently than those working in high-income countries.[15] These experts include practitioners, funders, and consultants that work across a wide range of geographies and have expertise in different sectors. This exercise uncovered four main areas where emerging-market differences might influence entrepreneurial and accelerator outcomes: those pertaining to ventures, entrepreneurs, entrepreneurial ecosystems, and accelerator programs (see Table 9.4). These four areas are addressed, in turn, below.

Table 9.4 Commonly held beliefs about entrepreneurship and acceleration in emerging markets

Emerging-market ventures are different
Emerging market ventures are less developed at application
Emerging market ventures are more developed at application
Emerging market ventures need less capital
Emerging-market entrepreneurs are different
Emerging market entrepreneurs have greater talent gaps
Emerging market entrepreneurs have less entrepreneurial experience
Emerging market entrepreneurs have less money to invest
Emerging market entrepreneurs are less confident of success and thus return on investment (ROI)
Emerging-market ecosystems are different
Emerging markets have less local equity investment
In emerging markets, success without acceleration is harder
Emerging-market accelerator programs are different
Emerging market accelerators make fewer direct investments
Emerging market accelerators are of lower quality
Emerging market accelerators have lower-quality networks

Are Emerging-Market Ventures Different? When asked to account for the specific challenges associated with accelerating ventures in emerging markets, experts shared numerous beliefs about systematic differences. Table 9.5 sheds light on the differences that pertain to the ventures themselves. Focusing on the implications of locating in different ecosystems, one important question relates to whether a venture's headquarters are located in the country in which it operates. In cases where leadership and decision-making are situated in one ecosystem while operations are housed in another, ventures have access to a more diverse set of ecosystem actors, but also face the challenges associated with managing distance and differing operational contexts. The first row of Table 9.5 suggests that it is rare for ventures operating in high-income countries to have headquarters in another country. While this may not be surprising, it is interesting to see that the same small percentage of emerging-market ventures applying to same-country accelerators have their headquarters in other countries. However, emerging-market ventures applying to programs in other countries are significantly more likely to have non-local headquarters. The majority of these ventures (roughly 60 percent) are headquartered in the United States, while another 24 percent are headquartered in another high-income-country. Therefore, many of the ventures in this second group have direct access to one local (and somewhat limiting) ecosystem and another that is arguably better-suited to support promising entrepreneurs. This difference should be kept in mind when we examine the effects of acceleration in different country settings.

Table 9.5 Venture differences across three groups

	Emerging markets, same-country program	Emerging markets, different-country program	High-income countries	Sig.
Different operations and headquarter countries	2.4%	10.6%	2.5%	$p = 0.00$
Legal form	For-profit, 83.6% Nonprofit, 7.1% Other, 5.2% Undecided, 4.0%	For-profit, 78.5% Nonprofit, 11.6% Other, 6.9% Undecided, 3.0%	For-profit, 75.3% Nonprofit, 14.2% Other, 7.4% Undecided, 3.1%	$p = 0.00$
Sectors (top 5)	Education, 15.9% Agriculture, 17.0% Health, 11.4% Financial services, 10.0% ICT, 7.3%	Education, 14.4% Agriculture, 19.1% Health, 9.0% Financial services, 8.3% ICT, 7.7%	Education, 21.3% Agriculture, 10.6% Health, 15.9% Financial services, 11.0% ICT, 6.0%	$p = 0.00$
Any intellectual property	41.5%	40.3%	46.0%	$p = 0.00$
Venture age	Average = 2.3 years	Average = 2.9 years	Average = 2.2 years	$p = 0.00$
Application revenues	Average = $32,802	Average = $62,806	Average = $51,232	$p = 0.00$
Application FT employees	Average = 3.8	Average = 4.9	Average = 1.2	$p = 0.00$

Another factor that might influence the commercial and investment performance of early-stage ventures is their adopted legal form. A recent study of impact-oriented companies working around the world suggests that those working in emerging markets tend to have stronger social orientations, and tend to be more deeply engaged with the traditional nonprofit sector.[16] This could manifest in a larger percentage of nonprofit ventures in the two emerging-market groups. However, Table 9.5 indicates that EDP ventures that operate in emerging markets, and especially those seeking acceleration in their home countries, are significantly less likely to operate as nonprofits. It is not clear whether the higher percentage of nonprofits in high-income countries reflects a true tendency within the more developed ecosystems or is simply an artifact of the accelerators that elected to join the EDP initiative. However, it does diminish concerns that emerging-market ventures tend to select the legal form that makes revenue generation and outside equity investment more challenging.

There are also differences across the three groups when it comes to sector participation. In the high-income-country group, there is a higher percentage of ventures in the education (roughly 21 percent) and health (roughly 15 percent) sectors. On the other hand, there are relatively more agriculture ventures in the two emerging-market groups (roughly 17 percent and 19 percent). However, this may have little relevance when it comes to explaining average commercial and investment performance differences. A series of ANOVAs[17] estimated on the full EDP sample does not reveal any significant differences across these five major sectors when it comes to the prior-year levels of full-time employees ($p = 0.49$) outside equity ($p = 0.49$) and debt ($p = 0.28$) reported on applications. When it comes to earned revenues, the average differences are marginally significant ($p = 0.06$), with the highest average found in the health sector ($68,821) and the lowest in the financial services sector ($29,355). For philanthropy, the differences are again significant ($p = 0.05$), with the highest average found in the education sector ($19,942) and the lowest in agriculture ($6756). Mapping these overall sector differences onto the differences reported in Table 9.5, there are only three places where sector participation might help to explain performance differences among emerging-market ventures. Earned revenues are higher on average for health sector ventures, which are less common in emerging markets. Philanthropic support is greater on average for ventures in the education sector, which are also less common in emerging markets. It is also smaller on average for agriculture ventures, which are more common in emerging markets.

Another factor relates to intellectual property, which is clearly linked to four of the five venture performance variables tracked in this book. On average, ventures with at least one patent, copyright, or trademark report roughly $48,000 more in revenues, 3.2 more full-time employees, $15,000 more outside equity, and $7000 more debt in the year prior to filling out their accelerator program applications. All of these differences are significant. At the same time, ventures working in high-income countries are significantly more likely to report owning protected intellectual property.

The experts that we consulted are split on the question of how well-developed emerging-market ventures are when they present themselves to accelerators. Some think that they are less developed in general, while others believe that they tend to wait longer before applying and are therefore more developed. The latter belief is partially supported in Table 9.5, which shows that emerging-market ventures that apply to accelerators run in other countries are older at the time of application (2.9 years). This difference may not be large, but it does give them an extra six months to lay the foundation for their ventures. The other two groups are quite similar on average (2.3 years for emerging-market ventures that stay home and 2.2 years for high-income-country ventures). To get a sense of how the different ventures made use of these early months, consider the two variables that indicate the amount of commercial progress made before acceleration. Consistent with their more advanced average age, emerging-market ventures that seek acceleration in other countries report significantly higher average revenues (roughly $63,000) and full-time employees (roughly five) on their applications. The emerging-market ventures that seek acceleration in their home country report the lowest average revenues, while the high-income-country ventures report the lowest number of full-time employees.

Are Emerging-Market Entrepreneurs Different? The second set of potential differences within emerging markets relates to the individuals who populate the founding teams. The information presented in Table 9.6 speaks to some of these differences. The first thing to note is that there are significant differences in the percentage of teams with multiple founders. Multi-founder teams are most common among the emerging-market ventures that apply to same-country accelerators (roughly 81 percent) and least common among the high-income-country ventures (roughly 72 percent).

Many experts think that emerging-market entrepreneurs have greater talent gaps than their high-income-country counterparts and that emerging-market entrepreneurs have less entrepreneurial experience. One way to infer skill or

Table 9.6 Founding team differences across three groups

	Emerging markets, same-country program	Emerging markets, different-country program	High-income countries	Sig.
Multiple founders on team	81.1%	76.5%	72.2%	$p = 0.00$
Average founder age	Average = 34.5 years	Average = 33.8 years	Average = 36.6 years	$p = 0.00$
Any prior founding experience	57.7%	63.8%	56.9%	$p = 0.00$
Any prior accelerator participation	29.2%	28.8%	27.9%	$p = 0.66$
Own money invested since founding	68.4%	67.3%	Yes = 66.6%	$p = 0.47$
	Average = $35,533	Average = $45,414	Average = $57,588	$p = 0.00$
Founding team gender	All men, 49.6%	All men, 44.7%	All men, 53.3%	$p = 0.00$
	All women, 11.3%	All women, 15.7%	All women, 18.8%	
	Mixed-gender, 39.0%	Mixed-gender, 39.6%	Mixed-gender, 27.9%	

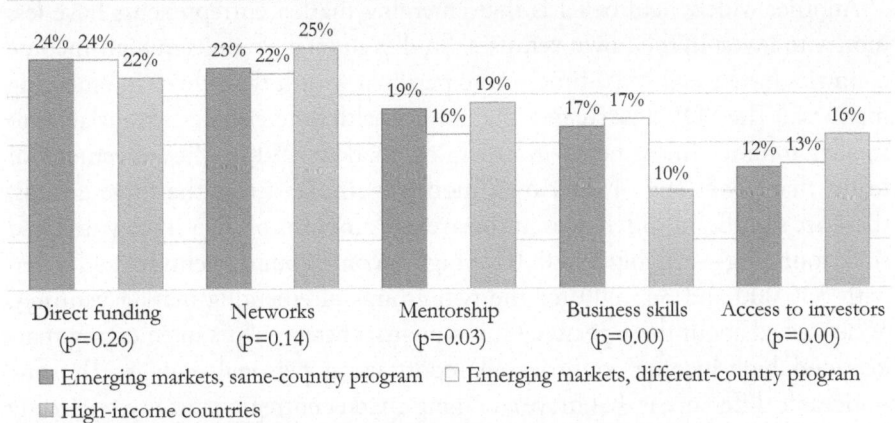

Fig. 9.1 Accelerator benefits ranked #1 across three country groups

capability gaps among the three groups of entrepreneurs is to look at how they prioritize the various benefits that are offered by accelerators. Figure 9.1 shows that the three groups of entrepreneurs place similar emphasis on the prospect of direct funding from the program. However, the two groups of emerging-market entrepreneurs place significantly more emphasis on business skill development. On the other hand, seeming more confident about their business skills, high-income-country entrepreneurs place more emphasis on possible relational benefits like building networks and gaining access to investors. This does not confirm the presence of talent gaps. Nor does it tell us exactly where emerging-market entrepreneurs think they are falling short. It does, however, lend an element of proof-by-consensus that entrepreneurs and accelerators in emerging markets are paying more attention to skills development.

Bolstering concerns about a skills gap, these same experts tend to believe that emerging-market entrepreneurs have fewer prior entrepreneurial experiences. When asked about instances where founding teams have great ideas but problems with execution, emerging-market investors often point to their lack of entrepreneurial experience: 'We often see great technical ability but significantly lower entrepreneurial ability.' In the EDP sample, however, the founding teams of emerging-market ventures report significantly more prior entrepreneurial experience, having established an average of 2.8 companies, compared with 2.3 in high-income countries. It will be interesting to learn why these prior entrepreneurial experiences are not being recognized by investors and other experts.

Another widely held belief is that emerging-market entrepreneurs have less money to invest in their own ventures. Studies show that adults in high-income countries have roughly 16 times more personal wealth than those in emerging markets.[18] The EDP data suggest that these wealth differentials do translate into smaller founder investments in emerging markets. While the percentage of teams that invest any of their own money is similar across the three groups, there are significant differences in the average amounts of own money invested since founding—roughly $58,000 for high-income-country ventures compared with $36,000 and $45,000 for the two groups of emerging-market ventures. When asked about these personal investments, entrepreneurs in emerging markets and high-income countries all report using personal savings. The one noticeable difference is that more emerging-market entrepreneurs invest directly from their paychecks on an ongoing basis. This is indicated by one emerging-market entrepreneur who says that 'I didn't have a lot of money to start with, but I put in everything I had – this was money I had earned from my job, as I had no savings, and my friends and family had no money to contribute.'

Are Emerging-Market Ecosystems Different? The third broad category of factors that experts highlight when talking about emerging markets relates to the local entrepreneurial environment. As we stressed at the beginning of the book, the ecosystem in which entrepreneurship plays out has major implications for the likelihood that a promising entrepreneur with a great idea will end up with a viable and growing company. Along the way, they must have access to the right kinds of capital and the right kinds of support services. One indication of the ability to receive support from the ecosystem is found in responses to the question about prior acceleration experiences. However, the first row of Table 9.7 suggests that the percentage of founding teams that report prior acceleration experience is almost identical across the three groups. While we need to learn more about the quality and location of these prior accelerator experiences, it is interesting that there seems to be a similar supply of support options in emerging markets.

The most striking contrast between the ventures operating in high-income countries and those in the two emerging-market groups relates to their ability to secure outside funding for their ventures. While prior investment differences are related to many of the differences already observed in this chapter—for example, less intellectual capital, lower earned revenues, and more prior entrepreneurial experiences—the investment differences reported in Table 9.7 seem decidedly out of proportion. The largest emerging-market deficit relates to outside equity investment. On their applications, the high-income-country ventures reported

Table 9.7 Ecosystem differences across three groups

	Emerging markets, same-country program	Emerging markets, different-country program	High-income countries	Sig.
Prior accelerator participation	29.2%	28.8%	27.9%	$p = 0.66$
Outside equity since founding	Average = $7104	Average = $6505	Average = $32,202	$p = 0.00$
Total debt since founding	Average = $3851	Average = $6697	Average = $11,220	$p = 0.00$
Philanthropy since founding	Average = $6131	Average = $15,156	Average = $21,504	$p = 0.00$

receiving an average of more than $32,000 of equity investment since founding. This is more than four times greater than the corresponding averages for the two emerging-market groups. Similar differences, although not quite as large, are observed for debt and philanthropy. If one indication of a supportive ecosystem is its ability to direct investment support to promising ventures, then these numbers indicate real gaps in the emerging-market ecosystems.

Many experts believe that emerging-market ventures simply require less capital. Recall that the EDP application surveys ask entrepreneurs about their plans for additional investment support over the next 12 months. Setting aside the small set of entrepreneurs with unrealistically high aspirations (see the discussion surrounding Fig. 3.4) and focusing on 12-month plans for debt plus equity investment, high-income-country entrepreneurs seek an average of roughly $610,000, which is more than double the corresponding average for emerging-market entrepreneurs who seek acceleration at home. This large and significant difference suggests that the demand for private capital is a lot lower in emerging markets. Of course, this might reflect real differences in growth potential, lower confidence among emerging-market entrepreneurs, perceived constraints in the local investment community, or the simple fact that a dollar of investment goes farther in emerging markets. Whatever the actual reasons, a difference of this size is worthy of additional scrutiny, especially since investment outcomes are going to be linked to the requests that are made by entrepreneurs.

Accelerator Effects in Emerging Markets

We have seen several ways that emerging-market ventures tend to differ from their high-income-country counterparts; for example, their work is distributed differently across sectors. Some of these differences probably make it more difficult for them to attract support; for example, they tend to have less earned revenue. Other differences should make them more attractive to supporters;

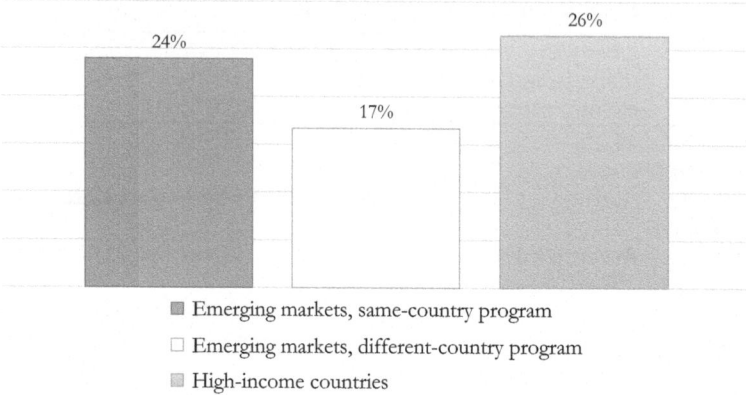

Fig. 9.2 Probability of program participation across three country groups

for example, they tend to be somewhat older and have more full-time employees. Irrespective of any positive, negative, or neutral differences, they are seeking help from accelerators when it comes to growing revenues and especially investment. We therefore conclude this examination of emerging-market ventures by looking once again at the one-year change variables, with and without acceleration, across the three groups of ventures.

Overall, roughly 22 percent of the EDP applicants were accepted to participate in the programs to which they applied. The acceptance rate is highest (roughly 26 percent) among entrepreneurs working in high-income countries. Zeroing in on the two groups of emerging-market entrepreneurs, Fig. 9.2 shows that acceptance rates are higher (roughly 24 percent) among entrepreneurs who apply to programs run in their own countries, compared with those who are more footloose (roughly 17 percent). It does seem to be somewhat more difficult for emerging-market entrepreneurs to get into accelerators. However, this disadvantage is mitigated for entrepreneurs who apply to programs run in their own countries.

Consistent with the analyses reported in Chap. 4, we examine year-over-year changes in revenues, full-time employees, outside equity investment, new debt financing, and philanthropic contributions—this time distinguishing two groups of ventures operating in emerging markets from those working in high-income countries. For the most part, the observations about accelerator effects for emerging-market ventures that stay in the same country are promising (see Table 9.8). Average increases for revenues (roughly $29,000) and full-time employees (roughly 0.9 employees) are significantly greater for the ventures that participate in accelerators compared with those that apply but are not accepted. For the three types of investment, participating ventures also

Table 9.8 Average accelerator effects across three groups

Emerging markets, same-country program	Participated (N = 230)	Rejected (N = 731)	Difference	Sig.
Change in revenues	$41,184	$12,547	$28,637	p = 0.10
Change in full-time employees	2.09	1.23	0.86	p = 0.08
Change in outside equity	$9374	$4611	$4763	p = 0.26
Change in total debt	$6035	$1780	$4236	p = 0.20
Change in philanthropic support	$3378	–$2207	$5585	p = 0.27
Emerging markets, different-country program	Participated (N = 160)	Rejected (N = 798)	Difference	Sig.
Change in revenues	$27,591	$17,655	$9936	p = 0.68
Change in full-time employees	1.60	0.14	1.46	p = 0.35
Change in outside equity	–$1688	$5822	–$7510	p = 0.28
Change in total debt	$1226	$1900	$674	p = 0.90
Change in philanthropic support	$10,998	–$1644	$9355	p = 0.10
High-income countries	Participated (N = 259)	Rejected (N = 722)	Difference	Sig.
Change in revenues	$3044	$23,187	–$20,143	p = 0.21
Change in full-time employees	0.55	0.33	0.22	p = 0.13
Change in outside equity	$22,955	$9831	$13,124	p = 0.29
Change in total debt	$11,119	$6092	$5026	p = 0.38
Change in philanthropic support	$4459	$9153	–$4693	p = 0.70

experience more growth, but the differences are not significant. The very small equity investment bump is problematic for growth-oriented ventures, especially given the small amounts of outside equity investment received prior to the program (recall Table 9.7). These one-year accelerator bumps are contextualized by comparing them to those observed in the high-income-country group. By far, the largest accelerator bump for emerging-market ventures that stay home relates to revenues. This roughly $29,000 revenue bump compares with a negative accelerator effect of roughly $20,000 for high-income-country ventures. However, these latter ventures experience a larger average equity bump of more than $13,000.

Once again, these average accelerator effects are muddied by the fact that accelerators tend to have opposing effects at the top and the bottom ends of the growth distributions. Figure 9.3 replicates the information presented in Fig. 4.1 after breaking the sample into the three groups. The right side of all four panels shows the expected dual effects of accelerator program participation in the high-income countries. A significantly higher percentage of the ventures that grow revenues and investment participate in accelerators. The same is true for the ventures where these four variables decline. This attests to a robust across-the-board accelerator effect in high-income countries.

A similar pattern of accelerator effects plays out down the left side of the four panels. In three cases, we see the opposing effects of accelerator participation

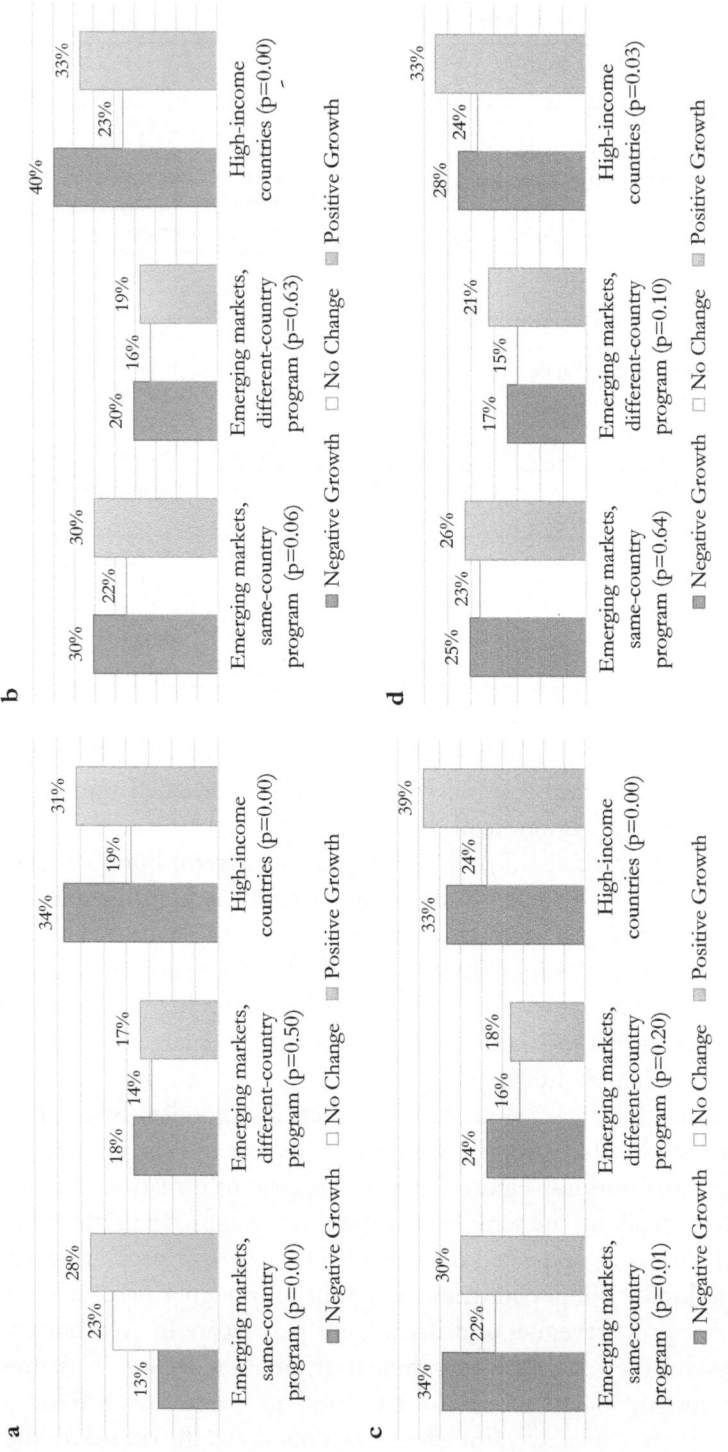

Fig. 9.3 Accelerator participation and negative-, no-, and positive (**a**) revenue-growth ventures, (**b**) equity-growth ventures, (**c**) debt-growth ventures, and (**d**) philanthropy-growth ventures across three country groups

among the ventures with positive-growth and negative growth outcomes, with the equity and philanthropy effects being somewhat muted. The latter differences across the negative-, no-, and positive-growth groups are not significant ($p = 0.64$). Once again, there is some cause for concern that accelerator effects in two of the spots where they are needed most—stimulating and channeling equity and philanthropic investment—are weak. The one positive observation among the emerging-market ventures that stay home relates to revenue growth. Here, there is a large and positive participation effect among ventures that experience positive revenue growth. However, there is no evidence that accelerators guide the under-performing ventures into the negative revenue growth category. This helps explain the large average effect of acceleration reported earlier. Taken together, these observations bolster those made earlier in the book. It seems that accelerators are better at driving investment growth in high-income countries and revenue growth in emerging markets.

Finally, the middle observations in the four panels show minimal accelerator effects among emerging-market ventures that seek acceleration in other countries. Across the board, the patterns resemble those seen in the high-income countries, but the size and significance of the effects are minimal. This provides some indication that it is more difficult for accelerators to have an effect on emerging-market entrepreneurs when their programs are situated in other ecosystems.

While differences among accelerator programs receive less attention, the expert panel holds a few beliefs about programs run in emerging markets. Some of them believe that emerging-market programs have fewer resources or are of lower quality than the established programs run in high-income countries. Others suggest that emerging-market accelerators make fewer direct investments in their ventures. The EDP program data allow us to look for differences in these three input variables: program cost, number of mentors, and total guaranteed investment for participating entrepreneurs. In all cases, there is no evidence of inferior resources for emerging-market programs. They spend slightly more per program (roughly $209,000 on average compared with $198,000) and they attract a similar number of mentors (53 on average compared with 61). Emerging-market programs also offer more guaranteed investment on average—roughly $123,000 compared with $95,000—to the entrepreneurs who participate in their programs, although this difference is not significant (Table 9.9).

Table 9.9　Resources spent on accelerator programs

	Program cost	Total mentors	Guaranteed investment
Emerging-market programs	$208,600	52.5	$123,458
High-income-country programs	$197,754	61.0	$95,059
Sig.	$p = 0.84$	$p = 0.52$	$p = 0.58$

(continued)

(continued)

There is no quantitative evidence that program quality differs between emerging-market and high-income-country accelerators. Homing in on one qualitative factor that might relate to program quality, some experts believe that emerging-market accelerators have less-established networks of advisors, mentors, and investors. Although 'they helped to develop my business' is the most common benefit that entrepreneurs identify as coming from these connections, 'they helped to expand my networks' is more commonly expressed by high-income-country entrepreneurs. This is evident in the following remark from one high-income-country entrepreneur: 'We gained an inside view to (the) healthcare industry, introductions to government officials.' Moreover, various conversations and interviews give the impression that emerging-market entrepreneurs are less likely to feel that connections made during a program help them grow their own networks. Program managers in emerging markets also tend to report having a harder time recruiting mentors and advisors. This suggests that the social capital benefits that should accrue during programs might be harder to develop and then sustain after the program. While these are speculations at this point, they warrant further scrutiny, especially because of the ties between driving equity into program participants and various factors that relate to social capital (see Chaps. 6 through 8).

Concluding Remarks

Because it is more important and more challenging to accelerate impact-oriented ventures in emerging markets, we must cultivate answers to two overarching questions: How are emerging-market entrepreneurs and ventures different? and Do they also benefit from acceleration? Before answering these questions, we must recognize that entrepreneurs in emerging markets can be further divided into two groups: those that seek acceleration services in their home countries and those that look elsewhere for these support programs. It turns out that this distinction influences the answers to both of the questions posed in this chapter.

Two salient anomalies emerge when we isolate the emerging-market ventures that apply to accelerators in their home countries. Relative to applicants from high-income countries, their commercial performance is mixed; that is, they have lower revenues but more full-time employees. However, their investment performance is severely impaired across all types of outside funding. For instance, their average prior-year revenues are more than 60 percent of those earned by high-income-country ventures, but the amount of equity or debt they have received since founding is less than one-quarter. These disproportionate differences suggest that emerging-market entrepreneurs have serious problems attracting investment that is commensurate with their early-stage performance. The second oddity relates to prior entrepreneurial experience. While it is widely assumed that emerging-market entrepreneurs are deficient in this respect, the EDP data suggest the opposite. This begs the question of why their prior founding experiences are being discounted—by investors and by the entrepreneurs themselves (who place the highest priority on developing business skills).

These are problems that high-quality accelerators, with their emphasis on closing knowledge, network, and capital gaps, can address. In this respect, it is comforting that emerging-market entrepreneurs tend to experience the same benefits that accelerators provide in high-income countries. The two biggest questions that remain for future research are: (1) Why is it that emerging-market acceleration is better at stimulating revenue growth than investment growth? and (2) Why are accelerators that engage emerging-market entrepreneurs from other countries not able to produce the same magnitude of effects? We return to both of these questions in the concluding chapter of this book.

Appendix: A Closer Look at Three Emerging Markets

To give an indication of the country-level differences that will become clearer as the EDP sub-samples grow within specific countries, Table 9.10 provides a first look at three emerging-market countries—India, Kenya, and Mexico. In some ways, the ventures and entrepreneurs in three countries are similar. A small percentage (from 3 percent in Mexico to 5 percent in India) of the ventures are headquartered in another country. There are also small differences in the percentages of nonprofit ventures. The average ages of the ventures and founders are also similar across countries. Moreover, the three groups have used this time to drive revenues to roughly the same level. The differences between roughly \$29,000 in Kenya, \$31,000 in India, and \$45,000 in Mexico are not significant ($p = 0.30$). Looking further down the table, a similar percentage of these founders (roughly two-thirds) invest a similar amount of their own funds into their ventures (between \$33,000 and \$44,000 on average).

There are also differences that warrant further scrutiny in future country-level analyses. The dominant sectors (by a fairly wide margin) are education in India, agriculture in Kenya, and health in Mexico. These differences might have more to do with the different focus areas of the EDP programs than actual differences in the underlying populations of ventures seeking acceleration. However, the magnitude of these differences makes them worthy of attention.

Table 9.10 Differences across India, Kenya, and Mexico

	India (N = 539)	Kenya (N = 597)	Mexico (N = 642)	Sig.
Different operations and headquarter countries	4.8%	4.2%	3.1%	p = 0.31
Legal form	For-profit, 85.9%	For-profit, 84.9%	For-profit, 84.4%	p = 0.10
	Nonprofit, 4.3%	Nonprofit, 6.1%	Nonprofit, 7.0%	
	Other, 5.8%	Other, 6.7%	Other, 4.4%	
	Undecided, 4.1%	Undecided, 2.4%	Undecided, 4.2%	
Sectors (top 5)	Education, 35.6%	Education, 8.1%	Education, 7.8%	p = 0.00
	Agriculture, 8.9%	Agriculture, 25.0%	Agriculture, 6.7%	
	Health, 12.7%	Health, 6.9%	Health, 21.3%	
	Financial services, 12.3%	Financial services, 7.8%	Financial services, 16.7%	
	ICT, 3.5%	ICT, 10.8%	ICT, 8.0%	
Any intellectual property	36.7%	38.4%	56.4%	p = 0.00
Venture age (application)	Average = 2.2 years	Average = 2.3 years	Average = 1.9 years	p = 0.15
Application revenues	Average = $31,206	Average = $28,779	Average = $44,609	p = 0.30
Application FT employees	Average = 5.0	Average = 3.1	Average = 3.4	p = 0.07
Multiple founders on team	80.0%	77.4%	82.8%	p = 0.06
Average founder age	Average = 33.9 years	Average = 33.8 years	Average = 33.9 years	p = 0.96
Any prior founding experience	39.0%	56.1%	68.4%	p = 0.00
Any prior accelerator participation	22.3%	32.7%	33.0%	p = 0.00
Own money invested since founding	68.8%	69.2%	Yes = 68.7%	p = 0.98
Founding team gender	All men, 66.7%	All men, 44.4%	All men, 49.0%	p = 0.50
	All women, 5.1%	All women, 15.5%	All women, 12.9%	p = 0.00
	Mixed-gender, 28.2%	Mixed-gender, 40.1%	Mixed-gender, 38.2%	
Outside equity since founding	Average = $13,251	Average = $3234	Average = $11,982	p = 0.02
Total debt since founding	Average = $3484	Average = $3469	Average = $7041	p = 0.19
Total philanthropy since founding	Average = $10,209	Average = $5236	Average = $9153	p = 0.68

There are other differences as well. Ventures in Mexico are significantly more likely to own some form of intellectual property (roughly 56 percent), while ventures in India are somewhat larger in size (5 employees). Indian entrepreneurs tend to be less-experienced, with only 39 percent reporting any prior founding experience, compared with roughly 56 percent of Kenyan entrepreneurs and 68 percent of Mexican entrepreneurs. India also has the lowest percentage of all-women and mixed-gender teams of the three countries.

Turning to variables that indicate the state of the ecosystems in the three countries, the likelihood that someone on the founding team received support from another accelerator prior to application is lowest in India (roughly 22 percent). However, investment conditions seem to be most problematic in Kenya, where ventures report the lowest levels of equity, debt, and philanthropic investment. The former equity deficit is significant. Further indication of the challenges experienced in Kenya is found in the percentage of applicants who seek acceleration in their home countries. Roughly 72 percent of the EDP applicants from Kenya applied to programs run in Kenya, compared with more than 92 percent in India. Mexican entrepreneurs are in between, with roughly 85 percent applying to Mexican accelerators. If the likelihood of applying to local programs is an indicator of confidence in the combination of local ecosystems and accelerators, then these significant differences suggest greater problems in Kenya than in India.

It is surprising that entrepreneurs in all three countries place similarly low emphasis on gaining access to potential investors (see Fig. 9.4). Only about 12–13 percent of entrepreneurs rank this benefit as number one. This may reflect an unfamiliarity with the network-based processes that tend to drive external financing outcomes or a lack of availability of investors across these

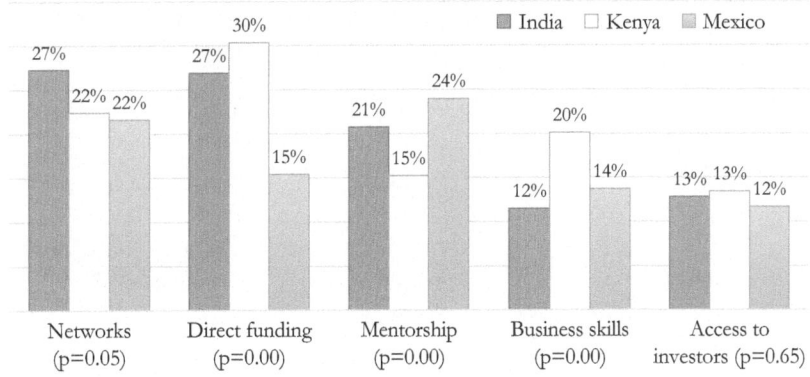

Fig. 9.4 Accelerator benefits ranked #1 for India, Kenya, and Mexico

three ecosystems. Given their problems attracting outside investment, it is not surprising that entrepreneurs from Kenya place the highest priority on obtaining direct funding from accelerators (see Fig. 9.4). Roughly 30 percent of them rank the direct funding benefit highest, compared with just 15 percent of the entrepreneurs in the Mexico sub-sample. They also place a greater emphasis on developing business skills relative to the other two groups of entrepreneurs. On the other hand, they are significantly less likely to place a high value on mentorship, with only 15 percent of them ranking this potential benefit first, compared with 21 percent and 24 percent in the India and Mexico sub-samples, respectively.

The final set of observations relates to the effects that accelerators have on ventures that operate in the three countries. With appropriate caveats for the fact that different percentages of entrepreneurs participate in same-country versus other country programs, and the fact that entrepreneurs tend to prioritize different accelerator benefits, the two panels of Fig. 9.5 provide plenty to think about as we design future country-level studies of the differential effects of acceleration. First, when it comes to revenue growth, there are

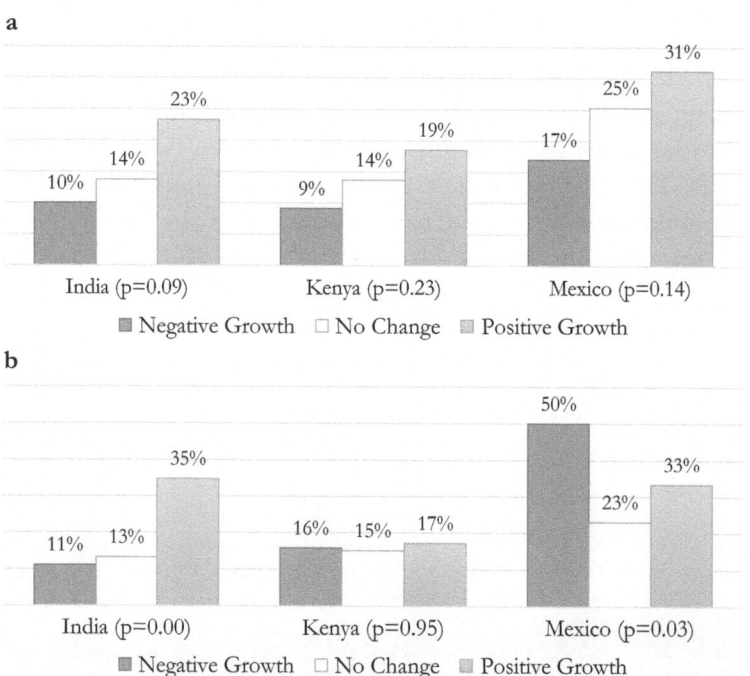

Fig. 9.5 Accelerator participation and negative-, no-, and positive (**a**) revenue-growth ventures and (**b**) equity-growth ventures for India, Kenya, and Mexico

similar positive cascades for the percentage of accelerated ventures across the negative-growth, no-growth, and positive-growth groups. In all three countries, there is a higher percentage of accelerator participants among the latter positive-growth group and a lower percentage among the former negative-growth group. Despite the many differences among entrepreneurs, ventures, and ecosystems, the overall emerging-market pattern reported in Fig. 9.3 is fairly consistent across these three emerging-market countries.

The results are not as consistent, and clearly not as positive, when it comes to equity growth. In India, the percentage of participants in the positive-growth category is significantly higher. However, there are no identifiable participation effects in Kenya. In Mexico, the percentage of accelerator participants in the positive-growth category (33 percent) is much higher than in the no-growth category (23 percent). However, the percentage of accelerator participants is highest in the negative-growth category (50 percent), indicating that accelerators are doing a better job pushing equity away from less promising entrepreneurs.

These initial country-level observations offer a glimpse into the types of analyses that should continue into the future.

Notes

1. See http://www.sehatkahani.com/
2. See http://www.safemotos.com/
3. SafeMotos Long Journey to Improve Road Safety in Rwanda. *AppsAfrica* (April 2015).
4. According to the Aspen Network of Development Entrepreneurs (ANDE), small and growing businesses are 'commercially-viable businesses with five to 250 employees that have significant potential, and ambition, for growth. Typically, they growth capital from $20,000 to $2 million.' See https://www.andeglobal.org/page/AboutANDESGBs
5. See https://genglobal.org/gec/about-gec
6. See http://www.infodev.org/about
7. For an overview of the PACE program, see *Accelerating Entrepreneurs: Insights from USAID's Support of Intermediaries.* United States Agency for International Development.
8. See https://www.galidata.org/accelerators/
9. *A Look Inside Accelerators: Building Businesses.* Nesta (February 2015).
10. *Accelerating Startups in Emerging Markets: Insights from 43 Programs.* The Aspen Institute.

11. This chapter relies heavily on materials that were originally written, with Abigayle Davidson and Genevieve Edens and a team of researchers from Deloitte, for a GALI report entitled *Accelerating Startups in Emerging Markets: Insights from 43 Programs* (May 2017).
12. See https://blogs.worldbank.org/opendata/new-country-classifications
13. When interpreting the various tables in this chapter, the reader must consider the overlap between the World Bank's income and region classifications. Virtually all of the high-income country ventures in the EDP sample operate in the United States or Canada, while the emerging-market ventures tend to operate in Sub-Saharan Africa, Latin America and Caribbean, and South Asia.
14. *Small and Growing Businesses: Investing in the Missing Middle for Poverty Alleviation.* The Aspen Institute (2012).
15. See Appendix A3 in *Accelerating Startups in Emerging Markets: Insights from 43 Programs* (May 2017).
16. Li-Wei Chen, Georgia Kossoff, Justin Koushyar, Wesley Longhofer & Peter W. Roberts. 2017. Developing a Better Understanding of Social Businesses in Lower-Income Countries. Working Paper.
17. Analysis of Variance (ANOVA) is a statistical technique used to analyze differences among group means in a sample. It is useful for comparing three or more group means while checking for statistically significant differences.
18. According to the *2016 Credit Suisse Research Institute's Global Wealth Databook*, average wealth in high-income countries is $150,000 compared to $10,000 in emerging markets.

10

Where's the Equity for Women Entrepreneurs?

Chapter 9 explored how accelerators are taking on the challenges associated with closing the knowledge, network, and capital gaps faced by entrepreneurs working in emerging markets. This chapter shifts attention away from where impact-oriented entrepreneurs work to focus on a group of entrepreneurs that is collectively under-appreciated and underserved, whether or not they work in less-developed ecosystems. In too many ways, the world has a hard time appreciating, supporting, and rewarding the contributions made by women.[1] This is the case when it comes to entrepreneurship, which is often construed as a male-gendered domain.[2] Women entrepreneurs are regularly subjected to gender-biased evaluations that cause many to shy away from pursuing promising entrepreneurial ideas. This occurs despite the fact that studies provide little systematic evidence that companies launched by women are less valuable or viable than those founded by men.[3]

While these entrepreneurial biases are problematic in the context of normal entrepreneurial processes, they border on unconscionable when it comes to impact-oriented entrepreneurship. In this domain, founder motivations clearly extend beyond that of providing attractive financial returns to investors. Instead, companies are started and supported because of the meaningful benefits they might provide to the planet and its people. And, many people will tell you that 'women social founders want to solve what they define as a social crisis: anything from poverty and malnutrition to human trafficking or recovery from war and genocide.'[4] In support of this bold assertion, research indicates that women business leaders already emphasize goals other than profitability. Two studies show that US companies with higher female board representation are more engaged in environmental and corporate social

© The Author(s) 2019
P. W. Roberts, S. A. Lall, *Observing Acceleration*,
https://doi.org/10.1007/978-3-030-00042-4_10

responsibility activities.[5] Another study finds that woman-led companies are less likely to lay off workers during recessions.[6] At a more fundamental level, a review of several economic experiments concludes that women tend to express more other-oriented social preferences than men, something that explains their inferior performance in individualistic games, while supporting the argument that they make great social entrepreneurs.[7]

To get a more tangible sense of the contributions that come from impact-oriented entrepreneurs who are also women, consider Rimidi, a healthcare sector startup that was launched in 2012 by a mixed-gender founding team led by Lucienne Ide. Rimidi's software helps clinicians personalize care for individuals who suffer from diabetes by leveraging patient-generated data, clinical information, and the latest practice guidelines.[8] The promise inherent in the founder and her idea were recognized by Village Capital selectors, who admitted Rimidi into their 2014 Health IT: US program. The potential was also recognized by the other entrepreneurs in that cohort, who chose Rimidi to receive one of the two peer-selected investments made at the end of that program. In the years since 2014, Lucie and her team continued to develop their business and were recently rewarded with a $6.75 million equity investment by a group 'which includes a strategic investment by Eli Lilly and Co., an investment from Turner Investments, and participation from existing investors Cox Enterprises, Village Capital, The Jump Fund, and JAMB Global.'[9] Sadly, the example of Lucie and Rimidi is an exception rather than the rule. In the last decade, a range of studies and reports document the challenges that women experience when it comes to attracting investment for their ventures.

Securing the investment required to scale an impact-oriented venture is almost always hard and, irrespective of gender, failure is more common than success. Simply stated, 'external finance is often not available in the form that a firm would like.'[10] However, just because it is generally difficult to raise capital does not mean that it should be more difficult for ventures that have women founders. Recent analyses of data from the Kauffman Firm Survey show that 'women started their firms with significantly less capital than men' and that 'women also went on to raise significantly smaller amounts of follow-on capital, both debt and equity.'[11] These observations, which are common in the academic and practitioner literatures,[12] support the claim that 'women entrepreneurs entering self-employment are disadvantaged by their gender.'[13]

This general bias that women entrepreneurs face when it comes to attracting investment is amplified for one particular, and especially important, source of early-stage finance—outside equity investment.[14] Consider the following statements:

- 'About 38 percent of new businesses in this country are started by women but only between 2 percent and 6 percent of those founders receive VC funding.'[15]
- 'During 2011–2013 more than 15 percent of the companies receiving venture capital investment had a woman on the executive team. Compared with our finding in 1999, when businesses with women on the executive team received fewer than 5 percent of all venture capital investments, this figure represents important progress.'[16]
- 'In the period from 2009 to 2014, CrunchBase records 14,341 U.S.-based startups that received funding. Of those, 15.5 percent, or 2,226, have at least one woman founder ... In 2009, 9.5 percent startups had at least one woman founder, but by 2014 that rate had almost doubled to 18 percent.'[17]

There is almost universal consensus around the observation that founding teams that include women have a harder time attracting outside equity investment. This is somewhat ironic given that equity is defined in two ways: 'justice according to natural law or right; specifically, freedom from bias or favoritism,' and 'the money value of a property or of an interest in a property in excess of claims or liens against it.'[18] This chapter merges these two definitions by revisiting the arguments and observations in the specific context of impact-oriented entrepreneurship and acceleration.

The Gender Composition of Founding Teams

Relative to men, women tend to struggle as entrepreneurs because their historical and current social roles create outsized knowledge, network, and capital gaps. This is why American entrepreneurs between the ages of 18–24 and 55–64 are much less likely to be women than men.[19] These biases are also evident outside of the United States, where women are also 'much less likely to be involved in entrepreneurship than men worldwide.'[20]

The EDP application surveys ask applicants to identify the top three members of their founding teams. We begin the analyses in this chapter by looking at the gender of each of the three founders listed in the application surveys. Do we see an adequate number of women-led businesses in these application pools? It turns out that this is not as straightforward a question as it may seem. While much of the research on gender in entrepreneurship focuses on individual founders, launching a venture is often a team effort. So clearly, all-men founding teams represent the counterfactual when considering the implications of being a woman entrepreneur. However, as we move away from the all-men

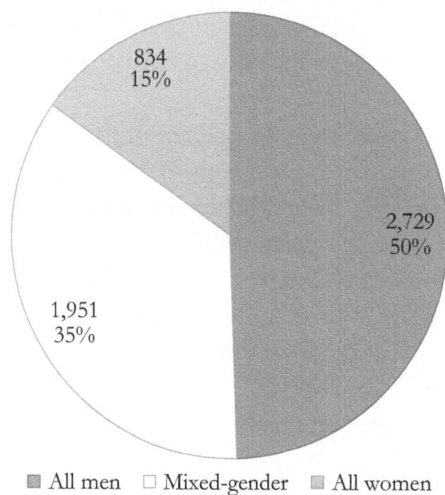

Fig. 10.1 Founding teams by gender category

founding teams, we face choices about how to identify women-led ventures. While much of the literature talks about the investment experiences of ventures with women founders, this category has (at least) two sub-groups: mixed-gender teams and all-women teams (see Fig. 10.1). Ventures with all-men founders represent just under half of the EDP sample. This leaves a slight majority with at least one woman reported among the top-three founders. Most of these ventures, roughly 35 percent of the sample, were founded by mixed-gender teams. Here, it is important to note that only 38 percent of the mixed-gender teams report a woman as the first founder, suggesting (but not confirming) that women may play a somewhat subordinate role on these mixed-gender teams. This leaves just 15 percent of the EDP ventures with all-women founding teams.

In the remainder of this chapter, we compare three categories of ventures: those with all-men founding teams, mixed-gender teams, and all-women teams.

Before taking a closer look at the many possible differences among ventures that were founded by teams with different gender compositions, it is instructive to look at how the stated impact objectives vary across the three groups. Table 10.1 homes in on the most commonly identified IRIS impact objectives covered in the EDP application data.

For two of these impact objectives, there are no significant differences in the reported emphases across the three gender categories. There are nearly the same percentages of ventures dedicated to income and productivity growth (roughly 27 percent) and to health improvement (roughly 19 percent) across

These percentages differ from the 'stylized fact' that women founders represent roughly 30–40 percent of all small companies:

- 'since the 1997 Index, the share of new entrepreneurs who were females has fallen from 43.7 percent to 36.8 percent.'[21]
- 'women-owned firms (51 percent or more) account for 39 percent of all privately held firms and contribute 8 percent of employment and 4.2 percent of revenues.'[22]
- '36 percent of all businesses are women-owned, and they account for 12 percent of all sales and 15 percent of employment.'[23]

This difference might be due to the fact that the current sample tilts away from conventional entrepreneurs and in the direction of impact-oriented ventures. It might also reflect the fact that previous studies tend to home in on the 'primary founder' when talking about women-led businesses. In the current sample, 1558 of the ventures list a women entrepreneur first among the three named founders. This percentage (29 percent) is much closer to those reported in the previous studies. Finally, it might reflect the fact that EDP data pick up entrepreneurs at a much earlier stage of development (typically less than three years since founding). This means that we might be seeing them before the biased early-stage selection processes have a chance to winnow women out of the sample.

the three groups of founding teams. The all-men founding teams are significantly more likely to focus on providing access to financial services and information, but less likely to focus on employment generation, community development, and capacity building. The all-women founding teams are significantly more likely to focus on providing access to education, equality and empowerment, and food security, but less likely to focus on agricultural productivity. Finally, it is interesting to see how the mixed-gender teams never stand out on their own, but typically lean in the direction of one of the two

Table 10.1 Reported IRIS impact objectives by founding team gender

	All men	Mixed-gender	All women	Sig.
Employment generation	29.1%	38.2%	38.6%	$p = 0.00$
Income/productivity growth	27.5%	27.5%	27.2%	$p = 0.99$
Community development	22.3%	26.7%	25.8%	$p = 0.00$
Access to education	20.9%	21.8%	26.7%	$p = 0.00$
Health improvement	18.7%	20.1%	19.5%	$p = 0.48$
Equality and empowerment	15.7%	17.4%	26.3%	$p = 0.00$
Agricultural productivity	17.1%	17.6%	10.7%	$p = 0.00$
Access to financial services	18.4%	12.1%	8.0%	$p = 0.00$
Capacity building	12.2%	16.0%	17.8%	$p = 0.00$
Access to information	13.9%	11.0%	11.2%	$p = 0.01$
Food security	11.4%	12.8%	8.0%	$p = 0.00$

gender groups. The mixed-gender teams present a similar emphasis on employment generation as the all-women teams, but a similar emphasis on access to education as the all-men teams.

The main takeaway from Table 10.1 is the imperfect mapping of founder gender to impact objectives. There are some impact objectives that tend to attract more women than men, such as providing access to education and supporting equality and empowerment. If women are having a harder time raising capital to establish and grow their ventures, then these impact areas are also being starved of the financial resources needed to translate promising ideas into growing companies.

Are Women Attracting Less Outside Equity Investment?

Early-stage ventures with women founders have a well-documented disadvantage when it comes to raising equity investment. This observation is replicated in the current sample of impact-oriented ventures (see Fig. 10.2). To get a sense of the cumulative investment deficits faced by founding teams that include women, we examine the total amounts of outside equity, debt, and philanthropic support that each EDP applicant reports since founding. Overall, the sampled ventures report an average of roughly $43,000 of outside equity investment. All-men teams average more than $53,000, while the mixed-gender team average is quite a bit lower (roughly $40,000). However, all-women teams report dramatically lower investment (just $16,000). Teams with all-women founders receive, on average, less than one-third as much outside equity as the ventures that have only men as founders. The differences that make up this equity investment cascade are statistically significant.

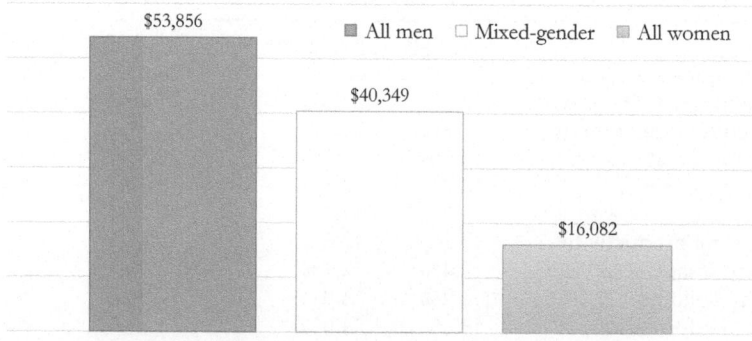

Fig. 10.2 Outside equity since founding by founding team gender

Some might worry that the differences presented in Fig. 10.2 represent two different dimensions. The first is a side-by-side comparison of founding teams that comprise women versus men when it comes to raising capital at or around the time when accelerator applications are lodged. The second is a historical fundraising differential that may or may not make these applications necessary. In other words, the entrepreneurs who have raised more money since founding might be more comfortable with their current pace of development and less likely to apply to accelerators. To ensure that the reported differences capture, at least in part, the former bias, we look at gender differences in the amount of outside equity investment reported in the previous calendar year. Once again, the ventures with only men as founders report the highest average ($20,879). This is roughly double the corresponding averages for mixed-gender teams ($10,973) and teams with only women as founders ($9486).

To provide additional context for the equity investment differentials, we look at other prominent sources of capital for early-stage ventures: debt, philanthropic support, and money invested by the founding team members. Debt and philanthropy represent important sources of capital for impact-oriented ventures. The average amounts of debt since founding ($31,316) and philanthropic support since founding ($50,483) are similar to the average for outside equity ($43,364). However, ventures with all-women founders are at the bottom of these two distributions, especially when it comes to debt financing. One other observation that stands out in Table 10.2 is the relatively strong performance of the mixed-gender teams in attracting higher levels of debt and philanthropy than the teams comprised only of men.

Table 10.2 Other investment sources by founding team gender

	All men	Mixed-gender	All women	Sig.
Total debt since founding	$23,964	$51,032	$9248	$p = 0.11$
	(13.7%)	(14.6%)	(10.0%)	$p = 0.00$
Philanthropy since founding	$27,734	$93,553	$24,165	$p = 0.05$
	(24.4%)	(29.1%)	(26.9%)	$p = 0.00$
Own investment since founding	$65,327	$88,351	$25,683	$p = 0.35$
	(67.5%)	(71.8%)	(61.2%)	$p = 0.00$

When it comes to the investments made by the founders themselves, the average differences between the three groups are large but not statistically significant ($p = 0.35$). While the mixed-gender teams are the most prolific investors in their own ventures—both in terms of the percentage making investments and the overall average—the average amount of own money invested by the all-women teams is less than half of that invested by the all-men teams, a ratio that is consistent with that reported for outside equity investments.

These equity observations become more nuanced when access to equity investment is disentangled from typical investment amounts. Consider the responses to the simpler 'Yes or No' question: 'Have you received any outside equity investment since founding?' The percentage of positive responses among teams of men (roughly 20 percent) exceeds the overall sample average and that reported by the mixed-gender teams (roughly 17 percent). However, ventures founded by all-women teams are less than half as likely to report receiving any outside equity investments (8 percent). Looking at the average amounts of equity raised by teams that have had some outside investment reveals an interesting pattern. Mixed-gender teams are only slightly less likely to report having any outside equity investment than their all-men counterparts. For those that do receive equity investment, the average amounts are similar (roughly $245,000 compared with roughly $272,000). All-women teams are much less likely to report outside equity investments, but those receiving some investment attract only slightly smaller amounts on average (roughly $206,000).

This suggests that the core problem for teams with women founders relates to gaining access to interested investors. Once outside investors have decided to make investments, the dollar values that flow to the different groups of ventures are quite similar (Fig. 10.3).

Another more nuanced pattern emerges by examining different equity investment sources. The EDP application surveys ask each entrepreneur, 'from which sources has your venture received this outside equity?' Two of the response options are venture capitalists and angel investors. Another two are friends or family and other individuals. We combine the latter two responses into a single variable that indicates whether the founding team received outside equity investment from their personal networks, and the former two options into a single variable that indicates investment support from more impersonal sources. The first panel of Fig. 10.4 shows that all-women founding teams are disadvantaged

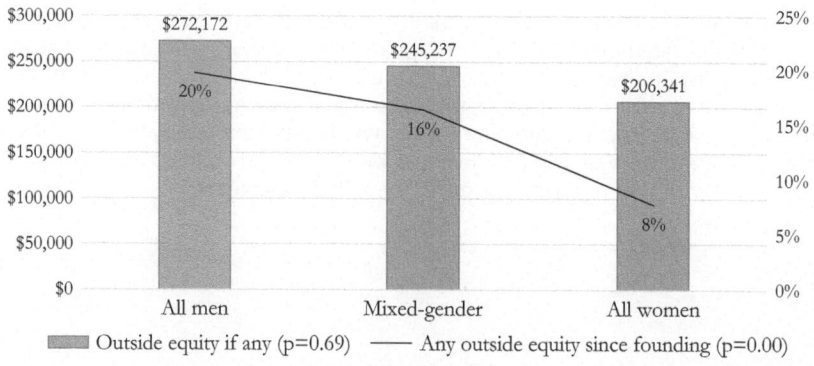

Fig. 10.3 Outside equity since founding by founding team gender—differences broken down

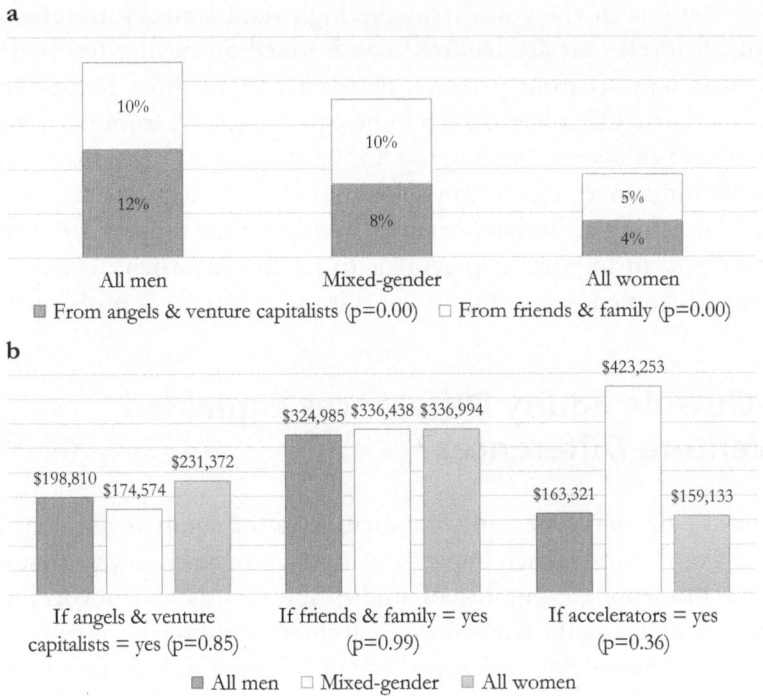

Fig. 10.4 (a) Sources of outside equity by founding team gender; (b) Levels of outside equity conditioned on access to source

among both groups of investors. The biases among angel investors and venture capitalists are consistent with the general belief that women have a harder time pitching to traditional equity investors—remember the concerns about pitch events expressed in Chap. 8. While success rates are low across the board, there is a success cascade that mirrors the cascade depicted in Fig. 10.2. Ventures founded by men have a 12 percent success rate with angels and VCs, followed by the mixed-gender teams at 8 percent, followed by the all-women teams at 4 percent. This differential success rate becomes critical once we see in the second panel of Fig. 10.4 that the average equity investment differences disappear once we focus on founding teams that received any investment. Once again, the problem for the women entrepreneurs seems to be one of opening doors.

It is interesting to see a similar pattern of problems among the friends and family networks. Although the gender cascade is not as steep, it is still significant. Roughly 10 percent of the ventures founded by men report receiving some outside investment from personal sources. This is the same as the percentage reported by the mixed-gender teams. However, only half as many ventures founded by all-women teams (roughly 5 percent) report receiving investments from these personal sources. This access deficit becomes serious in the context of the high (and similar) average equity investment levels that are reported conditioned on having received some investment support from personal networks. In all three gender groups, the entrepreneurs that begin with some equity support from personal networks report an average of roughly $330,000 of total outside equity; the miniscule differences across groups are not close to significant ($p = 0.99$). Clearly, launching an impact-oriented venture with support from friends and family is an important precursor to future investment support. The fact that all-women teams do not get this early support is problematic.

Are Outside Equity Differences Explained by Venture Differences?

This may be the first systematic examination of the equity investment biases faced by women who launch impact-oriented ventures. However, these observations stand among a number of studies and reports that uncover similar equity deficits among the women who start more traditional companies. After finding that women entrepreneurs differ in the ways they finance their new ventures, one of these studies suggests that investment differences might be attributed to the types of businesses started by, and the pre-founding experiences of, these entrepreneurs.[24] A more detailed summary of the various explanations that are proffered for these equity investment differences is published under the heading of 'eight myths' about women and equity capital[25]:

1. women-owned ventures are in industries unattractive to venture capitalists
2. women do not want to own high growth businesses
3. women do not have the right educational backgrounds to build large ventures
4. women do not have the right types of experience to build large ventures
5. women are not in the network and lack the social contacts to build a credible venture
6. women do not have the financial savvy or resources to start high-growth businesses
7. women do not submit business plans to equity providers
8. women are not a force in the venture capital industry

The first two myths align with the previous study and focus on the types of companies that women entrepreneurs are starting. To see whether the gender-based equity disadvantages in Fig. 10.2 are due to differential propensities to develop equity-friendly ventures, we take a closer look at the application pipelines. As we discuss the various patterns summarized in Table 10.3, we also check to see whether each variable is implicated directly in equity investment outcomes. We do this by isolating ventures founded by men and then checking to see whether the variable in question helps to explain the distribution of investment outcomes in this sub-sample of ventures that do not have women founders.

The first thing to consider is whether an impact-oriented venture commits to operate as a nonprofit entity. It is not surprising that the 410 all-men-founded ventures that applied to EDP accelerators as nonprofits report significantly ($p = 0.05$) lower equity investment levels than other legal structures: $5244 compared with $36,525 for the rest of the all-men-founded ventures. The open question is whether nonprofits are more common among the ventures with women founders. Looking at how the reported legal status varies across the three gender categories reveals that nonprofits are significantly over-represented among the mixed-gender and all-women founding teams. Roughly 7 percent of the ventures with all-men founders report the nonprofit status on their applications, compared with almost 14 percent of the mixed-gender teams and 17 percent of the all-women teams. Legal status must be accounted for when explaining the lower outside equity investment averages among women who start impact-oriented ventures.

The inferences are less clear when it comes to sector participation. Again, the data suggest that ventures operating in certain sectors are more appealing to equity investors. According to a simple ANOVA that examines equity investment outcomes among the all-men-founded ventures, there are significant differences between different sectors. However, it is not clear that these differences map onto the sector differences reported in Table 10.3. Among the five largest sectors in the current sample, the ICT sector reports the lowest average equity investment levels ($9408). However, when it comes to gender participation, this sector clearly tilts toward men. The second-lowest average equity investment level is found in the agriculture sector ($15,355), which is also less common for ventures founded by all-women teams. At the other end of the equity distribution is the health sector, where the average equity reported by all-men founding teams is $42,236. Here, the percentage of ventures is fairly consistent across the three groups. The two remaining sectors—financial services ($29,926) and education ($42,179)—are split when it comes to gender participation, with the former sector leaning toward men founders and the latter toward women founders. Thus, although equity investors demonstrate sector preferences when making their investments, these preferences do not track the gender imbalances that are evident in the EDP application data.

A third variable that is often linked with equity investment is intellectual property. Innovative ventures built around new proprietary technologies and practices are thought to offer more attractive prospects for future competitive advantage and growth. Therefore, possession of patents, copyrights, or trademarks is valued

Table 10.3 Ventures by founding team gender

	All men (N = 2729)	Mixed-gender (N = 1951)	All women (N = 834)	Sig.
Legal form	For-profit, 84.3%	For-profit, 75.5%	For-profit, 70.7%	p = 0.00
	Nonprofit, 7.2%	Nonprofit, 13.5%	Nonprofit, 16.7%	
	Other, 5.2%	Other, 7.1%	Other, 8.6%	
	Undecided, 3.1%	Undecided, 3.6%	Undecided, 3.8%	
Sectors (top 5)	Education, 15.6%	Education, 17.3%	Education, 22.8%	p = 0.00
	Agriculture, 15.7%	Agriculture, 16.9%	Agriculture, 10.4%	
	Health, 12.1%	Health, 12.3%	Health, 12.2%	
	Financial services, 13.5%	Financial services, 6.9%	Financial services, 4.8%	
	ICT, 8.4%	ICT, 6.1%	ICT, 3.8%	
Any intellectual property	44.3%	44.8%	33.5%	p = 0.00
Venture age	Average = 2.1 years	Average = 2.8 years	Average = 2.6 years	p = 0.00
Application revenues	Average = $42,604	Average = $62,788	Average = $32,717	p = 0.00
Application FT employees	Average = 3.2	Average = 3.7	Average = 2.0	p = 0.00

by equity investors. This underlying thesis is supported by the application data. The 1209 all-men founding teams that report having some intellectual property average $88,831 in outside equity investment since founding, compared with just $26,037 for the remaining 1520 all-men founded ventures. This difference is significant. The intellectual property designation also tracks the gender composition of the founding teams, where a significantly lower percentage of the all-women teams (roughly 33 percent) report having proprietary intellectual property, compared with almost 45 percent for the all-men and mixed-gender teams. It seems important to account for this difference when trying to understand and explain the equity investment differences in Fig. 10.2.

To continue this examination, we look at the average age of the ventures when they apply to accelerators. Among the ventures established by all-men founding teams, there is a modest positive correlation ($\rho = 0.10$) between a venture's age and the amount of equity it raises since founding. This might be due to the fact that older ventures have more time to raise funds, and more time to establish the observable characteristics that are attractive to equity investors. The much larger correlation between venture age and prior-year equity investment levels ($\rho = 0.60$) seems to favor the latter explanation. If older ventures attract more outside equity investment, it stands to reason that ventures with women founders might simply be approaching accelerators when they are younger and less developed; however, the data suggest the opposite. Ventures founded by all-women teams are older (2.6 years on average) than those founded by all-men teams (2.1 years on average), and the mixed-gender teams are even older (2.8 years on average). Thus, any differences in venture age would be consistent with a bias in favor of, and not against, women entrepreneurs.

Another set of signals that a venture is more investment ready is found in its recent commercial performance. This idea is also supported in the application data, where the amount of equity raised since founding (among the all-men founded ventures) is positively correlated with revenues ($\rho = 0.12$) and with the number of full-time employees reported in the prior year ($\rho = 0.07$). But, do ventures with women founders tend to report less earned revenues? The answer is yes and no. Compared with the overall sample average ($48,250), the all-men founding teams—those attracting the lion's share of the outside equity—do not report higher prior-year revenues. Instead, ventures founded by mixed-gender teams report the highest average prior-year revenues (roughly $63,000), while those founded by all-women teams lag behind (an average of roughly $33,000). A similar pattern appears when the focus shifts to full-time employees. The average for the all-men founding teams (3.2 full-time employees) roughly matches the overall sample average. The average for the mixed-gender teams (3.7 full-time employees) is higher, while the average for the all-women teams is quite a bit lower (2.0 full-time employees). This suggests that the recent commercial performance of ventures might help to explain the equity gap facing ventures with only women founders, but it cannot account for the gap faced by the mixed-gender teams.

Very few of these venture-level observations are consistent with the idea—or myth—that impact-oriented ventures established by women founders are at odds with the kinds of things that equity investors look for. However, this does not mean that the women entrepreneurs are actually seeking similar or larger amounts of private capital when developing their ventures. This is evident in Fig. 10.5, which reports the average amounts of equity plus debt and philanthropic support that the three groups of founders are seeking over the next 12 months. Notwithstanding the many similarities and differences reported in Table 10.3, the same gender-based cascade is observed for the short-term investment aspirations. The more than $310,000 average investment being sought by the men is almost three times greater than the roughly $115,000 sought by all-women teams. Once again, the average amount that is being sought by the mixed-gender founding teams is in between, but closer to, the all-women team average.

The last three columns of Fig. 10.5 provide an interesting contrast to the gender-based debt and equity cascade by showing that the average philanthropic support that is being sought is similar—and a lot smaller—for all three groups. These averages confirm what many observers already know; when thinking about investment in early-stage ventures, the dominant logic pushes entrepreneurs toward equity investment. What may not be as obvious is the extent to which this dominant investment logic is gender sensitive. While the all-men founding teams are looking for roughly ten times more equity than debt or philanthropy, the ratio for the mixed-gender teams is roughly five-to-one. For the all-women founding teams, the ratio is between two and three to one.

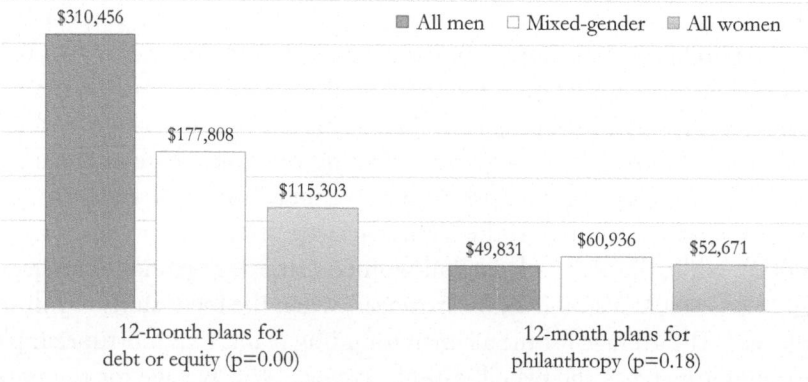

Fig. 10.5 Twelve-month investment aspirations by founding team gender

Looking at the venture-level data, it seems that the equity investment differentials are not clearly explained by tangible venture-level differences. However, women entrepreneurs do seek significantly less private investment than their male counterparts. This leads us to consider the third through sixth myths presented earlier, those related to educational backgrounds, prior entrepreneurial experiences, networks, and financial savvy. Perhaps the significant equity investment cascade is linked to differences among the entrepreneurs themselves. Women are thought to have fewer opportunities to develop the credentials and mindset that facilitate entrepreneurial success, especially the kind of success that attracts mainstream equity investors: 'Conventional wisdom suggested that women entrepreneurs were neither prepared nor motivated to found high-potential businesses. As a result, they [are] not good candidates for venture capital investors.'[26]

A Closer Look at the Entrepreneurs

On the EDP application survey, entrepreneurs are asked to list up to three founders and then provide specific information about each founder, including their gender and their prior educational, professional, and entrepreneurial experiences. To look for salient differences between the men and women who populate these founding teams, we created a founder-level file that describes 3783 women and 8859 men. The first row of Table 10.4 shows that men are more likely to be listed on the applications as the first founder; roughly 47 percent compared with less than 43 percent of the women entrepreneurs. This is due in part to the fact that there are more teams with only men listed as founders, and to the fact that roughly 60 percent of the mixed-gender founding teams list a man as the first founder.

We begin by looking at the average ages of the men and women listed as founders. After setting aside a few outliers, that is, founders older than 75, we see that the women and men are almost exactly the same age on average

Table 10.4 Women versus men founders

	Women founders (N = 3783)	Men founders (N = 8859)	Sig.
Named first	42.7%	46.9%	$p = 0.00$
Founder age	34.7 years	34.6 years	$p = 0.64$
Some graduate school	38.1%	39.5%	$p = 0.16$
Any prior CEO experience	22.7%	31.1%	$p = 0.00$
Prior founding experience (for-profit)	31.4%	47.2%	$p = 0.00$
Prior founding experience (nonprofit)	16.3%	17.8%	$p = 0.04$

(roughly 35 years old). Clearly founder age is not a factor when it comes to explaining large differences in outside equity investment. Nor are there meaningful differences when it comes to prior educational experiences. Three of the choices for responses to questions about the educational background of each founder are 'some graduate degree,' 'Master's degree,' and 'PhD.' Roughly 38 percent of the women and 40 percent of the men report having some graduate school experience. This insignificant difference ($p = 0.16$) suggests that outside equity investors are probably not being influenced by differences in education levels.

Differences begin to emerge when we look at prior career experiences. One of the founder background questions asks for 'information about the two more recent paid full-time jobs held by each of the above founders before launching this venture.' In addition to providing information about the employer type and country, respondents are asked to indicate the type of role that was occupied, including 'CEO or Executive Director' as one possible response. According to Table 10.4, a significantly higher percentage of the men in the founder sample (roughly 31 percent) report occupying these senior roles before founding their latest venture. This compares with just 23 percent for the women entrepreneurs. Women report a similar deficit of prior entrepreneurial experiences, especially for-profit founding experiences. Roughly 47 percent of the men in the founder file report that they started at least one other for-profit venture before their current project. On the other hand, only 31 percent of the women report these prior entrepreneurial experiences. A similar but much smaller difference is observed when it comes to prior non-profit founding experiences.

These observations suggest that men and women entrepreneurs are virtually identical when it comes to their ages and prior educational experiences. However, the men begin to separate themselves—in ways that probably matter to equity investors—when it comes to the caliber of their prior employment experiences, and the volume of their prior entrepreneurial experiences.

To consider a few more differences that pertain to founding teams, Table 10.5 transitions back to the venture-level data. The prevailing wisdom that equity investors prefer to work with teams of founders, rather than individuals, is supported in the EDP data. The all-men founding teams that report just one

Table 10.5 Founding teams by gender category

	All men	Mixed-gender	All women	Sig.
Multiple founders on team	71.4%	100.0%	45.1%	$p = 0.00$
Any prior accelerator participation	29.4%	30.0%	23.9%	$p = 0.00$

founder on their applications have an average of $27,614 of prior-year equity investment. This is less than half of the average reported by teams with two or more founders listed on their applications ($64,671). Looking across the three gender categories, we see that roughly 70 percent of the teams with men have multiple founders, compared with just 45 percent of the all-women teams.

A final way that entrepreneurs might become more investment ready is through prior experiences working with accelerators. However, the EDP data are equivocal when it comes to linking outside equity to prior acceleration. Among the 803 all-men-founded ventures that report prior accelerator experience, the average outside equity ($55,912) is only slightly higher than the 1926 ventures without prior acceleration experience ($52,999). Notwithstanding this insignificant difference, it is instructive to observe that the all-women founding teams are also significantly less likely to report prior acceleration (24 percent) than their all-men (29 percent) and mixed-gender (30 percent) counterparts.

A final thing to consider when comparing the three groups of founding teams is which accelerator benefits they prioritize when applying to programs. Figure 10.6 reveals two patterns that track the equity investment cascades that are giving us causes for concern. The emphasis placed on networking support and gaining access to investors are highest for men and lowest for the women entrepreneurs. In both cases, the mixed-gender founding teams are situated in between. On the other hand, the emphasis placed on finding mentors and developing business skills is highest for women and lowest for the all-men founding teams. Again, the mixed-gender teams sit in between. Each of these four sets of differences is significant ($p < 0.06$). These differences in internal versus external priorities become problematic when interpreted in the context

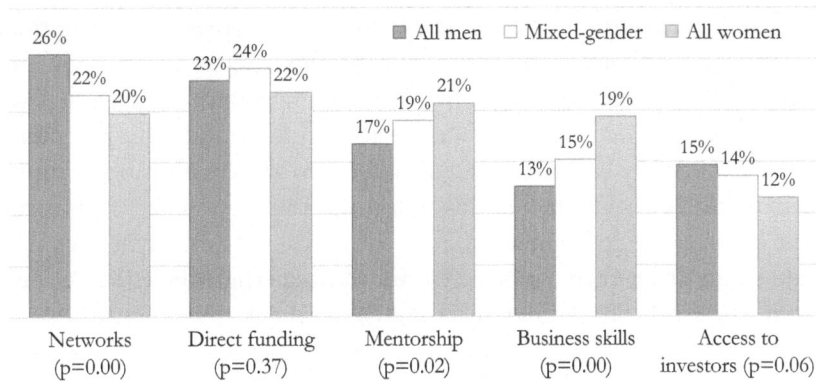

Fig. 10.6 Accelerator benefits ranked #1 by founding team gender

of one conclusion reached by the Diana Project in 2014: 'contrary to existing perceptions, many fundable women entrepreneurs had the requisite skills and experience to lead high-growth ventures. Nonetheless, women were consistently left out of the networks of growth capital finance and appeared to lack the contacts needed to break through.'[27] If this is true, then the women entrepreneurs in the EDP sample should be looking for support to expand their external connections, especially to potential investors. Instead, they are tending to adopt a more internal orientation, looking to find mentors and build skills rather than develop connections.

When viewed in tandem with the cascading levels of private investment that are sought across the three groups of founders, we are left with the impression that a main challenge when it comes to securing outside equity investment is that the women who start impact-oriented ventures are less inclined to adopt an aggressive external posture in order to please angel investors and venture capitalists, and more inclined to adopt an aggressive internal posture to develop robust foundations that support long-term venture development. If this is indeed the case, it raises real challenges for accelerator program managers, who must decide whether to meet women entrepreneurs where they are, or try to change their mindsets to more closely match the interests of current equity investors. Finally, because accelerators typically facilitate investments through mechanisms like pitch events and demo days (recall Chap. 8), program managers should also reflect on whether these individualistic promotional forums are suitable for the aspirations and orientations of women entrepreneurs.

Bringing It All Together

One of the goals for this book is to show how careful observation of entrepreneurs, ventures, and accelerators can help develop deeper and more nuanced understandings of the challenges that must be overcome to promote widespread impact-oriented entrepreneurship around the world. This potential for greater illumination is demonstrated in the two regression models summarized in Table 10.6. When thinking about the cause-and-effect relationships that lie behind the deficit that women entrepreneurs face when it comes to outside equity investment, it is important to disentangle the effects of bringing different kinds of ventures and different founder credentials to the table from the effects of women being discounted or downgraded in apples-to-apples comparisons. While falling short of providing definitive answers or actionable recommendations, moving from the first to the second model in Table 10.6 gives us much to think about. The first model is a simple regression

Table 10.6 Explaining equity since founding by gender category, with and without controls

	Coefficient	Sig.	Coefficient	Sig.
High-income country	$81,946	$p = 0.00$	$83,852	$p = 0.00$
Own investment since founding	–	–	$0	$p = 0.00$
Nonprofit	–	–	–$53,604	$p = 0.00$
Education sector	–	–	–$459	$p = 0.97$
Agriculture sector	–	–	–$1481	$p = 0.90$
Health sector	–	–	–$15,440	$p = 0.23$
Financial services sector	–	–	$11,983	$p = 0.39$
ICT sector	–	–	–$17,203	$p = 0.28$
Any intellectual property	–	–	$33,511	$p = 0.00$
Venture age (logged)	–	–	$35,651	$p = 0.00$
Application revenues	–	–	$0	$p = 0.00$
Application FT employees	–	–	$74	$p = 0.83$
Multiple founders	–	–	$26,597	$p = 0.01$
Some graduate school	–	–	$11,231	$p = 0.15$
Any prior CEO experience	–	–	$950	$p = 0.91$
Prior founding experience (for-profit)	–	–	$30,689	$p = 0.00$
Prior founding experience (nonprofit)	–	–	–$5209	$p = 0.58$
Mixed-gender teams	–$5380	$p = 0.53$	–$14,823	$p = 0.10$
All women teams	–$42,365	$p = 0.00$	–$19,288	$p = 0.11$
Constant	$23,468	$p = 0.00$	–$64,807	$p = 0.00$
N	5514		5445	
R-squared	0.02		0.06	

of equity investment since founding against the founding team gender variable. It replicates the gender-based cascade depicted in Fig. 10.2. Mixed-gender teams, but especially all-women teams, are disadvantaged when it comes to attracting outside equity. The only addition is a control variable that indicates whether the venture operates in a high-income country. Not surprisingly, average outside equity investment is greater for ventures that work in ecosystems containing a greater supply of equity investment.

The second model adds several variables that capture the confounding factors discussed in this chapter, focusing on those that are most plausibly linked to notable equity investment cascades. In almost every instance, the estimated effects are in the expected direction. Ventures receive significantly more outside equity investment when their founders invest more of their own money in the business, have proprietary intellectual property, are older and therefore more advanced, report more earned revenues, and have multiple founders with prior entrepreneurial experience. They receive less outside equity investment when they operate as nonprofits. While all of these effects are unsurprising, their inclusion in the model has an effect on how we think about the equity biases that women entrepreneurs face. Specifically, the estimated deficit for all-women teams relative to the baseline group of male entrepreneurs is still marginally significant (p = 0.11) but falls from roughly $42,000 to $19,000. On the other hand, the estimated deficit for mixed-gender teams becomes significant (p = 0.10) after increasing from roughly $5000 to almost $15,000.

This suggests that the problems that women face are different depending on whether they enter into entrepreneurship with or without male colleagues. In the latter case, much (but not all) of the problem, at least in the eyes of equity investors, relates to differences in ventures and founder credentials that are brought to the table. In the former case, true biases mask the fact that the multi-gender partnerships are actually bringing more attractive combinations of venture characteristics and founder credentials.

As we continue to mine the accumulating data for more nuanced observations of the underlying issues, it is also important to take a first look at whether accelerators are working for women founders of impact-oriented ventures—those working alone, with other women, and with men.

Do Accelerators Make Equity Investment More Equitable?

As the population of active accelerators expands, one of the questions that people are asking relates to whether they are offsetting the disadvantages that women entrepreneurs face when establishing and growing their businesses. In the eyes of many, accelerators are well-positioned to overcome the many barriers faced by women. After all, they are 'designed to address the networking, education and capital challenges all entrepreneurs face. These challenges are most acute for women and minority tech entrepreneurs, suggesting that incubators and accelerators could have the greatest impact on their ventures.'[28]

The EDP application and follow-up data allow us to consider how the effects of acceleration play out across teams with and without women founders. If accelerator programs are going to address the problems that women are facing, they must first admit mixed-gender and all-women founding teams at similar or higher rates. In this respect, it is comforting to know that the probability of participation is virtually identical across the three groups: 16 percent for founding teams comprised only of men and for mixed-gender teams, and 17 percent for the all-women teams. These very small differences are not significant (p = 0.72).

Then, the data should show that the positive equity investment bumps are greater for the two groups of founding teams that include women. In this respect, Table 10.7 delivers some good news and some bad news. The good news

Table 10.7 Average accelerator effects on investment by founding team gender

	Participated (N = 230)	Rejected (N = 731)	Difference	Sig.
All men	$15,552	$11,215	$4337	p = 0.60
	Participated (N = 160)	**Rejected (N = 798)**	**Difference**	**Sig.**
Mixed teams	$15,163	$2963	$12,200	p = 0.02
	Participated (N = 259)	**Rejected (N = 722)**	**Difference**	**Sig.**
All women	−$4417	$2019	−$6436	p = 0.70

is that participating ventures founded by mixed-gender teams are doing well on average. Comparing the ventures that participate in EDP programs with rejected applicants, the average one-year change for participants is more than $12,000 higher, and that difference between the two groups is significant ($p = 0.02$). This accelerator bump is almost three times larger than that experienced by ventures founded by men. However, this positive result does not extend to ventures with all-women founding teams. Here, the average one-year equity bump is actually negative. The average one-year growth in outside equity investment is more than $6000 lower for ventures that participate in accelerators.

Recall from Chaps. 4 and 7 that accelerators tend to have opposing effects at the top and the bottom ends of the equity investment growth distribution. Figure 10.7 shows how these opposing effects play out across the three gender groups. Starting in the middle, the mixed-gender founding teams reproduce this productive pattern of accelerator effects. Relative to the base case of no year-over-year change in outside equity investment, participating ventures are over-represented in the positive-growth sub-sample (33 percent relative to 20 percent) and in the negative growth sub-sampled (31 percent). The significant differences in the percentage of accelerator participants across the three sub-samples suggest that programs are identifying and rewarding ventures at the top end of the distribution while ushering the less promising ventures at the lower end in different directions. The same pattern is revealed among ventures founded by all-men teams. In this way, we conclude that accelerators work well for teams that have some or all men as founders. When it comes to all-women founding teams, however, the story is different. Although the negative-growth ventures are over-represented by accelerator program participants, there is no participant effect at the top end of the equity-growth distribution. There is the same percentage of program participants in the no-growth and positive-growth sub-samples. It seems that all-women founding teams are getting the discouraging feedback that leads to diminished equity growth. However, accelerators are finding and rewarding ventures that deserve more positive feedback and more positive equity-growth outcomes.

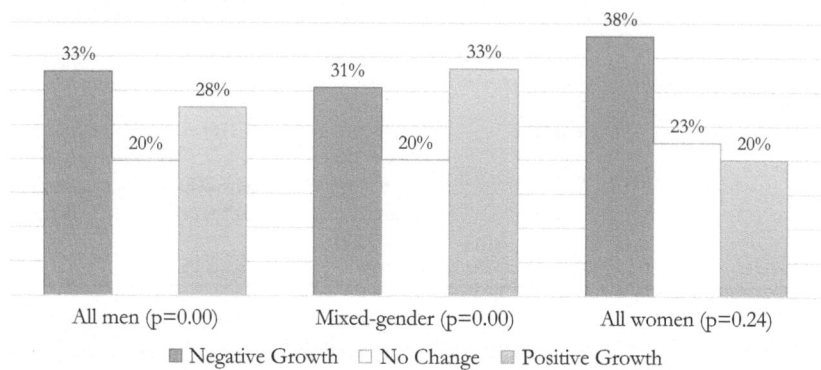

Fig. 10.7 Accelerator participation and negative-, no-, and positive equity-growth ventures by founding team gender

However, this is not to say that accelerators are not aware of the need to cater their services to be more appealing and effective for women. To get a sense of the program differences, we decomposed some of the program-level information presented in Table 4.6 to see how the different gender groups fared in the different programs. This exercise revealed that in 41 of the EDP programs, the average one-year change in outside equity investment was highest (or tied for highest) for ventures founded by men. The average equity change in these programs is $35,336. However, the ventures founded by the other two groups of founding teams did poorly in these programs. The average equity change was −$8592 for the mixed-gender teams and −$10,074 for the all-women teams in these same programs. In 38 of the programs, the average equity bump was highest (or tied for highest) for ventures founded by mixed-gender teams. The average equity bump for mixed-gender ventures in these programs is $45,749. Again, the other two groups of founders did poorly in these same programs: −$1665 bump for the men and −$1054 for the women.

It is interesting to see how programs can be run that cater to the equity investment needs of the all men and mixed-gender founding teams. It is also interesting to see how the programs that work for one gender group do not do well for the others. However, it is also important to note that the sample does not produce any good news for all-women founding teams seeking to raise additional equity investment. In the 22 programs where the average equity bump was highest (or tied for highest) for ventures founded by women, the average equity change for these ventures was negative: −$966. The other two groups did even worse in these programs: −$14,710 for the men and −$33,089 for the mixed-gender teams.

Accelerators are shifting to make their programs more women friendly. Village Capital is doing this through peer selection, and reducing its emphasis on demo days, Kinara Indonesia adjusted its workshops so they were longer, fewer,

(continued)

(continued)

and during the week rather than the weekend (so women could be at home with their families on the weekends). The question (and challenge) remains—to what extent can accelerators be an opening for women entrepreneurs into an ecosystem that was largely built by and for men? We encourage accelerators to consider gender-related design and the specific challenges faced by all-women teams throughout their programming.

Concluding Remarks

This chapter presents a series of observations that illuminate the challenges that women face when trying to secure investment for their ventures. The first thing to emphasize is that there are actually three gender-based groups of founding teams: all-men, mixed-gender, and all-women. In addition to being seriously under-represented in the sample, the all-women teams attract less than one-third as much outside equity investment as those with only men. Mixed-gender teams fall in between, but closer to the all-men teams. This is problematic for women entrepreneurs who do not have male business partners. It is also problematic for the impact areas that are dominated by these all-women teams, including access to education, and equality and empowerment.

Looking behind the investment outcomes, all-women teams and their ventures are different in ways that explain some of this deficit. They are more likely to establish nonprofit organizations and less likely to build ventures around proprietary intellectual property. They also tend to approach accelerators with less earned revenues and fewer full-time employees. While they have similar education levels, their teams have less work experience at very senior levels and less prior entrepreneurial experience. Taking all of these factors into account shrinks the estimated equity investment deficit considerably, although not making it disappear. This more nuanced observation does not trivialize the investment problems faced by women entrepreneurs. It simply instructs protagonists and supporters that the problems, and therefore the solutions, are more complicated. It is equally important to see what happens to mixed-gender founding teams when these covariates are taken into consideration. In many respects, their ventures should be more appealing to investors. For example, they have more earned revenues and more full-time employees. When this is factored into the equation, the revealed bias facing mixed-gender teams increases substantially. All of this suggests that, at the end of the day, the challenges faced by women entrepreneurs are twofold. Those who work without men face an underlying gender bias that is amplified by the fact that they also present less obviously attractive ventures and teams to investors. Those who work with men actually present more attractive investment options, but this attractiveness is masked by gender biases that have no business penetrating the world of impact-oriented entrepreneurship.

The final task for this chapter is to see whether accelerator programs are helping to address these two sets of problems. When considering these preliminary observations, we must remember that teams with women founders, and especially all-women teams, are different when it comes to their espoused aspirations, both in terms of private investment targets and expected accelerator program benefits. With this caveat in mind, the EDP data suggest that accelerators are addressing the investment deficits experienced by mixed-gender teams. However, there is no evidence that they are finding ways to increase the flow of outside equity investment into all-women teams. Whether this represents a failure in execution or a failure to identify the root causes of the problems faced by these different founders and ventures remains an open question—one that desperately needs an answer.

Notes

1. Claudia Goldin & Cecilia Rouse. 2000. 'Orchestrating impartiality: The impact of "blind" auditions on female musicians.' *American Economic Review*, 90(4): 715–741.
2. Helene Ahl. 2006. 'Why research on women entrepreneurs needs new directions.' *Entrepreneurship Theory and Practice*, 30(5): 595–621.
3. For instance, companies led by women tend to be smaller but are no more likely to go out of business. See Arnold C. Cooper, Javier Gimeno-Gascon & Carolyn Y. Woo. 1994. 'Initial human and financial capital as predictors of new venture performance.' *Journal of Business Venturing*, 9(5): 371–395; Arne L. Kalleberg & Kevin T. Leicht. 1991. 'Gender and organizational performance: Determinants of small business survival and success.' *Academy of Management Journal*, 34(1): 136–161.
4. More and More, Women are Combining Profit with Purpose to Create a Better World. *CNBC Online* (May 2017).
5. Post C., Rahman N., & Rubow E. 2011. Green governance: Boards of directors' composition and environmental corporate social responsibility. *Business & Society*, 50: 189–223; Marquis C. & Lee, M. 2013. Who is governing whom? Executives, governance, and the structure of generosity in large U.S. firms. *Strategic Management Journal*, 34: 483–497.

6. Matsa, D. A., & Miller, A. R. 2014. Workforce reductions at women-owned businesses in the United States. *Industrial and Labor Relations Review*, 67: 422–452.

7. Croson, R., & Gneezy, U. 2009. Gender differences in preferences. *Journal of Economic Literature*, 47: 448–474.

8. See https://rimidi.com/company/

9. *Rimidi Closes $6.575 Million Series A with Strategic Investment from Eli Lilly.* PR Newswire (July 2018).

10. Andy Cosh, Douglas Cumming & Alan Hughes. 2009. 'Outside entrepreneurial capital.' *The Economic Journal*, 119(540): 1494–1533.

11. Susan Coleman & Alica Robb. 2009. 'A comparison of new firm financing by gender: evidence from the Kauffman Firm Survey data.' *Small Business Economics*, 33(4): 397.

12. Gry Agnete Alsos, Espen John Isaksen & Elisabet Ljunggren. 2006. 'New venture financing and subsequent business growth in men- and women-led businesses.' *Entrepreneurship Theory and Practice*, 30(5): 667–686.

13. Susan Marlow & Dean Patton. 2005. 'All credit to men? Entrepreneurship, finance, and gender.' *Entrepreneurship Theory and Practice*, 29(6): 717–735.

14. Patricia G. Greene, Candida G. Brush, Myra M. Hart & Patrick Saparito. 2001. 'Patterns of venture capital funding: Is gender a factor?' *Venture Capital: An International Journal of Entrepreneurial Finance*, 3, 63–83; Candida Brush, Patricia Greene, Lakshmi Balachandra & Amy Davis. 2017 'The gender gap in venture capital- progress, problems, and perspectives.' *Venture Capital: An International Journal of Entrepreneurial Finance*, 20.

15. *Why VCs Aren't Funding Women-led Startups.* Knowledge @ Wharton (May 2016).

16. *Diana Report – Women Entrepreneurs 2014: Bridging the Gender Gap in Venture Capital*, Babson College (2014).

17. *Female Founders On an Upward Trend, According to CrunchBase*, TechCrunch (May 2015).

18. See https://www.merriam-webster.com/dictionary/equity

19. *Global Entrepreneurship Monitor: United States Report 2016*, Babson College (2017).

20. Maria Minniti & Carlo Nardone. 2007. 'Being in someone else's shoes: the role of gender in nascent entrepreneurship.' *Small Business Economics*, 28(2): 223–238.

21. *The 2015 Kauffman Index of Startup Activity: National Trends.* The Kauffman Foundation (2015).

22. See https://www.nawbo.org/resources/women-business-owner-statistics

23. See https://blog.dol.gov/2017/07/05/get-facts-women-business-owners

24. Ingrid Verheul & Roy Thurik. 2001. 'Start-up capital: Does gender matter?'. *Small Business Economics*, 16(4): 329–346.

25. Their research team examined each of these eight myths, showing many to be either outright wrong or undergoing substantial change. See Candida G. Brush, Nancy M. Carter, Elizabeth Gatewood, Patricia G. Greene and Myra M. Hart. 2008. The Diana Project: Women Business Owners and Equity Capital: The Myths Dispelled. Working paper.
26. *Diana Report – Women Entrepreneurs 2014: Bridging the Gender Gap in Venture Capital*, Babson College (2014).
27. *Diana Report – Women Entrepreneurs 2014: Bridging the Gender Gap in Venture Capital*, Babson College (2014).
28. *Creating Inclusive High-Tech Incubators and Accelerators: Strategies to Increase Participation Rates of Women and Minority Entrepreneurs.* JP Morgan Chase & ICIC (2016).

11

Accelerating Learning About Accelerators

The observations in this book leverage several years of collaboration among the EDP, GALI, and scores of accelerator programs working around the world. Between 2013 and 2017, these partnerships collected and collated application and follow-up data from thousands of impact-oriented entrepreneurs. These data have been used in sector reports, data briefs, and major publications, whose insights are read and applied by accelerator program managers, funders, and supporters to reflect on and make improvements to their programs. EDP accelerator partners also receive custom reports following each application period and in each post-program year, which helps them to manage, promote, and update their offerings. The various chapters in this book build on these research outputs by connecting the many pieces, updating with additional observations and analyses, and presenting insights to a broader audience.

Aligning an expanding global commitment to support impact-oriented entrepreneurs with a parallel commitment to collecting and analyzing data creates a foundation for widespread experimentation, plus the ability to learn from these many experiments. Based on patterns in the EDP data—complemented by numerous examples and interviews—we are starting to see how impact-oriented accelerators are addressing knowledge and network gaps, and then driving financial resources into ventures started by impact-oriented entrepreneurs, including those working in challenging ecosystems and those whose efforts are otherwise under-appreciated.

In this final chapter, we summarize several over-arching insights that might help program managers and supporters build stronger accelerators that will support waves of impact-oriented entrepreneurs into the future.

© The Author(s) 2019
P. W. Roberts, S. A. Lall, *Observing Acceleration*,
https://doi.org/10.1007/978-3-030-00042-4_11

What Have We Learned?

1. Accelerators have effects on impact-oriented ventures ... at both ends of the growth distributions.

Our main finding (from Chap. 4) is that accelerators influence the short-term commercial performance of the ventures that they support. Accelerator participants show better average growth outcomes across the board, even after accounting for prior-year commercial performance and program-specific effects. Aggregating the EDP observations to the program level shows that the NFF (described and analyzed in Chap. 5) into participating ventures (relative to rejected ventures) is positive. The roughly per-venture $30,000 funding bump is both important and statistically significant. Among the full sample of accelerators, $1 spent on programming translates into roughly $1.70 of additional earned, invested, borrowed, or donated funds for participating ventures. Moreover, the NFF bump exceeds the average per-venture operating costs in 33 of 52 EDP programs. While we caution against using short-term commercial performance growth as the *only* indicator of accelerator success, we do believe that it is *an important* indicator that is salient for a range of accelerator program stakeholders.

These average program effects mask two opposing effects that accelerators seem to have at the upper and lower ends of the growth distributions. Accelerators are charged with finding and selecting entrepreneurs who demonstrate some underlying potential. When true promise is revealed, their task is to ensure that the most promising entrepreneurs have the resources and support needed to grow their ventures. When the additional attention and scrutiny reveal major problems or flaws, their task is to encourage entrepreneurs to pause, pivot, or exit. Consistent with this latter winnowing function, the EDP data reveal accelerator participation effects at both ends of the one-year growth distributions. Compared with the 60–80 percent of ventures that experience no revenue, employee, or investment growth, participating ventures tend to be over-represented in the positive-growth *and* negative-growth groups. This suggests that accelerators have their intended effects at both ends of the promise spectrum.

When we focus on the top 50 ventures for one-year growth outcomes in revenue, employment, equity investment, debt, or philanthropic support, we see that roughly 37 percent of accelerated ventures make it onto the list, compared with only 21 percent of ventures that applied to accelerators but were rejected. This significant difference is one more indication that accelerators are indeed pushing cohort ventures into the upper echelons of short-term commercial growth outcomes.

2. All accelerators are not created equal.

Although these overall effects are promising for accelerator supporters, they mask considerable variability across programs. For the median program in the EDP sample, participating ventures experience an average revenue growth of just $13,000. At the same time, average revenue growth for the top program is $263,613. For the bottom program, average revenue growth is negative (−$344,447). Similarly, the median program experiences no change in average equity growth, but the data reveal extreme average outcomes of +$222,800 for the highest-performing program and −$77,000 for the lowest performer. Clearly, not all accelerators are created (and implemented) equal. Although much of this program-to-program variability is attributable to the different choices that accelerators make when building application pipelines, selecting entrepreneurs, and designing their programming, there are two general spaces where performance deficiencies seem to be systematic. EDP accelerators are not having much effect on emerging-market ventures that participate in (regional and global) programs run in other countries. This becomes problematic when the current supply of quality accelerator programming in a country is insufficient to support the demands placed by its promising entrepreneurs. The accelerator programs are also doing a relatively poor job when it comes to supporting ventures launched by all-women founding teams. This suggests that the entrepreneurs who have the biggest structural challenges navigating their ecosystems are also the ones who get the weakest support from accelerator programs.

3. The most funding-effective accelerators drive equity or revenues.

Looking closely at the 33 programs whose NFF outcomes more than cover the costs of running programs, we see that there are only two viable pathways: focus on growing revenues or driving outside equity investment. The few high-NFF programs whose dominant funding effects came through driving new debt or philanthropy end up with inferior NFF outcomes. This does not mean that debt and philanthropy are unimportant. It simply means that overall incremental funding growth for participating ventures is higher and more reliable when programs focus on helping entrepreneurs grow revenues or equity.

4. Some program design choices seem more promising than others.

The general question of whether accelerators work quickly gives way to more specific and nuanced questions about which program choices seem to work better. Here, the EDP data offer some nuanced insights that should be considered by individuals developing and supporting impact-oriented accelerators:

- *Money isn't everything, but it helps ... when deployed appropriately.* It is interesting and important to note that the high-NFF accelerators—those driving more incremental funding into participating ventures—actually spend less per venture on their programming. Moreover, they are no more likely to make direct investments into their ventures. However, the high-NFF programs that do make these direct investments end up with a significantly higher average NFF. This funding advantage holds after subtracting the direct program investments and also appears to stimulate additional net revenue growth. Both of these observations suggest that when high-NFF programs spend their money, they do so carefully and strategically.
- *Selectivity is not as important as inclusivity.* The intuition that selectivity is a sign of program quality does not hold true for the accelerators in the EDP sample. Rather, applicant pools for high-NFF and low-NFF programs are about the same size, as are acceptance rates into the two groups of programs. Nor do successful programs simply cherry-pick already high-performing ventures. In fact, the average prior-year commercial performance is actually lower among the high-NFF programs. We find that high-NFF programs seem to work harder and smarter when developing their applicant pools, recruiting from a wider set of sources and relying on referrals from their own cultivated networks.

The EDP data challenge a second intuition—that programs focusing on more marginalized entrepreneurs should not expect the same degree of commercial success. In fact, programs that report a preference for women or minority entrepreneurs are more likely to be found among the high-NFF programs. Although we are currently unsure about how or why this happens, the observation is still motivating for supporters of more inclusive entrepreneurship.

- *Entrepreneur selection is more art than science.* Accelerators fill a specific role in the entrepreneurial ecosystem—accelerating the performance of the *most promising* ventures. However, impact-oriented programs do their work among entrepreneurs and ventures where potential is not obvious or easy to discern. Therefore, the best programs spend a lot of thought and effort developing 'secret sauces' for entrepreneur selection. Our efforts to identify the main ingredients of the better selection sauces were largely unsuccessful. High-NFF and low-NFF programs do not differ much in the size or composition of their selection committees. Nor do they vary in terms of the emphasis placed on the quality of the team, idea, or venture. One interesting observation is that few high-NFF programs deploy pitches as part of their selection process, which is somewhat surprising given the current usage of pitch contests to engage investors at the end of most programs. Because the most obvious observables do not help us understand this critical component of the accelerator model, we encourage more innovative, and probably qualitative, research projects to give future program managers better guidance as they try to find the diamonds buried in the rough parts of under-developed ecosystems.

- *When it comes to accelerator programming, 'when' and 'where' matters more than 'what' and 'how.'* Many of the most concrete program choices—related to things like curriculum design and mentorship programs—do not vary systematically between high-NFF and low-NFF programs. However, we do find empirical support for the cohort-based approach, which is a key feature of the accelerator model. Programs in which entrepreneurs spend more time working together and on-site tend to do better than those where entrepreneurs spend more time working alone and remotely. Taken together, these last two insights challenge observers who desperately want to find the 'treatment effect' of acceleration among the hard and codified elements of program design. After all, it would be great if we could find a few well-defined silver bullets that could be replicated across programs working around the world. Instead, it seems that when difficult-to-articulate selection processes attract the right ecosystem stakeholders, including promising entrepreneurs, and then give them time and space to engage with one another, better accelerator outcomes ensue.

What Are the Next Biggest Questions?

After nearly five years of asking questions and collecting data, we are more confident that impact-oriented accelerator programs are moving a specific set of needles when it comes to supporting entrepreneurs. We also know that they vary in their ability to drive incremental financial resources into the ventures that are accepted into their programs. Finally, we believe that certain entrepreneurs (e.g., all-women founding teams) and certain ventures (e.g., some that operate in emerging markets) experience fewer benefits (again on average) from the accelerators that they have a chance to work with.

These foundational observations provide justifications for accelerator supporters to keep funding impact-oriented programs. Just as there are no sure bets when it comes to entrepreneurship, there are no sure bets when it comes to supporting entrepreneurs. But, when the overall average and median program effects are consistently positive, one can make a case that bets placed on accelerator programs will be sound. This does not mean that program managers should use the observations in this book (and in related research projects) as all-purpose justifications for funding any program. Nor does it mean that the governments, foundations, and corporations that fund accelerators should not ask specific questions when placing their funding bets. They must ask whether program managers have specific and defensible points of view on various design choices related to pipeline-building, entrepreneur selection, and programming. They must also ensure that program managers have strategies for validating these points of view and resources in place to conduct the relevant post-program assessments. Developing an ongoing appetite for asking the right questions and a companion capacity for generating evidence-based answers produces one more critical return on investment for accelerators. Not only can funders expect the documented positive effects at the center of the accelerator outcome distributions, they can also expect a sector-wide learning agenda that will help us understand what contributes to the variance around these average program outcomes.

We also propose that the two major categories of null effects in this book—those related to all-women founding teams and emerging-market ventures accelerated in other countries—should also motivate funders to continue supporting accelerators. The full value of these investments derives from the need for further experimentation and learning. Given the prevalence and felt need for effective regional accelerator programs in Africa, Asia, and Latin America, it is troubling that accelerated ventures in these kinds of programs are not currently able to raise the funding they need, even as they successfully grow their revenues. The diminished efficacy of current programs suggests that the underdeveloped funding ecosystems in these places require different kinds of stimulation. It is likely that these stimulants will involve different roles for impact investors, venture philanthropists, development finance institutions, *and* accelerators. Our colleagues at ANDE (and in several of its member organizations) are currently mapping entrepreneurial ecosystems in West Africa, Latin America, and India.[1] As accumulating evidence provides more accurate pictures of possible structural impediments, accelerator programs will be innovating their basic models to provide more targeted support to entrepreneurs. As convincing program innovations are presented, funders must be willing to support them, and researchers must be in place to observe and assess their efficacy.

At the same time, the espoused belief that accelerators are promising places for women entrepreneurs to address and overcome their unique obstacles is not widely supported. The EDP data allow us to compare two different categories of women-led ventures—that is, those with all-women and mixed-gender teams—with the largest group of all-male teams. The problems faced by the all-women teams are obvious. They are not coming to accelerators with the same observables and credentials, and they are not getting anything that resembles an appropriate share of outside equity investment. The issues faced by mixed-gender teams are more nuanced. According to the EDP data, they should be *more* attractive to equity investors because, for instance, they demonstrate stronger revenues. However, we still see outside equity funding flowing disproportionately to the all-male teams. The persistent sore spots when it comes to investing in promising ventures started by women provides another justification for more learning-based experimentation. The best way to crack these generations-old gender biases is to develop and fund more programmatic experimentation while ensuring that plans are in place to validate, and then replicate, the more successful program features.

Overall, the current answers to some of the bigger accelerator questions are not sufficient given the importance and scope of the work that impact-oriented accelerators are being asked to do. In this spirit, as we bring the book to a close, it is important to remind ourselves about the big questions that we have not yet tackled.

1. Will the short-term effects of acceleration on commercial performance hold in the medium and long term?

The short-term observations in this book are optimistic for those who aim to unlock the potential trapped in underperforming impact-oriented ventures, both for-profit and nonprofit. It is exciting to know that, on average $1 spent on an impact-oriented accelerator can be expected to deliver more than $1.70 of additional financial resources—revenues, equity, debt, and philanthropy—for ventures going through the program. It becomes more exciting as future research projects—quantitative and qualitative—help us understand the effects of specific programmatic changes that might refine the basic accelerator model and generate better and more reliable short-term commercial effects. However, we must recognize the fact that the full value from an immediate burst of acceleration only emerges if the higher velocity can be maintained or improved in subsequent years. In this respect, evidence of immediate growth is a necessary-but-insufficient condition for longer-term growth. The good news is that the EDP is on a trajectory to begin looking at the important question of whether we see continued commercial performance growth in participating ventures. With another year of data collection under its belt, the EDP program should have a critical mass of data to allow for rigorous analyses of second-year follow-up data.

2. Are there systematic relationships between long-term societal impacts and short-term (and medium-term) commercial performance?

The real holy grail when it comes to assessing whether accelerators are helping to change the world is to see whether their short-term (and medium-term) effects on commercial performance translate into the social and environmental benefits that entrepreneurs and impact investors, along with accelerator program managers and funders, are seeking. This takes us back to a key question that we sidestepped in Chap. 3, where we chose to focus on one specific performance domain. For practical reasons, and for reasons that relate to the primary theory of change for most accelerators, it is important to know whether they are having an immediate effect on the commercial trajectory of impact-oriented ventures. The mainly positive observations throughout the book provide both comfort and motivation to begin thinking about the bigger and broader questions.

In many respects, this foundational question is more straightforward because it simply requires a combination of time plus the commitment to keep collecting (and providing) financial data. The second, and arguably more important, question about societal impacts is more problematic. Consistent with our observations about the variable impact objectives that are subsumed under the broad heading of impact-oriented ventures, very few impact-oriented entrepreneurs are consistently and systematically documenting their impacts. This lack of impact measurement is not entirely surprising, given the complexity of measuring social performance and the relatively nascent stage of most of these ventures. However, it does leave the question of whether these promising entrepreneurs are able to convert their good intentions to actual social and environmental impact.

Researchers must find innovative ways to test the implicit belief that fostering improved commercial performance among impact-oriented ventures actually produces greater societal impact. For sure, this remains an ongoing challenge for anyone interested in impact-oriented entrepreneurship—how do we demonstrate the long-term social or environmental impacts of the ventures that do scale?[2] One way to tackle this challenge is to collect additional data about impacts by establishing stronger and more consistent social performance measurement systems that foster comparability. For example, Acumen works with companies in its energy portfolio to measure the impact of energy access on incomes, wellbeing, and kerosene usage in rigorous impact evaluations.[3] In cases where interventions are more complex and involve behavior change, we may need to be pragmatic and focus on measuring basic outputs and activities.[4] Here, existing efforts like those being developed by IRIS and B Lab are taking positive steps. We are also tracking the emerging efforts of the Poverty Probability Index,[5] Lean Data,[6] and satellite imaging.[7] Practitioners are also experimenting with other initiatives like the Goldilocks Initiative by Innovations for Poverty Action[8] and the Impact Management Project.[9] As different stakeholders develop promising methodologies for tracking actual social and environmental impacts, accelerators will play important roles in promoting a broader and more consistent understanding and application of impact measurement.[10] It is up to the broader research community to leverage these many efforts in future studies that work to link the acceleration of commercial performance to societal impact.

3. Are we paying too much—or not enough—attention to outside equity investment?

Early on in this book, we made reference to a streetlight bias when arguing for the need to examine the behavior and performance of accelerators that work outside of the highly visible technology sector in places like Silicon Valley. A similar bias might be emerging when it comes to financing early-stage ventures. Because the whole world focuses on equity investment, we are only examining the drivers of outside equity investment. In this book, we spend a lot of time focusing on the people and places that attract the lion's share of outside equity investment. Consistent with this obsession on equity investment and its importance for high-growth companies, we spend an equal amount of time figuring out how to get angel investors and venture capitalists matched with promising impact-oriented ventures, especially those founded by marginalized entrepreneurs (e.g., Chap. 10) and those working in emerging markets (e.g., Chap. 9).

It seems obvious that we should continue this line of inquiry in order to produce more equitable and appropriate distributions of outside equity investment. At the same time, we might also want to consider whether we need more innovative thinking when it comes to funding impact-oriented ventures. The thousands of entrepreneurs in the EDP data attest to the explosion of new ideas and business models when it comes to using markets to address major societal problems. However, there has not been a similar explosion of novel ideas when it comes to investment vehicles. One promising thread of experimentation—and one that aligns with the observations made in this book— relates to revenue-backed financing.[11] Chapter 5 showed that a major component of the NFF is outside equity growth. Most of the incremental investment that flows into accelerated ventures comes in the form of outside equity investment. However, we also find that overall NFF is highest for programs whose dominant NFF component is net revenue growth. It seems that when ventures prove their ability to bring in revenue, investors are more confident about their current and future prospects.

This does not tell the whole story. Other observations in Chap. 9 corroborate prior research studies[12] by showing that early-stage equity investment is scarce in many emerging markets. We also know, and showed in Chap. 10, that equity investment has some structural aversions to women entrepreneurs. The singular emphasis on equity investment leads us to wonder if accelerators and entrepreneurs are missing out on other sources of finance, like revenue-backed financing. If there was more documented experimentation with risk-adjusted finance that tracks the things that women and emerging-market entrepreneurs are good at—that is, growing revenues—then accelerators might consider experimenting with these.

Where Are We Going?

We are writing this book as we close out the first phase of GALI. In doing so, it is important to remember what got us here in the first place. The path was initially set by the growing number of entrepreneurs who want to address major social and environmental challenges with for-profit companies or market-oriented nonprofits. As more entrepreneurs started walking this path, it became obvious that the differences baked into their innovative ventures make it harder to identify and close the knowledge, network, and capital gaps that hinder their performance and momentum. These ecosystem challenges pulled a growing number of support programs, like accelerators, into the journey. The combination of impact-oriented entrepreneurs experimenting with their own time, talent, and treasure, plus accelerator program managers and supporters chipping in with their social and financial capital, creates a lot of excitement about the ability to accelerate the progress of impact-oriented ventures in entrepreneurial dead spaces around the world. However, until 2013, there was no collective capacity to ask and answer questions related to the efficacy of these various entrepreneurial experiments and investments.

In the middle of 2018, the global context for broad-based entrepreneurship is in better shape, mostly because the stocks and flows of impact-oriented entrepreneurs and accelerators are robust and, in many cases, more experienced. As the various figures and tables in Chaps. 3, 4, 5, 6, 7, 8, 9, and 10 demonstrate, we are now able to look at many of these efforts and learn something about what is and is not working in the world of impact oriented entrepreneurship.

We must keep looking at the various (new and established) accelerators that are continuing to support promising entrepreneurs. As we continue to look and continue asking questions, we must recognize the fact that the models that we will be estimating in the coming years are going to get complicated. Just think for a moment about the innumerable interactions between all of the variables introduced in this book. Accelerator programs will continue to try moving a number of different needles, including those related to short-term and longer-term commercial, social, and environmental performance outcomes. The ventures that they end up working with will vary on a number of critical dimensions. The same will be said about their founding teams. When designing their programs, managers will make a range of different choices as they build pipelines, select entrepreneurs, and work to close knowledge network and capital gaps. If we try to address all the combinations and permutations in a single tell-all study, we would need enough data to address an almost infinite number of outcomes-ventures-entrepreneurs-programmatic choice interactions.

Thankfully, the world does not really need this kind of grand unified model of accelerator effectiveness. Instead, it needs answers to the many more specific questions that underpin the particular initiatives that accelerators, foundations, impact investors, and governments are undertaking to support impact-oriented entrepreneurship around the world. For example:

- Village Capital wants to know whether a commitment to peer selection fosters an accelerator environment that is more supportive for women and minority entrepreneurs.
- The Omidyar Network wants to know how philanthropic and commercial capital can be appropriately combined to stimulate growth in impact-oriented ventures.
- Nesta wants to know more about the flows of entrepreneurs seeking support across different countries.
- The Mastercard Foundation wants to know how to best accelerate the commercial performance of African ventures started by young entrepreneurs.

- The Lemelson Foundation wants to know the most effective ways to support hardware- or invention-based entrepreneurs, compared with those that are developing software-based ventures.
- Acumen wants to know which impact measurement approaches (e.g., B Lab, Lean Data) are most useful for social enterprises in emerging markets.

Instead of looking for all of the answers in a single—academic or practitioner—study, we need a broader commitment among a broader set of researchers to keep asking and answering the most relevant questions as they come up. To answer these questions, we also need to keep collecting and analyzing the quantitative and qualitative data that sit behind the findings presented in this book. With an expanding set of questions and data from an expanding sample of accelerator programs and entrepreneurs, programs like GALI will continue to encourage and support the growing roster of researchers who are collectively producing answers to the questions that are critical to our field.

As we expand these efforts, we must remain aware of blind spots in our sampling processes. This means seeking out programs that are different by design, targeting different types of entrepreneurs (such as those not seeking high-risk equity investment in order to become the next unicorn). We must also find ways to modify our research processes so that they can tease out the subtle-but-important nuances across regions and cities within emerging-market countries.

Concluding Comments

There is a growing parade of individuals and organizations that are passionate about the potential for entrepreneurship to contribute to economic development. In truth, it does not take much to get excited about the many benefits that come with successful acts of entrepreneurship. Just think about the long list of invaluable products that people now take for granted: cars and airplanes, medicines and vaccines, refrigerators, and computers and cell phones.[13] Now think about the similar long list of critical services, such as DNA testing and magnetic resonance imaging, banking and microfinance, or email and social media.[14] All of these product and service innovations were brought to the world by talented and persistent entrepreneurs. To see the link between cultivating more entrepreneurial successes and broad-based economic development, simply think about the many societal problems waiting to be solved: those related to poverty and environmental degradation.

There are also long queues of entrepreneurs with creative ideas that could address one or more of these major problems. To get a feel for these numbers, start with the roughly 13,000 founding teams that applied to EDP accelerators between 2013 and 2017, and then consider the hundreds of programs that are not working with the EDP research team.[15] If the best of these entrepreneurs can be identified and then supported with financial and non-financial investments, then many of the societal problems that currently seem intractable might be replaced by market-based solutions that will one day be taken for granted. This requires entrepreneurial conversion rates that resemble those seen in places like Silicon Valley. However, most of the world's impact-oriented entrepreneurs are not white men from northern California. They are often women and minorities, two groups that are overlooked or underestimated when it comes to entrepreneurial potential. They often live and work in regions and sectors that are not synonymous with high-growth entrepreneurship. Because of this, they do not have similar track records when it comes to converting entrepreneurial potential into positive company growth outcomes. Every time one of these promising ideas withers before having a chance to develop, the world loses a claim on a future taken-for-granted product or service.

Thankfully, there is another growing parade of individuals and organizations that are similarly passionate about the role that accelerators can play to offset the outsized challenges associated with being an underestimated entrepreneur working on an overlooked problem in a marginalized country, region, or city. The best of these accelerators excels when it comes to identifying unexpectedly (by many) promising entrepreneurs and then running them through programs that close the many knowledge, network, and capital gaps that stand between an entrepreneur's potential and their future business success.

If these pipelines of promising impact-oriented entrepreneurs and impact-oriented accelerator programs are both large, then why do we need a book like this one? Simply stated, the parade of researchers who actively study the links between entrepreneurship, acceleration, and socio-economic development is not very long. As a result, the ratio of active learning to programmatic experimentation is woefully inadequate. If we do not stimulate more and better analyses of the full range of ecosystems and accelerators, then future entrepreneurs will not benefit from the lessons that rigorous research can provide.

The impact-oriented entrepreneur's challenges are in many ways more difficult than those facing more traditional entrepreneurs. Consider the basic fact that many of the solutions to problems that benefit poor people or the planet lack an obvious revenue model.[16] This makes it difficult to cover the operational expenses of a growing venture, let alone attract outside investments of private capital. Add to this the problems associated with underdeveloped ecosystems and the broader set of barriers that come with that. The problems faced by this targeted group of entrepreneurs are carried into the accelerators that are set up to support them. Just as impact-oriented entrepreneurs are experimenting and tinkering with new ways to tackle societal challenges, impact-focused accelerators are devising new approaches to help these entrepreneurs. To be able to keep up with these amazing entrepreneurs and accelerators, we must do a better job of learning from their efforts. We must develop a better understanding of the underlying cause-and-effect relationships. We must communicate these observations back into the sector, so that each new experiment can learn from the prior successes and failures.

And this is where the parades and lines are not so long. This book joins a small and slow-growing list of reports and studies that carefully examine the efforts and outcomes of impact-oriented accelerators, and of the ventures that they support. It also grounds an open call to researchers! To continue learning, we must keep asking questions about pipeline-building, entrepreneur selection, and accelerator programming. We must also keep collecting the (qualitative and quantitative) data that speak to these questions. If we do this, and develop a pipeline of research that is at least as promising as the pipelines of entrepreneurs who are applying to impact-oriented accelerators around the world, then we will be better-positioned to get the most of the accelerator programming that aspires to get the most out of the entrepreneurs who are trying to change the world.

Notes

1. http://www.whysgbs.org/what-are-ecosystems/
2. Ebrahim, Alnoor, and V. Kasturi Rangan. 'What impact? A framework for measuring the scale and scope of social performance.' *California Management Review* 56, no. 3 (2014): 118–141.
3. See Acumen. 'Energy Impact Report' (2017). Available at https://acumen.org/energy-impact-report/
4. Innovations for Poverty Action Goldilocks Toolkit Case Study: Splash (January 2016). https://www.poverty-action.org/publication/goldilocks-case-study-splash
5. https://www.povertyindex.org/
6. https://acumen.org/lean-data/
7. Innovations for Poverty Action Goldilocks Toolkit: Micro-Satellite Data: Measuring Impact from Space. (February 2016). https://www.poverty-action.org/publication/micro-satellite-data-measuring-impact-space
8. https://www.poverty-action.org/right-fit-evidence

9. http://www.impactmanagementproject.com/

10. Lall, Saurabh. 'Measuring to Improve Versus Measuring to Prove: Understanding the Adoption of Social Performance Measurement Practices in Nascent Social Enterprises.' *VOLUNTAS: International Journal of Voluntary and Nonprofit Organizations* 28, no. 6 (2017): 2633–2657.

11. See Ross Baird and Bryce Butler. 'Looking Past Equity Investments.' *Forbes* (August 2017).

12. Bruton, Garry D., David Ahlstrom, and Tomas Puky. 'Institutional differences and the development of entrepreneurial ventures: A comparison of the venture capital industries in Latin America and Asia.' *Journal of International Business Studies* 40, no. 5 (2009): 762–778.

13. See Daniel Stone. 'The 10 Inventions that Changed the World.' *National Geographic* (June 2017).

14. See A World Transformed: What Are the Top 30 Innovations of the Last 30 Years? *Knowledge @ Wharton* (February 2009).

15. The Entrepreneurship Database Program at Emory University: 2017 Year-End Data Summary.

16. Jyoti Sharma. 2017. 'Avoiding the neoliberal trap in social entrepreneurship: Seven lessons for walking the tight rope between social welfare and business.' *Stanford Social Innovation Review* (October 2017).

Glossary

Accelerator program Time-bound programs that work with cohorts of entrepreneurs to provide mentorship and training, with a special emphasis on connecting early-stage ventures with investors.

Commercial performance Overall financial performance of a venture, as measured by revenues and/or external investment received.

Debt (new borrowing) The amount of money borrowed by one party from another.

Developed country The World Bank's Country Income categories classify countries into four groups based on gross national income (GNI) per capita: High income, upper-middle income, lower-middle income, and low income. In this book, developed countries refer to the high-income economies.

Early-stage venture Typically, companies that have started business operations and are generating revenue, but are not yet profitable.

(Earned) revenues The amount of money that a company actually receives during a specific period. It is the top line or gross income figure from which costs are subtracted to determine net income.

Emerging market The World Bank's Country Income categories classify countries into four groups based on gross national income (GNI) per capita: High income, upper-middle income, lower-middle income, and low income. In this book, emerging markets refers to all upper-middle income, lower-middle income, and low-income economies.

Entrepreneur An individual who founds and runs a small business, assuming all the risks and rewards of the venture. The entrepreneur is commonly seen as an innovator, a source of new ideas, goods, services, and business/or procedures.

Entrepreneur selection The processes used by accelerators to select entrepreneurs for each cohort. Typically, these processes include a review of applications, followed by more qualitative assessments through interviews and site visits.

© The Author(s) 2019
P. W. Roberts, S. A. Lall, *Observing Acceleration*,
https://doi.org/10.1007/978-3-030-00042-4

Entrepreneurial ecosystem A combination of interrelated factors like access to finance, policy, human capital, access to markets, support, and culture that affects the emergence and growth of entrepreneurship in a specific region.

Entrepreneurship Database Program A program run out of Emory University that works with scores of accelerators to collect standardized data during the application process. It then follows up with annual surveys administered to all program applicants, including those who participated in accelerators and those who did not.

Founding team The group of entrepreneurs primarily responsible for launching a new venture.

(Full-time) employee An individual employed, on average, for at least 30 hours of service per week, or 130 hours of service per month.

Global Accelerator Learning Initiative A collaboration between the Aspen Network of Development Entrepreneurs and Emory University designed to explore key questions about enterprise acceleration, such as: Do acceleration programs contribute to revenue growth? Do they help companies attract investment?

Impact Investor Individuals making investments into companies, organizations, and funds with the intention to generate social and environmental impact alongside a financial return.

Incubator An organization engaged in supporting early-stage ventures by providing access to shared resources such as office space, management training, and legal and accounting services.

Intellectual property A category of property that includes intangible creations of the human intellect, and primarily encompasses copyrights, patents, and trademarks.

Net Flow of Funds (NFF) A variable that recognizes the four ways that funds flow into early-stage ventures; they can be earned (revenues), invested (outside equity), borrowed (debt), or donated (philanthropy). For an accelerator program, the NFF measures the average of participants' one-year growth in revenues plus investments minus the corresponding average for ventures that were rejected.

Outside equity investment Capital raised through the sale of shares in an enterprise. It essentially refers to the sale of an ownership interest to raise funds for business purposes.

Philanthropy Charitable giving to human causes on a large scale. Philanthropic funding is provided as a gift, and not required to be paid back.

Pipeline building Activities conducted by accelerators to attract a strong pool of applicants to their programs. These activities may include roadshows, advertising, word-of-mouth recommendations, and promotion on social media.

Silicon Valley A region in Northern California which serves as the global center for high technology, innovation, and social media.

Social capital Broadly refers to those factors of effectively functioning social groups that include such things as interpersonal relationships, a shared sense of identity, a shared understanding, shared norms, shared values, trust, cooperation, and reciprocity.

Social or environmental impact Positive, measurable changes that address important social or environmental challenges.

Streetlight effect An observational bias that occurs when people only search for something where it is easiest to look.

Index[1]

A

Africa, 2, 9, 17, 133, 135, 137, 138, 160n13, 192
All-male teams, 66, 193
All-women teams, 164, 166–171, 173, 174, 177, 179, 180, 183, 184, 193
Analysis of Variance (ANOVA), 37, 144, 160n17, 171
Angel investor, 3, 168, 169, 178, 195
Applicant pool size, 93–94, 109
Aspen Network of Development Entrepreneurs (ANDE), v, vi, 4, 20, 56n12, 107, 159n4, 192

B

B Impact Assessment, 39
B Lab, 34, 195, 198
Business model, 2, 3, 34, 51, 69, 108, 114, 195

C

Capital gaps, 6–9, 15, 43, 45, 84, 119–133, 155, 161, 163, 196, 197, 199
Cohort, 2, 6, 9, 18, 31, 33, 45, 49, 66, 69, 71, 83, 85–86, 89, 93, 95, 98, 100–103, 108–110, 115, 119–125, 129, 130, 132, 162, 189
Commercial performance, 6, 8, 46, 49, 50, 60, 61, 63, 65, 67, 72, 154, 173, 174, 188, 190, 193–195, 197
Corporate accelerators, 17, 25

D

Debt, 6, 16, 24, 34, 37, 40, 43, 44, 46, 47, 49, 62–65, 67–70, 72, 76–80, 88, 95, 121, 131, 144, 145, 149, 150, 154, 157, 162, 166, 167, 174, 188, 189, 193
Demo day, 1, 9, 18, 24, 84, 120, 128, 130, 178, 182
Donor, 20, 22, 72, 96, 110

---

[1]Note: Page numbers followed by 'n' refer to notes.

© The Author(s) 2019
P. W. Roberts, S. A. Lall, *Observing Acceleration*,
https://doi.org/10.1007/978-3-030-00042-4

E

Early-stage finance, 15, 16, 162
Emerging market, v–vii, 6, 9, 18, 21,
    22, 24–26, 29n42, 42, 59, 60,
    70, 72, 85, 107, 133, 135–159,
    161, 189, 192, 195, 196, 198
Emory University, vi, 4, 33–35, 56n12
Employment, 2, 8, 14, 15, 26, 38,
    45–50, 61, 66, 69–72, 75, 83,
    140, 141, 165, 166, 176, 188
Endeavor, v, 5, 15, 16, 18, 33, 45, 66,
    109, 121
Entrepreneurial dead spaces, 3, 5, 7,
    16, 33, 133, 196
Entrepreneurial ecosystem, 1, 3, 4, 7, 9,
    15–16, 18, 25, 59, 85, 107, 136,
    141, 190, 192
Entrepreneurship Database Program
    (EDP), 4–10, 25–26, 31–55,
    60–63, 65, 66, 68, 70, 71, 77,
    81, 82, 84, 85, 89–91, 94, 96,
    97, 100, 102–105, 107, 112–
    114, 116, 120, 121, 124, 125,
    128, 132, 133, 137–140, 144,
    147–150, 153, 155, 157,
    160n13, 163–166, 168, 171,
    175–178, 180–182, 184,
    187–190, 193–195, 199
Equity, 4, 6, 10, 15–18, 23, 24, 34, 37,
    40, 43–49, 60, 62–65, 67–70,
    72, 75–81, 88, 89, 95, 104, 115,
    120, 121, 129, 132, 144, 145,
    148–150, 153, 154, 157, 159,
    161–184, 188–190, 193,
    195–196, 198
Ethiopia, 2, 102

F

500 Startups, 3, 11n6
Follow-up data, 8, 35, 60, 66, 180,
    187, 194
Foundation, v, 2, 6, 18, 22, 26, 33, 46,
    76, 145, 178, 187, 192, 197, 198

Founders, 1, 3, 4, 6, 10, 11n6, 14, 15,
    17, 32, 34, 37, 40, 42, 45, 46,
    48, 52–53, 64, 69–71, 101, 103,
    108, 113, 116, 133, 135, 145,
    148, 155, 161–168, 171,
    173–175, 178–182, 184
Founding team, 10, 38, 42, 69, 70, 76,
    103, 108, 109, 113, 114, 116,
    119, 120, 130, 132, 133,
    145–148, 157, 162–169,
    171–177, 179–183, 189, 191,
    192, 197, 199

G

Global Accelerator Learning Initiative
    (GALI), vi, vii, 4, 5, 7, 20–22,
    24, 29n39, 29n40, 33, 56n12,
    71, 75, 82, 94, 107, 132,
    136, 139, 160n11, 187,
    196, 198
Global Accelerator Network, 20, 45
Global Entrepreneurship Monitor
    (GEM), 32
Global Impact Investing Ratings
    System (GIIRS), 39
Grants, 16, 18, 24, 33, 40, 46, 59, 121,
    129, 131
GrowthAfrica, 2, 4, 38, 97, 102, 112,
    121, 137

H

High-income country, 9, 21, 22, 25,
    29n42, 42, 70, 85, 133,
    137–142, 144, 145, 147–151,
    153–155, 160n13, 179

I

Impact investor, 16, 20, 40, 56n13,
    192, 194, 197
Impact measurement, 39, 40, 194,
    195, 198

Impact-oriented accelerators, 2–7, 10,
16–18, 23–25, 27, 33, 40–42, 45,
49, 60, 82, 99, 109, 120, 128,
130, 187, 190, 193, 199, 200
Impact-oriented entrepreneurs, 7, 14,
15, 21, 23, 26, 31, 43–45, 59,
61, 94, 96, 119, 132, 139, 161,
162, 187, 194, 196, 197,
199, 200
Impact Reporting Investment
Standards (IRIS), 34, 38–40,
56n13, 56n15, 140, 164,
165, 195
Incubator, v, 19, 22, 60, 61, 136, 180
India, 2, 13, 15, 20, 65, 101, 137, 140,
141, 155–159, 192
Intellectual property, 42, 66, 69, 71,
108, 145, 157, 171, 173,
179, 183

K
Kauffman Firm Survey (KFS), 32,
34, 162
Kenya, 2, 3, 13, 14, 98, 102, 137, 138,
140, 155–157
Knowledge gaps, 3, 6–9, 15, 16, 43,
44, 84, 119–133, 155, 161, 163,
187, 196, 197, 199

L
Latin America, 9, 17, 77, 85, 93, 97,
101, 133, 138, 192
Lower-middle income country, 137
Low income country, 137

M
Marginalized, 4, 16, 17, 31, 38, 96,
101–105, 128, 131–133, 190,
195, 199

Mentor, 3, 16, 18, 19, 59, 84, 86–88,
96, 103, 119–121, 125–127,
130, 131, 153, 154, 177, 178
Mentoring, vi, 2, 9, 17, 24, 45, 101,
121, 127, 132
Mentorship, 1, 43, 72, 120,
126, 127, 130–132, 136,
158, 191
Mexico, 2, 3, 20, 32, 36, 65, 97, 100,
103, 137, 155–159
Microclinic Technologies, 13
Mixed-gender teams, 10, 157,
164–169, 171, 173, 174, 177,
179–184, 193

N
Nairobi, 2, 97
Net Flow of Funds (NFF), 75–91, 94,
109, 128–130, 188, 196
Network Gaps, 3, 6–9, 15, 16, 43, 44,
84, 119–133, 155, 161, 163,
187, 196, 197, 199

P
Pentorship, 2, 3
Philanthropic, philanthropy, 5–7, 16,
22, 23, 27, 29n42, 33, 34, 37,
43–47, 49, 56n18, 60, 62–65,
67–70, 72, 73n11, 76–80, 88,
89, 95, 108, 131, 144, 149, 150,
153, 157, 166, 167, 174, 188,
189, 193, 197
Pipeline, 6, 8, 61, 72, 84, 90, 93–105,
131, 132, 170, 189, 192,
197, 199, 200
Pitch, 1, 18, 24, 84, 112, 113,
115, 120, 128, 130, 169,
178, 191
Points of Light Civic Accelerator, 2,
33, 37

R

Regression, 37, 66, 67,
    73n10, 178
Revenue-backed finance, 196
Revenues, vi, 6, 8, 10, 15, 19, 23, 26,
    32–34, 37, 40, 45–50, 60–63,
    65–71, 75–81, 83, 88, 89, 95,
    100, 104, 108, 115, 116,
    129–132, 144, 145, 148–151,
    153–155, 158, 165, 173, 179,
    183, 188–190, 192, 193,
    196, 199

S

Seed Accelerator Rankings
    Project, 45
Selection, vi, 8, 9, 32, 35, 36, 62, 71,
    72, 84, 89, 90, 107–116, 131,
    132, 165, 182, 190–192,
    197, 200
Selection committee, 70, 86, 109–111,
    115, 116, 191
SheEO, 6, 101
Silicon Valley, v, 1, 3, 4, 16, 85, 137,
    195, 199
Simpa Networks, 13, 15
Social Enterprise @ Goizueta,
    4, 56n12
Social impact, 34, 38, 108
South Africa, 2, 20, 31, 32,
    137, 138
South Asia, 3, 9, 77, 85, 160n13
Southeast Asia, 9
Start-Up Chile, 6, 59

T

Techstars, 1, 11n6, 94, 107
The Toilet Accelerator, 5
Togo, 13, 14
t-test, 37

U

Uganda, 2, 36, 102, 137, 138
United States (USA), 2, 3, 14, 36, 59,
    101, 115, 122, 127, 133,
    136–140, 142, 160n13, 162, 163
Upper-middle income country, 137
USAID, 60, 136

V

Venture Capital, 16, 69, 73n11, 139,
    163, 170, 175
Village Capital, 1, 2, 4, 17, 33, 36, 38,
    75, 82–84, 94, 96–98, 101, 108,
    113, 120, 121, 128, 137, 162,
    182, 197

W

Wanda Organic, 2, 3
Women entrepreneurs, 10, 72, 103,
    161–184, 193, 196
World Bank, 9, 31, 136–138, 160n13

Y

Y Combinator, v, 1, 3, 11n6, 17, 33,
    42, 59, 94, 107